MERRICK POSNANSKY is Professor Emeritus of History and Anthropology at the University of California where he has been a faculty member since 1976. After completing his Ph.D. in Archaeology at Nottingham University, Posnansky taught in Africa for 20 years, where he worked as Curator of the Uganda Museum, Director of African Studies at the University of Makerere and Professor of Archaeology at the University of Ghana. In 2007 he was a Senior Fulbright Professor at the University of Makerere, Uganda.

AFRICA AND ARCHAEOLOGY

AFRICA AND ARCHAEOLOGY

Empowering an Expatriate Life

MERRICK POSNANSKY

The Radcliffe Press

LONDON • NEW YORK

Published in 2009 by The Radcliffe Press
6 Salem Road, London W2 4BU

Distributed in the United States and Canada Exclusively by Palgrave
Macmillan, 175 Fifth Avenue, New York NY 10010

ISBN 978 1 84511 994 2

A full CIP record is available from the Library of Congress

Library of Congress Catalog card: available

Printed and bound in Great Britain by
CPI Antony Rowe, Chippenham.
Copy-edited and typeset by
Oxford Publishing Services, Oxford.

FSC
Mixed Sources
Product group from well-managed
forests and other controlled sources
Cert no. SGS-COC-2953
www.fsc.org
© 1996 Forest Stewardship Council

In memory of my wife Eunice, the love of my life, and for our three beautiful daughters Sheba, Tessa and Helen

Cairo

TOGO Denou
        Notse
Lome   BENIN
Begho
GHANA   Ouidah
    Legon
Fort
Ruychaver

Dufile
Wadelai
UGANDA
Bigo
Beyeyorere
Nsongezi

Addis Ababa

Makerere
    Magosi
    Nyero

Mogadishu

KENYA
Lolui Island
    Nairobi

RWANDA
Nyabusora

Lake
Victoria
Lanet
Olorgesailie

TANZANIA   Kilwa

Lubumbashi

Pretoria

△ Consultancies
◻ University Teaching
● Sites Excavated /
   Field Schools

Lenton
Priory
              R. Trent
Swarkeston
Lockington
Ingleby   Nottingham

Lamport
        Cambridge

0   50   100
              M.
0   50   100
         K.M.

500   1000
              M.
500   1000
         K.M.

JS

Map by Jack Scott.

Contents

Illustrations

Acronyms and Abbreviations

CMS	Church Missionary Society
ILO	International Labour Organization
IMF	International Monetary Fund
LAUSD	Los Angeles Unified School District
MAMA	Museums Association of Middle Africa
OAU	Organization of African Unity
OPEC	Organization of the Petroleum Exporting Countries
UCLA	University of California, Los Angeles
UNDP	United Nations Development Programme
UNESCO	United Nations Educational, Scientific and Cultural Organization
UNIP	United National Independence Party

Preface

A T THE OUTSET I decided that this should not be a chrono-logical account of my life. I have read too many histories that are cluttered with useless material merely to achieve chrono-logical comprehensiveness. I want to present what I feel was important to me, what was important when I wrote about it, not necessarily when it occurred. I am aware that my memory is not as good as it was – I look at some of the lists I kept of people to whom we sent Christmas cards and the names mean nothing to me; and I have so many photographs of people I cannot place. I rather hoped that putting events down on paper would jog latent memories. I never kept a diary or journal when I was travelling or in the field, which I now regret, so except for those parts of my professional career for which my papers and book chapters provide insights into my activities, I have to rely on my memory.

I do not even have the luxury of letters. I kept up a continuous correspondence with my mother from the time I went to college until she died, but unfortunately the residue of my letters to her were destroyed shortly after her death in March 1975. I do have some letters from friends and sisters over the years, but am too lazy to work through them at this stage. Somewhere I even have a few letters from three girlfriends I had before I got married, but I have not looked at them since I received them. I feel that my love and sex life should not be written about except for the abiding love I still have for my late wife Eunice, a love at times scarred by insecurities, but continuous and important to us both.

I decided intentionally to look at my life in a thematic way, to adopt six major themes – family; education; race and religion; my career; Hani, where I engaged in my most productive and happy fieldwork; and Africa.

The length of the various chapters is no indication of their relative importance. I have perhaps left too much out of my family origins, but hope that my sister Ruth in Israel, spurred by some wonderful titbits from the Posnansky family web page, will make use of what Leonard and I have written to provide a more readable account, for she is the best writer of us all. For details of my early history in Bolton, and of my memories of my parents and their early lives, my mother was an important source. I was fortunate to have had a sabbatical year in England in 1974 and to have spent time with her talking about her youth. For my father's origins I am grateful to my distant cousin Maurice Jenkins, who visited Bolimów in Poland from where our family hailed and who stimulated my 'roots' visit in 1996. I owe much of what I know about my wife Eunice's Uganda background to a trip we made to her family in 1996 when she knew she had Alzheimer's but bravely went back to say goodbye.

I have good reason to be thankful in my life to more people than I can name. I owe my greatest debt to Eunice, who patiently and lovingly put up with my travels, excavating, lecturing and being away from home. She was an African woman with all the multifarious skills and qualities that implies; she was a teacher, cultivator, caregiver and companion in the fullest meaning of those words and I did not fully appreciate all her wonderful gifts until she succumbed to Alzheimer's. Her legacy, our three beautiful and gifted daughters, Sheba, Tessa and Helen, the joy of my life, have been more than children; they have been friends and I am pleased they all inherited the travel bug. In my wider family my brother-in-law Sidney has always been good-humoured, full of jokes, enterprising, innovative and a real family man. My nephew Nicholas has many of the same qualities and has been a wonderful companion; he shares some of my quirks, including a passion to collect things we do not really need, but has been helping me enjoy every minute of what we were doing.

I realize that in my memoirs I have focused very much on my own life and feelings, but I was fortunate along the way to have some great friends. Those who have influenced me most have been good listeners against whom I could bounce ideas, who could dissuade with a glance rather than a rebuke, enthuse when I felt abandoned, and encourage through their example and help.

Among those to whom I am most indebted, but whom I may have failed to acknowledge in the text as mentors, were the late Ron Hendry at Nottingham who passed on his love of cricket and gave me a sense of purpose and feeling that all men are equal; Bill Bishop, a good companion in East Africa and always genial, ebullient and realistic; Jean Sassoon who helped me realize that I could make a contribution to African archaeology; the late Peter Kenyon and his wife Marilyn who were supportive and provided me with a receptive audience; Valerie Vowles at the Uganda Museum who was the best ethnographer I ever knew; and Colette and Hugh Hawes who shared their love of Africa and belief in mankind's finer human creative qualities.

In Ghana Seth Dankwa has been a supportive friend who effortlessly introduced me to so many aspects of Ghanaian life; Bossman Murey, whose efficiency and loyalty have always been an inspiration; the late Peggy Appiah who has shared her love for Asante art, proverbs and life and always provided welcoming hospitality; the people of Hani who accepted me as their 'prof' and taught me so much. In the United States I am grateful to all my doctoral students from whom I have learnt as much as I have given, especially Toni Adedze who has been a close friend. In recent years I have been particularly indebted to Dennis Laumann, now at the University of Memphis, who taught me not to take myself too seriously, to get rid of documents I did not really need, and who punctured with humour some of my firm beliefs that I had held for far too long; and also Chris Ehret, who has shown so much patience, is a scholar of integrity and whose enthusiasm grows with age. Finally, I would like to thank Selina Cohen of Oxford Publishing Services for her editorial help in preparing this book for publication.

Introduction

T HIS IS A BOOK ABOUT my life rather than an account of everything that has happened in it. It is a personal story rather than a record of the times in which I lived. Central to my life has been a sense of expatriation, looking at the world from outside rather than thinking of my life as central to it. I was born in England but my father was born in, and lived his early years in, Eastern Europe. My children were born in Africa and my grandchildren in the United States, to where my wife and I moved in 1977.

I often experience conflicts of identification, if not identity. I look to different worlds, yet feel fairly detached from all of them. In this sense I am a man of the world rather than of a particular country. I keep returning, either explicitly in my chapter on religion and race, or implicitly in my discussions on Africa and education, to what it means to be an expatriate. For much of my life, even before I had ever heard of the word or knew its meaning, I have regarded myself as an expatriate, the dictionary definition of which implies a conscious act of withdrawing from one's country or citizenship. For me the word suggests something less conscious, a sense of not fully belonging to the dominant society or community in which I live. I did not consciously withdraw from the society, but the society in which I lived did not in my own mind quite accommodate me.

This is a universal problem that becomes more acute as people compete in what is often assumed to be a shrinking world. Who rightfully belongs and who does not? Many native-born inhabitants of France and Australia are at present feeling detached from the society into which they were born. For me, being an expatriate is more about feeling than being.

As a child I was consciously Jewish; our community was small and we kept largely to our immediate family and congregation. Although I went to a tolerant Church of England school and wore the school uniform proudly, I did not participate fully in its life, prayers or the entire recommended curriculum. Because I went to synagogue on

Saturdays I missed out on sports, much of which took place on Saturdays – swimming in the morning and watching football in the afternoon. Our small Jewish community kept us separate from the larger Gentile world, so when other young people dated or went to dances, I stayed at home, not necessarily because of a predisposition to being celibate but because the opportunities for me to take part in outside activities were more limited.

I participated more at college and related to my age peers, my hall and my discipline. There, so long as there was no language barrier, social mobility depended as much on intellect as on class. I nevertheless still sometimes felt isolated. I was self-consciously Jewish and, at Cambridge, felt self-conscious about having been to a newer university. I felt acutely aware of being first-generation British without deep roots or neighbours who remembered my forebears; my family certainly had no attics full of family memorabilia. I lived at a time when being foreign or having a different religion could cause misunderstandings, and in a world just emerging from conflict and facing the inherent problems of colonialism.

As a young man observing the dissolution of the empire I became acutely aware of the expatriate experience, especially of English expatriates in India. In fact, one Anglo-Indian friend of mine at university had never been out of India until he was 20 years old.

High status, economically well-off British people were able to enjoy two worlds, the world from which they came and the world in which they worked overseas. Normally, however, they married or retired back to Britain. One of my early historical heroes, Samuel Baker, fell into this category, as did many European explorers. They often served in the army overseas, and/or planted tea on estates in Ceylon, experiences that whetted their appetites for a more unrestricted existence thereafter.

A true expatriate is a person who leaves his or her original homeland for good, who looks back either with anger but more often with fond memories, and who always remains somewhat remote from the new host country. In Africa, being an expatriate, coming from the land of the rulers rather than from the mass of those ruled, carried a certain cachet. In many ways we were more British than the British we had left behind, but our affection was for a Britain frozen in time, a Britain filled with class distinctions where former captains and majors still kept their ranks. A similar expatriation occurred among East Africa's Asians who kept up their finer social differences and biases even when these were becoming blurred in their own newly independent countries. It was as if time had stood still for the British, as if pop culture had never emerged in the 1960s. Being in a minority brought us together, gave us a sense of self-preservation and of our last little spurt of power. In many ways we regarded ourselves as representing civilization, so resented the increasing lack of interest in the 'empire and colonies' back in England. We were a minority that had known since the late 1950s that our days were numbered, that our cosy way of life was endangered.

It was also dawning on many people in Africa that the expatriates among them were not necessarily the best, brightest or even most representative of the ruling colonial authority. In the interwar years, many high fliers joined the Indian civil service, with tropical Africa regarded either as a place in which to farm on a large scale or as a stepping stone to better postings.

My early jobs increased my sense of separateness. In Kenya, in that I worked for a parastatal organization outside Nairobi, which was where the expatriate community was centred, I lacked the security of belonging to a government service and had no club affiliations. In Uganda, however, where I worked at the Uganda Museum, also a parastatal, there was strong camaraderie among the British who did not work for government and for whom Entebbe was the central focus; in fact, in some ways we felt superior to our counterparts in Nairobi's overly expatriate community. Home leaves reinforced the expatriate experience, as did reading newspapers from Britain and listening to the BBC. It was surprising how strongly we longed for foods from home. Even as late as the 1980s and 1990s, when I was in Ghana, a small fish and chip shop in an Accra suburb, run by a Ghanaian woman married to an Englishman who had spent time in England, became a magnet for British expatriates who also craved mushy peas, cider, shepherd's pie, baked beans and scones.

When independence came to these African countries, expatriates stopped feeling that they belonged. They emphasized their separateness by sending their children to school in England, by accentuating their English ways and by looking for upcountry hotels in the Kenya Highlands that still catered to their British ways. I was more conscious of British sport outside Britain than in it. Expatriates were possibly the staunchest British monarchists; they loved royalty and the paraphernalia of Britain, including tea cosies, tea time and video tapes of British comedies.

Working in African universities was a rather schizoid experience. We not only preserved an inherited British system and had ties with British universities, but we also developed new loyalties to other Britons in African territories in similar personal and professional positions. There were few British archaeologists in tropical Africa, but those of us who were there retained remarkably strong links with one another until we retired, mostly through the exchange of reprints of papers and Christmas cards. It was not until the 1980s that London University appointed an archaeologist for Africa and, as late as 2002, Cambridge became the first university to appoint an Africanist archaeologist, Dr David Phillipson, to a special chair in African archaeology. This separateness probably explains why small but vigorous African archaeology associations developed in Britain and America where other areas with more practitioners failed. Half a century ago British archaeologists in Africa felt isolated, neglected and cut off from their home country. It was in some ways an expatriation of neglect rather than of choice.

In America I became a citizen so that I could belong, vote and make my voice heard, but in some ways I felt even less at home there because I lacked the buffer of a resident British community. Los Angeles has long had a British community. Many of the early Hollywood stars were British; English sports such as cricket were played and numerous shops and public houses catered to the culinary needs of a resident British population of over a quarter of a million. But that population is dispersed and if one did not belong to the British Chamber of Trade or frequent the public houses to enjoy English ales or play darts, then one remained an isolated minority.

Being Jewish in a city with more than half a million Jews was no consolation. The Jews of Los Angeles belong to tight communities committed to their temples. Old world synagogues were called temples in the new world and acquired appurtenances like conference rooms, boutique souvenir shops and libraries. I found it difficult to melt in the melting pot, to blend into the cocktail of cultures. Perhaps America is better suited to receiving poor, oppressed people eager to forget their past and willing to adapt fairly rapidly, and less well suited to immigrants with their own rich history. This problem has led to the *ad infinitum* hyphenating of groups into such categories as African-Americans, Chinese-Americans, Mexican-Americans and Vietnamese-Americans. It is difficult for first-generation Americans to be really American, so many non-English speaking new immigrants move into bilingual or even monolingual neighbourhoods. Having grown up without baseball, proms, American radio and foods, even distinctive American clothes, makes it difficult to blend in with the natives.

My Third World experience, as well as my prejudices against and suspicions of the current Israeli government, made absorption into the Jewish community difficult. I was not used to belonging to a community, to accepting rather than discussing community norms. Americans believe that theirs is the most democratic society in the world, but for a newcomer bearing a heritage of European socialism, as well as strong beliefs in social justice, economic equality and anti-imperialism, America's social and political norms are difficult to accept without questioning and those who question them are not readily accepted. This is a paradox the expatriate who consciously chooses to become American has to face. There is so much to wonder at and admire in America, particularly the different freedoms from constraint, yet there are constraints that expatriates readily experience but Americans do not always recognize.

I had intended to include a separate chapter on travel, for my travels have been, and continue to be, an essential part of my life's journey. Travelling for me has always been an adventure, a learning experience rather than a series of holidays. I always felt that travel should be instructive. Perhaps it all began at school with geography field trips that forced me to look at the landscape, to understand what I was seeing and how the physical and human landscape was formed rather than just enjoying the beauty. How human activity shaped the landscape over time became more obvious once I started human geography and later archaeology at college. Houses and buildings are cultural artefacts and with historical architecture, albeit classical architecture, part of my A-level elective in art at school, I began to analyse, my children would say over analyse, everything I saw. My wish to analyse is linked to my collecting instinct, a need to add to one's pool of knowledge. At college I traced architectural history by visiting cathedrals and old houses, as well as by looking through antique stalls in town markets.

Travel provided me with the adventure of seeing new vistas and gaining new information, in much the same way I suppose as a train spotter adds engine numbers to his or her already considerable collection. Going up to Cambridge in 1952 and wandering around the Haddon Museum added an ethnographic dimension. Earlier visits to the Musée de l'Homme in Paris in 1950 and 1952, and watching some of their ethnographic films, had already aroused my interest in people who lived in different environments from my own. Some museums have a lasting impact and the Musée de l'Homme was significant for me in a way I did not realize at the time.

As a student I travelled around England, France, the Netherlands and Norway. When I went to Africa I made the most of my opportunities by visiting 29 different countries on that continent alone, as well as visiting other countries when we went on leave every two years. In 1966 I visited Japan for the first time. It was important to me as a scholar because it enabled me to see some of the variability of world culture. I think it steered me away from diffusionist theories, for I saw similarities with Africa that could only have occurred through independent development. Over the years I learnt a great deal from trips to places like Egypt, Lebanon, Greece and Malta, which reinforced my belief in the importance of the eastern Mediterranean and the strength of cultural contacts and trade.

Lecturing at an African-Caribbean summer school in Jamaica in 1977 expanded my interest in the African diaspora, in African-American studies in the United States, in developing new courses and in subsequently visiting Puerto Rico, Haiti, the Dominican Republic and Cuba. We have enjoyed quite a few trips in the United States, including a cross-country journey to Virginia, and several tours of New Mexico and Arizona, during which I absorbed a lot of American archaeology, particularly about the Anasazi. In the west I enjoyed numerous trips to ghost towns, missions and historical sites in places like Virginia City, Sonoma, Bodie and Sitka. All my travels have been wonderful learning experiences and reading and teaching have provided constant feedback.

When I reflect on travelling I realize that it is too broad a subject to be contained within a single theme. It is a palate that has coloured my life and, from time to time, given me an independence of spirit. The awareness it has brought of the basic humanity that exists throughout the planet has shaped my political views and made me realize that, while I have always lived in favourable environments, the vast majority of the world's population find their surroundings forbidding and their future frightening.

Three of my most significant visits were to Israel, to which I went on five occasions, South Africa and India. I thought that visiting Israel would deepen my grounding as an archaeologist, whereas in fact it gave me a more intimate insight into the problems of colonialism, which I had only studied from an historical perspective. There was much to praise and to sympathize with on both sides of the central issue of occupation, but it was difficult to think of any solutions. South Africa not only gave me insights into the richness of Africa's cultural heritage, as seen from the fabulous cave sequences and rock art, but it also demonstrated the fragility, and at the same time the paradox of strength, of the European experience. India was altogether different and it bowled me over. I had never witnessed such a kaleidoscope of cultural experience. The richness and array of buildings on the Portuguese sites of Goa and Bassein helped give Portuguese Africa a truer, more provincial perspective. The artistry of the sites ranging from early Buddhist stupas at Sanchi, through Hindu temples at Khajuraho to Muslim fortresses, tombs and palaces at Agra and Delhi, was a real eye opener. I was struck by the appropriateness of much of the technology in modern India, for example taxis able to seat six people made from scooters, as well as easily assembled village water pumps and grain mills. I realized that Africa would do well to learn more from well established, flourishing societies like India or rapidly developing economies like Korea and Taiwan. World economic forces, historical experiences and language have all made emerging Africa too beholden to the old colonial powers and the new behemoth of the United States.

All my life I have been involved in education – either my own or that of my students, whom I regard as my extended family. I have benefited from living in three parts of the world in which education is very different – England, Africa and the United States. The happiest times of my life, and in many ways the most challenging, productive and memorable parts of my career, were at Makerere University College in Uganda from 1962 to 1967 and at the University of Ghana from 1967 to 1976. My role as an archaeological educator was more important to me than my career as a research archaeologist. In the United States I tried to influence educational practice through my work in education abroad and participation in discussions on the role of higher education in Africa. In retirement I have enjoyed the luxury of being able to be more reflective, to use my career, reading and time in Africa as a fulcrum for unravelling questions about slavery, imperialism and colonialism.

As race and religion played a large role in my life I felt that they should be separated as specific themes. Being Jewish in an English Christian environment, being English, Jewish and an expatriate in an African social world and crossing many barriers to marry an African,

Christian, Ugandan wife have all been part of an immutable and enriching experience. That chapter is divided into three parts – England when religion was important in my life, Africa when race became important because of my reactions to the colonial experience and marriage to Eunice. Our myriad experiences as a married couple and my observations on the white experience in Africa are not unique but they are important in defining my attitudes. In the final section I deal with the United States when neither race nor religion impinged directly yet both were important determinants of my behaviour and beliefs.

My professional interests began as a collector fascinated by stamps, later by coins and finally by archaeology. My initial footsteps as a scholar were taken in 1948 when I gave my first professional paper to a local numismatic society on coinage reforms in the ancient world. From the beginning I was interested in what the objects could tell us about society rather than about the objects. From the summer before I entered university in 1949 I worked as a volunteer archaeologist on a Mesolithic site. The first digs I directed were on medieval sites. My interests were eclectic and have remained so. Human origins, recent local history and what I used to call bygones intrigue me. I have worked on early Stone Age sites and in my old age I have returned to stamps, trying to separate policy and motive from images.

My initial interest was in museums rather than full-time field research. I had connections with the University of Nottingham's Margidunum Museum, which was dedicated to Roman Samian ware, and began an active museum involvement at the National Parks of Kenya. My most productive time was as curator of the Uganda Museum (1958–62) when I started the Museums Association of Middle Africa. I have since then been interested in organizations that draw people together to enhance their cultural conservation, most recently through the Arts Council of the African Studies Association and the West African Archaeological Association.

My somewhat spasmodic career as a field archaeologist always had an educational component and I enjoyed taking students into the field. I dug at college on all manner of sites, including the earliest human ones at Hoxne near Cambridge in 1953, as well as on medieval and Dark Age sites in Nottinghamshire and Derbyshire. It was curiously in my spare time rather than as part of my core research that I developed the interest in historical archaeology that was to play such a major role in my later career. I enjoyed the social camaraderie of the dig, the outdoor activity and the opportunities it gave to experience new places. The economic approaches of my first major mentor, Graham Clark of Cambridge, greatly influenced my career and it was he who convinced me that if I wished hard enough to become an archaeologist and persisted then I would eventually get a job. He was right and I did not have long to wait.

Later on Sir Mortimer Wheeler became the main influence on my career as an archaeologist. Although he never taught me, I learnt a great deal from his books, particularly his *Archaeology from the Earth* and *Flames over Persepolis*. Through his rigorous methods he demonstrated that fieldwork was an art, that photography was important and that a world approach was indispensable.

He made me realize that archaeology was exciting, creative and humanistic. I thoroughly enjoyed my interactions with him when he visited Uganda and appreciated his hospitality and anecdotal wisdom at the Atheneum when I visited London. In Uganda I developed my own approach to archaeology. This involved using oral history to locate sites and to interpret social and political life on the kingdom sites of the last half millennium, particularly at Bigo, which was associated with the semi mythical Bacwezi state. It was an approach that influenced my students both in West Africa and the Caribbean.

Between late 1964 and 1970 I dug very little. At that time I was more consumed with being an educator, deciding what and how to teach African archaeology in Africa and introducing African studies at the university level.

From 1970 until 1981 I was active in Ghana, particularly at Begho, then later in Togo and Jamaica. Since 1981 I have been less actively involved, but have still worked with my students at their doctoral sites, run training programmes and gained vicarious pleasure from my participation. My interests turned to ethno-archaeology, which enabled me to work on my own and thus avoid logistical and managerial problems and the hassle of raising funds. The 1980s were also a time when my main focus was on restructuring the UCLA Institute of Archaeology and on developing University of California Abroad, first in Togo and later in Ghana.

While I worked a little in Benin in the early 1990s, my main interests lay in cultural conservation and in finding out what went wrong in African museums and antiquities services after the years of great promise in the 1960s. This was also when I wanted to look at how Africa fitted into the world and realized the importance of comparative studies. Such interests took me to Cameroon, India,

1. Ethno-archaeology at Hani, Ghana, interviewing a farmer in his field house. Mr S. Dankwa immediate right of Merrick.

South Africa and Cuba. For a time I had plans for a major historical archaeological project dealing with the Portuguese in the sixteenth and seventeenth centuries in both the Gondar region of Ethiopia and the Cape Verde islands. I abandoned these plans when the truth began to seep in that my love and responsibilities to Eunice and my weakening health following a 1996 bypass and deteriorating diabetic condition meant that I could no longer engage in major fieldwork.

My most enduring passion has been my association with the Brong Ahafo village of Hani in Ghana. I first went there in 1970 in search of the medieval town of Begho, the location of which was uncertain up to that time. I dug Begho on seven different occasions between then and 1979, but mainly became enmeshed in the life of Hani, the successor village of the medieval town. Its people became my people. I was elected *Ahohohene*, chief of strangers, in 1975 and took my role seriously. I realized that if I wanted to understand the past I needed to know what linked the past to the present and to understand how Hani people articulated with their environment. What began as a training exercise for students became a long-term commitment. I wanted to know how and why material culture changed, and what events external to the village, such as the national economy, political changes or environmental forces, had the most impact on the villagers' lives.

For more than 28 years I cooperated with two friends from the

University of Ghana, former staff members from the archaeology department, Bossman Murey and Seth Dankwa. After I left Ghana at least one of us, but more often two or all three of us, visited the village 13 times to compile questionnaires, to study crafts, farming and collecting activities, or just to watch the village and its people evolve. At one time I knew all the villagers by name, I had been in their homes and, though I knew little of their language except at a rudimentary level, we were able to communicate. In my combined total of 50 weeks there over 22 visits I gained a feeling of intimacy that I have never had for any other neighbourhood. I hope that I will do justice to that relationship by writing up my data in a more comprehensive form than is possible here.

I am an Africanist who does archaeology rather than strictly an archaeologist or historian. When asked about my professional identity I always put my African expertise above my disciplinary training. Africa has been my abiding interest since I arrived in Kenya in 1956. I still follow the economic and political news with interest. I see the world through African eyes, which has often brought me into contention with relatives and friends whose approach, particularly to Middle Eastern or American issues, is more parochial than mine. Our house is like a museum with pictures from Africa on the walls and artefacts and crafts scattered around. When I went to Africa I envisaged staying for two to three years and then returning to the UK, but Africa gets into one's system. I was fortunate to go when I did, for I experienced the colonial and independence periods. I often hated the climate but adjusted to it. I enjoyed the leisure, being able to master the more limited written sources and the opportunity, in countries with small elites, to make a difference, to become and be respected as an expert. Each of my African experiences was very different.

In Kenya I was able to see game, to live in a national reserve in close proximity to Maasai herders and, as the only foreigner in the area, to lead a colourful life. It was exciting for someone of my age. I travelled a lot, camped rough, climbed Kilimanjaro, visited the coast and learnt and used Swahili. It was a great learning experience and Kenya was a wonderful field laboratory for African geology and the environment. To rehabilitate Olorgesailie as a tourist site and build a field museum I drew on my experiences as a student in geography and geology and learnt practical skills that have proved invaluable. I met many of the greats in African geology and archaeology who passed through Kenya and made many long-term friends. I learnt to teach in an African setting and got my feet wet in African art. Being on my own I read and read and at that time the literature on Africa was limited enough for one to master a lot in a very short time. But in many ways Kenya was constricting. I disliked the colonial situation, had little freedom to expand intellectually and was fairly lonely as the warden of the prehistoric sites of the Royal National Parks of Kenya with its limited budget and rather unsympathetic boss for whom I had little respect.

Uganda was altogether different. As curator of the museum and in charge of archaeology, I had a free hand to learn a great deal about a country the size of England. I became a polymath and was at my most intense intellectually and socially. I remember one period when I went out on 60 consecutive evenings. I often worked well into the night at the museum, particularly in its dark room, which was not air-conditioned. With the help of a wonderful staff I created a vibrant and dynamic museum, put on numerous temporary exhibitions and scheduled lectures. I was able to introduce archaeology as a university discipline, ran training programmes in the field and lectured for the university extra-mural programme. I was enthusiastic, excited and accomplished a great deal, but wish I had written more. Uganda was an exciting place to be educationally and politically. I knew all the major politicians apart from one short-term military leader in 1985; in fact, I met every president, prime minister or head of state from the late 1950s into the present century.

We built our own house overlooking Lake Victoria, where our older children were born, and there was a lot going on to remember and describe. I loved Uganda, was very productive and saw a great deal of the country. By serving on several planning boards at the University of East Africa, I helped influence the future, particularly in the field of graduate education when I was director of the African Studies Pro-gramme and chairman of the Joint Board of Graduate Studies.

Could Uganda ever be topped? Ghana where, hesitantly missing Uganda, I started off and where Eunice, without a job and having just lost a baby, was at first very unsettled, turned out to be the happiest and most formative period of our lives. I still associate myself primarily with Ghana. I was able to create a full department of archaeology with teaching at all levels, we developed a research centre at Hani and ran many happy and productive field schools with participants from many countries. I loved the cut and thrust of a small liberal arts college. We had some marvellous home leaves travelling in Europe and most of all we were made to feel really happy. As mentioned above, I accomplished a lot, but somehow there was more to it; everything came together in a remarkable way. Ghanaians are the friendliest people among whom we have ever worked; I felt less like an expatriate and Eunice learnt and loved her new career as a librarian. We planned to stay a long time, but health problems, economic uncertainty and an invitation to accept a permanent post in the United States intervened.

We were unsettled in the United States at first. Our marriage and family were at their most vulnerable and we were economically challenged. Once we had adjusted, however, my Africanist opportunities exploded. I travelled to Africa every year and attended the annual African Studies Association conference and met old associates from Africa. I participated in numerous African ventures, which included serving on the curriculum committee of the 1986 public television series called *The Africans*.

I liked the flexibility of the American university system, which enabled one to teach virtually anything one wanted to teach. I branched out into African technology, Caribbean history and slave trade studies. Graduate teaching allowed me to explore new horizons through the work of graduate students in Jamaica, Togo and Benin. My association with the African Studies Center gave me access to links with universities in Africa and made it possible to develop education abroad programmes.

There were of course disappointments. Not least among these was the difficulty I experienced in maintaining any strong link with Francophone Africa. This problem stemmed partly from my own stupidity in failing ever to learn French adequately, but we nonetheless had some great conferences and meetings on Togo, both in Lomé and Washington. I served as director of the James S. Coleman African Studies Center, but it was a rather unsuccessful time for many reasons. One pleasurable, but ultimately fruitless, endeavour was our attempt to establish a productive working relationship with Japanese Africanists. Although I travelled to Japan and Korea to meet fellow Africanists, we held some good workshops and at one point the prospects, which I hope can be exploited in the future, looked promising, there were problems. Over the years I became interested in higher education in Africa and in various aspects of cultural conservation. While I like to think that I contributed to an ongoing dialogue, I suspect that my role may have been more to create background noise than to provide the leadership that such issues demand.

Chapter 1

Family

I KNOW VERY LITTLE about my family's origins, but I do know that, like other immigrant Jews with turbulent eighteenth- and nineteenth-century histories in the Russian Pale, it was subjected to changes of residence and, in the last half of the nineteenth century, the requirement to adopt a regular surname[1] over and above one's Hebrew name consisting of a personal name plus one's father's name. From conversations in Bolimów , from where my father came in 1897, and from the records of the Jewish voluntary fire service, there were Posnanskys[2] in the town in the early 1900s. My father, Simon Posnansky, known to his family and friends by his Hebrew name of Zachariah, sometimes also gave his origins as Lowicz, a large town 16 kilometres west of Bolimów and a main stop on the rail line from Poznan to Warsaw. Like far too many young people, I regarded my parents as immortal and never asked them about their history until it was too late. My father was uncommunicative and died in my teens when I was more interested in my career, my identity and in testing the parameters of parental control. Also, during the war and postwar period of austerity, my father, already nearly seventy, worked 60 to 70 hours a week and when at home was usually rather tired. Our Jewish community never made the news. It survived for nearly 65 years and yet no news items about its existence ever appeared in the *Bolton Evening News*.[3]

My parents' families originated in that great pool of Western Jewry, eastern Russia and Poland. We cannot trace our family further back than the mid-nineteenth century with any certainty, so I have no idea from where my great grandparents originally came. The earliest name in our maternal family tree is Miriam Cohen, my mother's grandmother who was born towards the end of the first half of the nineteenth century. Her husband died early but not before she had given birth to at least five children during the 1870s, none of whom reached their fiftieth birthday.

The family came to England in the last quarter of the nineteenth century. Sarah Bryna, the eldest daughter, married my grandfather, David Cohen, around 1901 in Manchester where my mother was born in 1902. Sarah was David's second wife. He already had nine surviving children from his first wife Annie and had lost at least two more in infancy. Born in 1851 he had come to England in 1867 at the age of 16, using the dowry of his first wife, who was four years older than he was, for travel expenses. His new wife, born in Russia in 1872, was close in age to several of his children. Eventually, his father and one of his brothers also came to Manchester. His father had the distinction of being president of the Fernie Street[4] synagogue for more than 25 years and his brother Pinhey was the first person to be buried at Urmston cemetery.[5]

David Cohen worked as a glazer for Baxendales, a plumber's merchant in Manchester, but lost his job when he fell fixing a skylight. There was no workmen's compensation in those years and, after several years of unemployment, he moved to Bolton in 1912. He worked for a few years as an itinerant glazer for the Bolton Corporation and later, walking around with a pack of glass on his back, as a freelance worker repairing casement windows, which were mainly of a standard size. He was possibly the last itinerant glazer in the greater Manchester area. He never owned a house but lived in rented terrace houses, the last two on Bark Street. My father Simon Posnansky and his wife Devorah, Sarah Cohen's younger sister, also lived on Bark Street. Bark Street was close to the cotton mills and horse-drawn drays laden with everything from beer barrels, bales of raw cotton, huge spools of undyed thread, or two hundredweight sacks of coal[6] would clatter along the cobble street every day.

When my father moved to Star Cliffs in 1922, he found the neighing horses, crowing cocks and barking dogs of suburbia disturbed his sleep more than had the thunderous noise of the iron-banded wheels of the horse-drawn drays. Unlike his father-in-law he owned his houses, first at 13 Bark Street, where he had a cold and draughty tailoring workshop in a wooden shed, and later, from 1918, at 46 Bark Street, by which time he had rented a new workshop and finally a shop front at 11 Crown Street. Tragically, his old wooden workshop burnt down on the night he married my mother in 1917. This was a bad time for my father and mother, for he realized in 1917 that his parents – refugees, tired-out human flotsam shuttling between advancing and retreating armies as the eastern front between Germany and Russia shifted every few months – had died of typhoid dysentery.[7]

My father woke my mother in the middle of the night shortly after they had got married to say that his father had just died. Nearly six months later they heard that his father had indeed died the very night he woke with the strange premonition.

My father, Simon Posnansky,[8] who was born in 1877, learnt his trade as a tailor from his almost blind grandfather. He often told me how he would earn a half or quarter kopek (a tiny copper coin like an English farthing) for threading five of the old man's needles. Some of his relatives were cobblers and traders. An uncle kept geese that still feature on the marshy meadows along the River Rawka[9] that runs to the north of the town. His mother Minnah came from the eastern part of the Pale, probably Lithuania, but we have no idea how she met my grandfather. Our known history has its roots in Bolimów where my extremely orthodox paternal grandfather Yehuda Michael spent most of his time studying the Torah, only occasionally working as a cap maker or doing odd jobs to bring in a little money. He visited England for six months with a view to emigrating with his family, but found that the Jews there lived too English a life and did not practise their religion in a rigorous fashion. He regarded the society as *traif*, too unclean for his family.

My father's relationship with his father left him with an ambivalent feeling towards books and study. He admired scholars but also felt that the only way to get ahead was to have a trade and make money. He was always cautious; he could have bought the whole building in which his shop was situated, but was afraid of investing his savings or taking on a mortgage. He distrusted banks and kept large amounts of cash, in fact the equivalent of a year's salary at the time of his death, in a safe in his bedroom. His caution derived partly from a bitter experience around 1906 when he opened a small grocery store that failed because he was too lenient with customers asking for credit.

He had few recollections to share about his home town apart from harsh winters with freezing temperatures and damp river mists spreading across the fertile flood plain and rich loess farming land. One disturbing image was of frozen sparrows falling from telegraph lines during a particularly brutal winter. Like everyone, he lived in a single-storey split log house with few rooms and no running water. Shabbos ceremonies and the close community in Judaism kept up their spirits. It was a reasonably integrated *stetl* with Jews making up about 20 per cent of the population and, by the 1920s, participating in its political life.

Jews had lived in Bolimów, a town of between 3000 and 4000 people, since 1797 and, as late as 1939, there were still about 50 Jewish families there. Of these, a dozen were Manns and Jenkins, to which the Posnanskys are related, with several first cousin marriages being recorded. My father's three sisters had moved to Warsaw in the 1930s shortly after my father and his brother Morris made their last visit to Poland in 1930. His only other visit had been in 1922 when he and his brother went there to erect tombstones for their parents.[10] On that visit they described their family as so poor that they left all their clothes with them. In gratitude, one relative gave my father a gold five-rouble coin from the tsarist period. As I collected coins I felt very pleased when he gave it to me before he died, but sadly it was stolen from our house in Northridge in the 1980s. In the interwar years a two-storey custom-built brick synagogue was erected, which now houses a police station. The whole Jewish community was deported to the Warsaw Ghetto in 1941 and finally to Auschwitz.[11] There were only four Jewish survivors of the Holocaust, all children and they did not return.

In the late nineteenth century Bolimów was an economically and socially constrictive place from which many young people fled. Like all young men, my father was conscripted into the tsarist army and posted to Odessa in the Crimea. The army paid for billets for the Christian soldiers but the Jews had to fend for themselves. They had to rely on the large Odessa Jewish community, which, being the most Westernized in Russia at that time, probably regarded Polish conscripts as country bumpkins. They spoke Russian whereas most of the Polish Jewish soldiers only spoke Yiddish. He remembers being so hungry in the heart of winter that he and his friends dug up frozen carrots and other root crops out of the ground to eat. Both he and his younger brother Moshe (Morris) were in the cavalry, but certainly not in a riding capacity.

During a leave in 1897 he ran away through Germany, was robbed *en route* and arrived in Manchester penniless. There, he stayed with his cousin Sarah Steinman, borrowed enough money to buy a pair of shears for 7s 6d, and by the end of the week was solvent. He worked long hours, often from 8 a.m. to 8 p.m. six days a week, with little chance to observe Jewish holidays. He moved to Bolton in 1906 and, until he bought his first house on Bark Street, worked with another tailor and rented a house on Bullock Street. His houses in Bark Street were small, narrow, dark and cramped, with outside plumbing and

heating only in the kitchen. He kept the house when he moved to Star
Cliffs and I remember collecting rent as a teenager. I could never
imagine how eight or nine people could have lived there.

Life was tough for Jewish women and when my father's first wife
Devorah died giving birth to her eighth, but sixth surviving, child in
1916, she was worn out. The baby was named Dora after her mother.
For a time her sister Sarah helped look after the baby, the other five
children and her own four children, but she suffered from a kidney
disease then known as dropsy and was in poor health. She and her
husband David hatched up the idea that their eldest child Dora, my
mother, should marry Simon to care for the young family. She
promised to help my mother, who was then only 14 and unaware of
the seriousness of her illness, with the work. When my parents
married in a civil ceremony in 1917, the registrar asked my mother if
she *had* to get married. She thought he was asking her if she was
pregnant, so she said no. Within a year her mother was dead and she
was married to a man 25 years her senior who did not love her. I
never saw my father hug or even kiss my mother and, as was customary at the time, they had separate beds. She inherited a family of
cousins of whom two, Ray and Barney, nearly her own age, resented
her. The sense of loss lingered for the youngest children and ultimately led to acrimony when my father died. After my mother had her
first daughter Brenda in 1922, her stepchildren, three of whom were
married by 1930, felt that the attention given to the second family
really belonged to the grandchildren, their own daughters. Even after
70 years, hurt over missed affections still lingers.[12]

Dora, known as Dolly, was a bright, serious child who loved reading, especially contemporary novelists like E. M. Forster, Howard
Spring, Arnold Bennett and Louis Golding. She had high hopes for the
future and by 1915 had become a pupil teacher in her school. This
was wartime when most male teachers had been conscripted and too
few women were entering teacher training colleges to ensure adequate
staffing, particularly of impoverished urban schools, but marriage
shattered her dreams. Her teenage memories are of moving home four
times, of the deaths of her mother and aunt and of marrying a man 25
years her senior whose English was limited and who neither read nor
wrote in English and had little comprehension of what it was to be a
teenager brought up attending English schools and knowing little
Yiddish. Her memories were of hard work, of 'schlepping' fish home
from market that she then had to scale, fillet and cook for Friday night

2. My parents, Dora and Simon in 1942.

and the Sabbath, of plucking chickens, of constantly washing clothes in boilers and forever ironing them.

At times she had help but it was neither consistent nor of her choice. She felt tired and depressed; in fact after my father's death in 1948, depression frequently afflicted her, often for years on end. She felt she had never had a life of her own or a chance to mature. She dreamt of a different future. Reading and later listening to BBC plays on the radio became an escape. She taught us to value the public library and curiously I owe my name to her love of books. At one stage she enjoyed short stories and Leonard Merrick, who wrote from Paris in the 1920s, was an author she especially liked. My older brother was called Leonard, even though his Hebrew name was Yehuda Michael, and when I was born I was to be named Meir after a deceased uncle on my mother's side. My father wanted to call me Mervyn, but my mother objected. In the end she decided to call me Merrick, a name I have always enjoyed and through life I have only met a handful of other Merricks.

Another of her interests was cooking. She was a natural cook, using her head rather than cook books. She made fabulous cakes, *kuchen* (cinnamon raisin bread), wafer thin crêpes for blintzes, delicately flavoured *tzimmes* (carrot stew) simmered for hours overnight, and perfect beetroot jam (*angermache*) at Pesach. She cooked all sorts of *kugel* for puddings – *lokshen*, potato, matzos – and rhubarb concoctions to die for, including some with glorious light sponge cake on top. Every Jewish festival found her ready with the right foods – potato latkes for Chanukkah, *hamentaschen* for Purim and perfect sponge cakes and *kichels* (hard cookies) for Pesach. Soups were another of her achievements – chicken soup with butter beans and homemade *mandl*, *rossel* soup, light borsht with lemon and eggs, and particularly filling lentil and barley soups. She believed in long cooking at low temperatures. The vermicelli she dried on the clothes hanger in the kitchen is an abiding memory. Cakes and pies were her forte. There was nothing she could not do.

Using a graphite, cast-iron, coal-heated oven without temperature controls or a thermometer, she was a virtuoso. The boiler behind the kitchen fireplace heated 20 gallons of water, but since the hot water got used up quickly, we all took baths on different nights of the week. From 1922, when the family moved to Star Cliffs, her scullery served as her kitchen and the actual kitchen became our family room. The scullery was five feet wide and twelve feet long with minimal storage and high shelves on which to keep seldom used pans and bar soap left to harden for longer usage. There was a small gas stove with burners one had to light with matches. She had a wonderful five-gallon copper jam-making pan. Sadly, in a fit of patriotism, she answered the wartime call for copper scrap and gave it away. But, glory of glories, the scullery had a window at the narrow end from which she could look out at little more than a stone-flagged yard and green painted wooden fence across Cope Bank to the hawthorn and other trees beyond and watch the changing colours of the skies. This view of the outside kept her spirits up. Until the last decade of its use when she bought some laminated covered ready-made units she had had to depend on badly built wooden cupboards. Cockroaches were a menace until the late 1940s when the floor was sealed with a bituminized red compound.

Siblings and childhood

Her first child, Brenda was born in 1922; Leonard followed in 1925. His birth depleted her of calcium, so she got gum and tooth problems and ended up having all her teeth removed. Dental care was primitive, even a generation ago; teeth were pulled out with abandon and there was virtually no root canal surgery, capping or bracing in England. My father died having never had anaesthesia for his fillings. He also lost many teeth and in the late 1930s was fitted with a bridge of seven teeth. He wore the bridge for a week, but it troubled him and he put the teeth in a green paper bag on his dresser, which was still there when he died. Freda was born in 1927 and I appeared on the scene in 1931. I recollect key events in my childhood, even my birth, but my daughters say it is impossible. I remember being in my mother's bed with a light blue bedspread with the sun filtering and flickering in through the moving boughs of the giant elm outside the window. My next memory is of my father buying me a tin truck and playing with it on the chequered linoleum of the kitchen. I cut myself, was taken to hospital with blood poisoning that turned to septicaemia and spent three weeks in hospital. I was then a little under two years old and lost the ability to walk. I remember the nurse visiting and screaming. I also remember being taken out of the hospital and being held in a nurse's arms in front of the Bolton Royal Infirmary and my picture being used on a collections' envelope in late 1932 or 1933.

In pre-National Health days patients had pay for their health care. My mother contributed weekly, through the newsagent, to a communal insurance. For those who had no money and could not draw on 'insurance' there was charity. Most money was collected on 'flag' days when paper flags, bearing the name of the charity, were sold to passers-by in the street in the same way as money is collected by selling red poppies before Armistice Day. Other money was collected through distributing envelopes that people could fill with small change, for many people did not use cheques until the 1940s.

I have happy memories of playing on the stretch of ground we called the tip that lay between our house and the nearest terrace houses on Holly Grove. The tip was an undulating expanse of slag from old iron workings and the waste from cleaning out the clinker from cotton mills. I particularly enjoyed the tip in the summer when the corporation cut the long grass and we imagined it was a haystack. Freda and Leonard saw me as too small to include in their games, but nobody worried then that we might be abducted.

While the mid- and late-1930s was for many people a period of economic depression, unemployment and personal deprivation, it was probably when my parents were happiest. Our father's older four children were married and our mother presumably felt that she and her children provided the family focus. In 1938 the house was redecorated and the front room panelled and lit with candle-like wall lamps and a wheel-shaped chandelier. We could afford a maid who lived in the attic, which was indescribably cold in winter and hot in summer. It had a sloping roof and was accessible only through a steep stairway behind a landing door. Until I used it for making model aeroplanes and chemistry experiments, it had been the room of one of my half sisters. A storage space in the eaves off the attic housed old photographs of the family from Poland, but alas these were considered unimportant, so were forgotten and abandoned.

We went on annual holidays, always with a heavy trunk that was a struggle to get down to the taxi; my father often hired a car to take us to our seaside destination. Nobody, but nobody we knew considered going on holiday to a non-seaside location. When Brenda got married in 1947 and we learnt that they were going to tour southern England, I was astounded that they could regard that as a holiday. Holidays were hard work for our mother, for only once or twice did we go to an actual hotel. Normally, we went to a boarding house with cooking facilities, so prepared our own food.

My father was a creature of habit. As befitting a tailor he dressed well and at all times wore a waistcoat with a gold watch chain. His shoes, which were always black, were well polished and he wore different ones each day. The grey spats he wore above his shoes were fitted with a special spat hook to allow him to fasten them tightly. He wore summer, winter and spring-weight top coats according to the season. He came home for lunch, which must have been a rush, but so did most people as offices and shops traditionally closed then for an hour. He normally came home around 7 p.m. At lunch and dinner time he would walk to the drinks cabinet in the front room to pour himself a shot of Old Navy rum, wearing out a recognizable path in the carpet. He was not a drinking man, but would occasionally call in at the Grapes pub near the shop for a drink.

He could read Yiddish written in Hebrew script and every now and then got a batch of newspapers from the USA, particularly *The Forward*, which in summer he would read on the front doorstep. I remember seeing Babe Ruth mentioned in the newspaper and failed to understand how a grown man could be called Babe. I think my father thought he was a Jewish baseball player. We had a wind-up gramophone for which one had to change the metal needle for every record change and he had several records including one of High Holiday chanting and another with humorous songs including one about a drunken cantor. Our total record library was only about 20, all scratched, of which the most played was 'Tiptoe through the tulips'. Except for playing cards with *lansleit* on a Sunday night, usually whist or rummy, my father had few diversions.

It was with some reluctance that my mother, who was fond of the cinema, would persuade him to take her to a film, but once the war started that rarely happened. Mother, however, often took me to the cinema, which I greatly enjoyed. I particularly remember Nelson Eddy and Jeanette Macdonald singing musicals and historically-based films such as *Beau Geste*, the *Four Feathers* and *Gunga Din*. Retail shops, though not workshops, closed for half a day each Wednesday and my father took the opportunity to go to the Turkish baths, which were at the time quite popular with businessmen. He occasionally went on holiday with his brother Morris after his wife Rachel died prematurely in 1940. The most exciting of these trips was a cruise in 1938 to the Canary Islands via Gibraltar. He brought back a rather poorly made cane *chaise-longue* with all sorts of appendages and seating adjustments, which became his pride and joy and in which he would sit on the few warm Sundays in the garden. It took up a lot of space in the corridor and became a bone of contention with my mother when it began to disintegrate. He also brought home a tiny little lion made of ivory, which in some ways became my first real link to Africa. Money was tight and my mother resented asking for small sums and not being trusted with a larger expense account. She felt she had no money of her own.

The Second World War
This period of family stability lasted until just before the war when my mother developed diabetes and was hospitalized for two weeks. At that time diabetes was a real trauma. Insulin had been discovered in 1922 and was administered with a metal syringe and reusable needles that had to be sterilized between injections. Because of the thickness of the needles my mother had bruises all over her injection areas. Plastic syringes and short micro-thin needles now obviate most such problems. Managing diabetes was time-consuming. My mother kept her syringe and needles in surgical spirit in a stainless steel box. We had no refrigerator so she kept the insulin on the windowsill and had to buy new vials every fortnight. Only one type of insulin was available. Blood glucose testing meant urine testing, not with the paper sticks that change colour that were common when I developed diabetes in the 1980s, but with liquids one had to heat using products like Benedict's solution, which changed colour. She also had periodic blood tests at the hospital. There must have been times when mother had highs and lows without realizing it, so failed to make the

readjustments needed to avoid the complications so common at the time. She became blind at 65 and her half sister Sarah had a leg amputated; mother was always frightened that the same fate awaited her. Aunt Toby developed kidney and heart problems in her fifties. Mother had to change her diet, weigh her food and balance fats, proteins and carbohydrates. At that time doctors recommended a quite high fat and protein diet. For such a good cook, changing her diet overnight but continuing to bake and create rich foods for her family must have been a real challenge.

The war brought instant stress. At first we had to tape all the windows and stick net on them to limit breakage from bomb blasts and to provide blackout. Air-raid wardens would visit our house if chinks of light showed through poorly closed curtains. We adapted the dank cellar mother had used to store potatoes and apples into an air-raid shelter by building an extra concrete wall and installing lighting. My half brother Barney was called up as a special constable rather than a soldier, so he stayed at home, but it meant my father having to do two jobs. Running the shop became more complicated as cloth was only obtained with permits. Customers had to bring in clothing coupons introduced at the beginning of the war. As father could not read the regulations for himself this was a strain. Bespoke tailors had to comply with rules to decrease the amount of cloth in a suit by reducing the trouser ends to 19 inches in diameter, by omitting turn-ups and by reducing flaps and lapel sizes. In retrospect, it was pointless because bespoke tailors bought cloth by the suit length, so the rules only meant more cloth in the waste bin. Father was called before the local magistrate, the shoe seller Mr Beswick, and fined £55 for a turn-up infringement. This was as much as the cost of more than 12 bespoke tailor-made suits. He was very upset.

Food rationing was introduced from 1939 – 1s 2d worth of meat per person (a few ounces of good meat or a lot of fatty or bony meat); 8 oz butter, margarine and cooking fat; 2 oz tea; 8 oz sugar; 4 oz jam or marmalade; and 1 oz cheese per week. From 1941 a points system was introduced that allowed one to choose other foods like biscuits, cereals and canned goods. At different times the amount of the ration was adjusted and bonuses given at Christmas. The distribution of eggs was controlled and each person received only about 30 a year. At times the situation brought touches of comedy. My father did not cook but liked to make his own breakfast, which often involved cooking oatmeal porridge overnight in a double pan left to cook slowly over the embers of the fire. He was also drawn to the dried egg introduced in about 1942, which was off ration. It had to be carefully mixed with water to avoid lumps and often turned out rubbery, but once he mistook the tin of mustard powder for egg powder. Because she was diabetic, mother was allowed extra rations of cheese and eggs. Nowadays such foods would have been regarded as too high in cholesterol or fat to be recommended for diabetics. The general health of the population improved during the war because people ate more complex carbohydrates and vegetables and less meat, sugar and fat. Maternal mortality dropped and with the special distribution of milk at school, of concentrated orange juice and cod liver oil, and vitamin and mineral enriched flour and cereals nutritional deficiencies were avoided.[13]

Transport was limited, bus schedules curtailed and at night headlamps emitted only small slits of light. People went out at night far less. In Bolton we were fortunate as we still had double-decker electric trams, which I took to secondary school from 1942. They rattled and their steel wheels on steel rails were noisy, but we missed them when they were withdrawn soon after the war. We rarely travelled, so it was a shock to see streets full of rubble when we visited Manchester soon after its fire bombing in 1941. Holidays were out, which must have been hard for my parents, though articles were published extolling the virtues of holidays at home.

Even for a small boy war was not unexpected. For a year the news has been full of Hitler's demands, concessions, atrocities, insubordination and renunciation of agreements. We were keen listeners to what we then called the wireless and I have vivid memories of walking with my siblings to get the wet battery, as heavy as a modern car battery, charged at a store nearby to keep the wireless running. At first most people did not want war. Britons had terrible memories of the First World War only 20 years earlier when more than a million Commonwealth soldiers were killed. Many men had come back maimed. My brother-in-law Nat, my oldest half sister's husband who had been in the Levant in 1917 and 1918 , kept having recurrences of malaria; and the father of John Orrell, my best friend at secondary school, died from his wounds ten years after the war. There were so many widows and single women with no prospects of marriage. People still remembered the effects of poison gas, with men lying in wet blankets for years while their skin healed. There were still no antibiotics. Books and magazines contained numerous pictures of the destruction of European towns.

Everyone mourned someone, yet what had the war accomplished? Many people were still poor; economic and social development had been set back and jobs were still difficult to obtain. With relatives in Poland and the *Jewish Chronicle* having sensitized us to the true nature of fascism, we followed events closely. We knew that war was imminent, that Britain had not stood still, that air-raid shelters were being built, that the air force had expanded, that barrage balloons were being raised and that refugees from Germany had been welcomed. We were on holiday in St Anne's when war was declared. We listened to Neville Chamberlain on the radio and were riveted. We realized that we were in for a long haul. The immediate impact was the arrival in our schools of evacuees from London and the south of England – many of them refugees and cockney kids who spoke 'funny'. We were issued gas masks and soon ration books, and it was apparent that quite a lot of planning had been undertaken between the appeasement of Munich and the invasion of Poland.

Though the war introduced strain into our lives it was a period of important changes. The last two of our half sisters left the house, first Sarah, who had been out of work, joined the Wrens (Women's Royal Naval Service) and Dora, who was a hairdresser, moved to Derby to practise with her sister Anne. When the war persisted she became a tram conductor, or clippie as they were known colloquially, and later a tram driver, the first woman to do that job in the Midlands. Towards the end of the war she became a plane spotter who sat with silhouettes of enemy planes and when they came over she counted the different types and phoned in the information. My sisters provided me with a vicarious experience of the war – Sarah brought home bits of shrapnel and Dora gave me details of different planes and helped me develop my hobby of building 1/72 scale models and collecting photos of different aircraft. It was a time of austerity that we grew to accept as a normal condition.

The hostilities hardly affected Bolton. There were few air raids and after a time our father refused to sleep in the cellar, even when the sirens sang out their shrill warning. On several nights we stood outside our house watching Manchester burning from the incendiary bombs the Germans had dropped. Father was very concerned about our wellbeing, particularly after Ruth, our baby sister was born on 5 November 1942, the day we heard news of the victory of El Alamein by General Montgomery in the Western Desert and of the first great victory by the Soviet armies in repulsing the Germans at Stalingrad.

These events signalled to us that the war would be won and for the first time church bells rang.

Father used to look for black market eggs, for he insisted that mother and Ruth should have an egg every day for breakfast. Mother had stored such items as sugar, tinned fruit and soap in 1939 when there was a threat of war and these supplies helped us weather the wartime shortages. We still managed to go on the occasional holiday to nearby seaside spots like Blackpool and we longed to know what the illuminations would be like after the war. However, we never again went as a whole family, normally mother, father, me and Ruth, once she was born. I remember father trying to talk to some Polish airmen and feeling inadequate when he could not remember any of the Polish he knew as a second language as a child. Brother Leonard helped out on a farm near Preston in the summer months and wanted to continue in agriculture, but his grades were not good enough to postpone national service and he had to join the army in 1943. Our half brother Barney was invalided out of the special constabulary in 1944 after a serious bout of pneumonia brought about by duty on foot patrol in the worst winter of the century. He never really recovered. One lung eventually had to be removed and during his sickness father supported his own and Barney's family until Barney died of meningitis in 1947. It was a great strain and was one of the causes of my father's relatively rapid decline.

Depression, deaths and disintegration

In 1947, during that grim period immediately after the war, father died of kidney failure. Though the war in Britain was stressful, there had at least been a sense of shared hardship. Class barriers weakened, women did men's work, there was a heightened sense of volunteerism; in fact, it was a cheerful time of upbeat songs and cheeky jokes, of full employment and of optimism for better postwar times. Before the war there had been unemployment and quite a lot of xenophobia. I remember people saying that if higher wages were given to poor people they would use it for drink, that if baths were installed they would use them for coal. What really happened during the war was that rations improved people's health and, encouraged by double summer time, many people had allotments on which they grew fresh vegetables. With whole families working they could afford to improve their homes and they became house proud.

Before the war we children were frightened to walk in the 'valley', an area of small terrace houses about a quarter of a mile from our house, in case the kids there threw stones at us or at least hurled insults. It was alleged that policemen even refused to go there unless there were three of them. Their houses were shabby, the men hung around the door of the pub looking unkempt and surly and many of the children, often without shoes, were dressed in rags. During the war people began to paint their front doors in bright colours, hang pretty curtains, grow flowers in planters and dress smartly. Drinking declined, for it was no longer the only way to alleviate misery.

After the war, the winter of 1946–47 was terrible. Even as late as March, when our eldest sister Brenda got married, there was snow into which my cousin Monty dropped her while trying to carry her to a taxi that could not get close enough. At this time rationing was tightened and extended to coal, heating oil, flour and many other products we had been able to buy freely in the war years. At Brenda's wedding, the small children who ran out from the ceremony to the reception area were the first to be served with pre-mixed gin and fruit squash, which the waiters had presumed was fruit squash.

Besides the austerity of the postwar period when change seemed glacial, our family suffered many setbacks. In 1946 father finally heard that none of his family in Poland had survived the Holocaust – in all 39 of his sisters, brothers-in-law, their children, grandchildren and close cousins had perished. He had tried to get news through the Purple Cross, a special unit of the Red Cross dedicated to tracking down survivors, and the waiting had been very trying. In December 1946 his overweight sister Toby died in Leeds of kidney failure and diabetes, not to mention Barney in 1947. Running the shop, working long hours and facing up to the deaths of relatives took their toll.

One pleasurable time for him was the wedding of our youngest half-sister Dora to Sol, an American, in Derby in 1944. They had a son, father's first grandson after 12 granddaughters, and left for America in 1945. This was a time when many British women were going to America as GI brides. Father hoped to visit the USA, which he saw as the land of the future and was impressed by the vigour of Jewish life evidenced from reading the Yiddish newspaper, *Forward*. The US impact had been fast but emphatic. In the north of England many people repeated the mantra that what was wrong with the Americans was that they were 'over paid, over sexed and over here'. But as kids we chased after them hoping for gum. Older relatives wanted cigarettes and drink, but they introduced more than gum, sweets, silk stockings and cigarettes in soft paper packets. They brought lively dance music. Swing and big dance bands became popular and were still popular when I went off to college in 1949. They brought gimmicks of all kinds and accelerated Britain's move towards adopting all manner of goods to improve one's daily life. They demanded ice, which we did not use since home refrigerators were still a novelty. After the war their drinks like Coca-Cola began to edge out Dandelion and Burdock, or Sasparella,[14] which had previously been our popular ones. We had never seen so many canned products and certainly not canned drinks. American films increased in popularity as the British film industry churned out very good patriotic war films, but not musicals with glamour girls.

Soon after Dora's departure father learned for certain that Sarah had married out. It was a blow. Intermarriage at that time was taboo and she was the first in our family to do so; he had not seen her for five years. Sarah had been the best educated of his daughters, but badly affected by the 1930s Depression. The war gave her activity and excitement, freedom from the restrictions of the small-town atmosphere of Bolton's closed Jewish society, and a chance to be her own person. In 1947 a motorcycle knocked father down at the side of the road near home. He was not badly hurt but the succession of mishaps left him feeling low. When Freda became engaged to her first cousin Sidney and a family wedding was in the offing in 1948 he cheered up a bit, made a suit and bought a new hat and shoes to wear to the Shabbos service in Hanley, the groom's town. On the Saturday before the wedding, he came back feeling ill and, after 36 hours of convulsive hiccoughs brought on by kidney failure, died a few hours after Freda's wedding. Within two years our family was reduced from seven at home to just four. I went off to Nottingham University in 1949 and Leonard got married in 1953, so within five years only mother and Ruth were still at home.

Mother went into a deep depression. She felt that, having been a drudge and wife since childhood, her life was basically over and that she could do nothing useful. Father had died without signing his will. The doctor suggested he sign it on his deathbed, but the family felt it would be too hard on him. It was a tragic mistake, for the children of his first marriage challenged his estate. This was a year before the law was changed that would have allowed mother to keep the house and half his assets. As it was, the house became part of an estate worth little more than £5000 that had to be split 18 ways. Mother kept custody but not ownership of the house, but the few rundown houses father owned, including 46 Bark Street, had to be sold when property prices were low. Relations between the two halves of the family were strained and several, including some of Barney's children, had nothing more to do with us for over 50 years. Leonard, then 23, an inexperienced tailor and just out of the armed forces, took over the business and did not appoint Ray's husband Nat, who had worked for father for over 20 years, as manager. This resulted in him branching out on his own. Within a few years dad's tailoring firm had collapsed and in the mid-1950s Leonard became a furrier in the business his parents-in-law owned. By the early 1950s four of our half sisters and ten of their children were living in the Los Angeles area. Our family had disintegrated. Curiously, I became the catalyst that eventually renewed contact when I visited UCLA for the first time in 1966.

Though I came home during vacations, my stays there became progressively shorter once I went to university. For the first few Christmas breaks, I worked at the Bolton post office for £1 a day, first sorting letters and later delivering them. I loved meeting people I had never known and exploring the neighbourhood. One summer I worked for Parks and Gardens cutting grass and clipping hedges on council housing estates. My two middle-aged, working-class colleagues taught me a great deal about life. In fact, I learnt so much that they gave me a little certificate at the end of six weeks. They used to send me with their enamel tea cans to collect hot water because young housewives seemed more receptive to me and would offer me milk and an occasional biscuit. Although we were unsupervised, we worked very hard and it was a rewarding experience. For part of the vacation I would go to Freda and Sid's house where mother and Ruth spent a lot of time – the great attraction being their small black and white TV set.

University was, however, a busy time. In seven years I only once had a vacation in which I did not travel, have a holiday job, or take part in an excavation or geographical field school. I was slowly loosening my family ties and Bolton had little to offer me. With fewer visits, I lost touch with relatives. I now occasionally regret that I did not get to know more about my father's cousins or my mother's half sisters and brothers. In hindsight, I should have done more for my mother and sister Ruth, but friendships at college became more important to me and the few romances I had were in Nottingham. My mother visited me in Nottingham twice in six years, but no one visited me at Cambridge. Looking back it is difficult to remember how complicated cross country travel could be in the 1950s when few people in our family owned cars. Visits to both Cambridge and Nottingham involved one or more changes of train.

In my early days in Africa family involvement was minimal. I wrote to my mother once a fortnight and to my sisters and brother only occasionally. In those days no one telephoned England, for it would have involved booking a call 24 hours ahead, waiting in the tele-communications centre for it to come through and then talking on a crackly line. A three-minute call cost nearly as much as a day's work. The first time I called abroad was in 1965 when Eunice was in Australia. Satellite technology began to change the situation in the 1980s, by which time I was living in the United States. I did not go on leave until 1960 and after dashing madly around seeing family and friends, as well as shopping for items unavailable in Africa, I was happy to get back to Africa. I had by then realized that Africa was my new home and that was where I would make my own family.

Eunice

We met at a Uganda Club dance I had organized in April 1959. I had taken another partner but that relationship was going nowhere. Eunice was with some American friends and I was fascinated. It was rare to meet an African woman on equal terms. I had always thought of myself as a bore because I found small talk difficult and I had not had a great deal of success with women. Academic work had been the sublimation for my sex drive. Eunice seemed to respond to my enthusiasm. We danced despite dancing being my weakest suit. I cannot carry a tune or rhythm; I dance out of step and concentrate too much on my footwork. But Eunice was tolerant even though her open-toed shoes made her very vulnerable. We enjoyed ourselves.

My companion had gone home early with friends so I took Eunice back to Makerere College School where she stayed with Joyce Masembe because it was too late to go back to Gayaza. I remember talking for hours in the car. We arranged to meet again, which we did often that year. Our pleasures were simple. We sat by the lake at Entebbe, walked in the botanical gardens, visited the earthworks by Lugard's fort[15] in Mengo and, to set schoolgirl tongues wagging, strolled through the attractive grounds of Gayaza High School. We visited friends, danced at Top Life in Mengo or had tea at home. At that time our group of friends included several Americans, notably Jill and Hap Funk from the US consulate, and some Asians, particularly Neela Korde whose parents invited us to the best Indian food I have ever tasted. We were usually together only at weekends. On Sundays Eunice had to go back to Gayaza early because the teaching staff prayed together for the success of the coming week after dinner at 8 or 9 p.m. and she was very conscientious.

We were circumspect or perhaps naïve, for Eunice and I never spent the night together until we began to go on safaris upcountry 18 months after we had met. If she stayed overnight it was at her brother Lukonge's house near Namirembe – once much to her inconvenience when all the wheels of her Volkswagen were stolen, a not uncommon experience in Kampala where it was customary to remove windscreen wipers for safety during fine weather. There was no telephone for teachers to use at Gayaza so we communicated by letter. I still think that letters are better suited for people in love than telephone calls or even e-mails. They demand that greater effort, a little extra thought, a chance to wax lyrical and be poetic. At times, particularly on Saturdays when it was late, I would follow Eunice's car to the Gayaza turnoff 11 miles from my house. It was exciting to drive back late at night on a fairly empty road and glimpse serval cats, owls, the occasional small antelope and other wild animals in my headlamps. Eunice once came up to visit me on my excavation at Bigo with Roland Oliver, whose book on missionaries in East Africa she had read at college. Her Volkswagen Beetle was probably the smallest car ever to have made the rough road to Bigo at that time.

Eunice's family history was typical of Baganda but with some unusual twists. Much of it I did not know about when we married in February 1961 and only slowly did a fuller picture emerge, some details not until I accompanied her on her last visit to Uganda in 1996. Her father Yoeri Lubega came from the Ssingo area in north Buganda. In the 1890s this was a troubled frontier zone with war raging between the largely Christian kingdom of Buganda and the Bunyoro kingdom to the north. The British had brought the rump of General Gordon's (later Emin Pasha's) old army, made up of Nubian mercenaries from central Sudan, down from northern Uganda as a paid fighting force. They had two functions – to keep the peace between feuding chiefs in the Buganda religious wars that pitted Catholics against Protestants and Muslims against both in a fluid sequence of unholy alliances, and as an armed force to protect British interests. In 1897 these Nubian soldiers rebelled against the British;

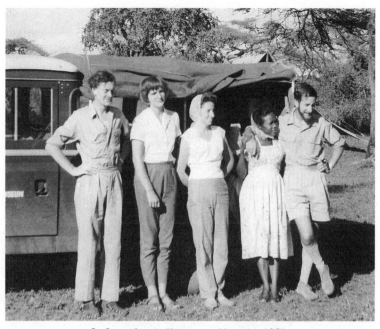

3. On safari in Karamoja, Uganda, 1961.

for a time the kings of both Buganda and Bunyoro joined them and there was chaos.

In 1891 or 1892 Eunice's grandfather, Muswangali, went off to fight the Bunyoro, leaving his pregnant wife Damali behind. On his return he found that his village had been raided and his wife was missing. Some years later he learnt from a visitor that his wife had been spotted in Masindi, a small town in Bunyoro and that she had a small child with her. He travelled the 80 miles to Masindi, redeemed his wife and arranged to go back to reclaim his son, Yoeri, Eunice's father. He collected sufficient funds to return and redeem his son. In 1900, the Uganda Agreement was signed, which formalized the British protectorate and freed all slaves obtained as a result of the recent wars. Eunice's father always hid the fact from his immediate family that he had been born into slavery and the story only came to light when elders related stories of his life at the naming of his son Seguya as his heir at a clan ceremony in 1978. Yoeri was one of the first students to attend King's College school in Budo, the first Protestant boys' boarding school in Buganda founded in 1906. Missionaries realized that conversion could only come about through education.[16] Rather than resisting this influence the Baganda readily cooperated and many of the earliest students were drawn from the Baganda elite. The British used well-educated Baganda to spread their influence to other parts of Uganda where they served as missionaries, ministers, clerks and schoolteachers. Yoeri was a school teacher and travelled and worked in several areas of northern Uganda before retiring early to be a coffee farmer at Nakwaya where Eunice was born in the nearby clinic of Kiboga in 1927.

Yoeri married Esita Yakimu on 23 January 1915. Esita came from quite far away, so, apart from her mother Tezira Nautome who lived with them in her later years, we know very little about that side of the family. Eunice was the fifth of ten children, four girls and six boys born between 1922 and 1940. Yoeri alo had three children by another woman, but it was not until 1996 that I knew of their existence. She was a small child and spoke little about her youth, but wrote tellingly about her schooling in a book edited by Roger Bannister.[17] Her father was strict and maintained a traditional household in which he and his wife had separate rooms. His mother-in-law slept outside the main house. He and his sons, once they were old enough, ate separately at a table in the main room. His wife and daughters ate later on mats in a different room.

Like many Baganda he was a small coffee farmer and grew most of his food in the *lusuku* or garden around the house. The banana grove provided *matoke*, the staple food of the Baganda, and served as a place for family burial. Our third daughter, who was stillborn, rests there. Coffee prices[18] were good and, though poor, he could support his family. He enjoyed hunting and participating in the coffee cooperative, but never forgot he had been a teacher and spent time teaching English to his children at home. He was concerned about their health and appearance and had a little scoop, a device common throughout Africa at the time, with which he took out excess earwax. One day he dug a little too deep and from childhood Eunice remained deaf in one ear.

Eunice spoke little about her childhood, but one event stood out. When she was about four, a paternal great aunt died and she was named as her heir and had to go to a special ceremony to receive her inheritance. They travelled a long way and she grew excited at the prospect of what she might inherit, but was quickly brought down to earth when she discovered it was a rusted metal case and a *kikoyi*, a striped wrapper worn under the traditional woman's *basuti*. It was threadbare and too big to wear. Such material impoverishment confused her and she began to cry. That the great aunt's family now regarded her as an adult, knelt before her, gave her locally made banana beer to drink and called her 'mother', made things worse.

Being aware of the stigma of poverty, her father bought land in his children's names and Eunice was given about 20 acres of farming land in Ssingo.[19] Eunice spoke little about her mother, though she remembered, with some lingering resentment, that she called her 'big head' because she was a forceps baby. Curiously, our first child, Sheba, also had a forceps delivery, but Eunice never called her big head.

Fortunately, unlike many African parents of the time, Eunice's father believed in educating girls and, after a year at the Nakwaya village primary school, Eunice was sent to a boarding school her older sister Esther attended at Ndejje, 40 miles away. The trip to school often entailed a two-day walk. Occasionally, they would get a lift in a truck or their father would cycle over rough roads and tracks with the two girls perched precariously on his bicycle. Eunice loved Ndejje, especially the songs she learnt from a missionary named Dorothy Allen. Ndejje gave her discipline, a sense of duty, modesty and respect, and a love of the sacrifice of missionary service.

At Gayaza and King's College Budo she made close friendships that continued as her cohort moved on to university at Makerere and into government office and politics. Her choral experience of singing with the Nightingales at Budo was particularly enriching and led to her participation in the annual performance of Handel's *Messiah* and madrigals at Oxford where she spent a year after graduation taking her diploma in education at Lady Margaret Hall.

Eunice was among the first female students at Makerere and was the first woman to graduate in East or Central Africa, though others had graduated abroad. She threw herself into women's and girls' education, both before we married and later when she became the first Ugandan woman to direct women's education at the Ministry of Education. She was co-opted onto many boards and committees, including the Infantile Malnutrition Committee, which sought to improve the nutrition of babies once they were weaned. Her favourite committee, however, was the Uganda Association of University Women of which she became the first African president in 1964. In that capacity she worked closely with many other women's groups. She spent a lot of time on a project to ensure the legal rights of all Uganda women to their inheritances.

She was also active on a committee to help needy girls obtain a secondary education and each year several girls were interviewed for boarding school scholarships. Eunice's capabilities as a mother, busy education official, keen gardener, enthusiastic dressmaker, choral singer, homemaker and loving wife with a lively interest in African politics impressed me greatly. She travelled to conferences in Kenya, Zanzibar and Tanganyika, attended Organization of African Unity meetings in Addis Ababa and Nigeria, each time bringing back wonderful clothes and gifts for the family, and in 1965 represented Uganda on a four-month mission to Australia. I was proud of her and admired the way she gave up a high position in Ugandan education to accompany me to Ghana in 1967. Some friends and family were disappointed with her choice because they felt she could have advanced further by remaining in Uganda, but political events, the Obote revolution, the destruction of the Buganda government and the exile of the Kabaka and his family had left her troubled and happy to explore life in West Africa. One passion we shared was a mutual interest in new cultures, travel and seeing how our world connected with others. This travel bug was something we passed on to our children in different measures.

It took her a while to settle down in Ghana. Because she was a Uganda national she could not get a job as an educational administrator; the stillbirth of our daughter in late August 1967 set her back badly and she missed her friends, family and voluntary activities. She noticed that wherever I moved I found fellow Englishmen, Jews and archaeologists, but she, as a Ugandan woman, felt like an exotic flower plucked from its soil. In 1969 I persuaded her to enrol in the new postgraduate library studies programme at Legon. She loved the experience, respected her teachers and, before she knew where she was, she was pregnant again with our daughter Helen, whom she also named Namulindwa, 'the long awaited one'. On graduation she worked at the central library in Accra for a year with very supportive colleagues. In 1972 she transferred to the Balme Library at the university where she also made many good friends. Before long she was encouraged to serve on the council of Volta Hall, the only women's college, and served for two years as a tutor appreciating the sisterhood of fellows and students. She was happy in Ghana and it was a wrench to move to Los Angeles in 1977.

Settling down in Los Angeles was made easier by having three loving sisters-in-law who, despite having had little contact with them for 25 years, welcomed us into their fold. Getting a permanent job, which I discuss in another chapter, proved difficult, as did the pace of life, the consumerism, high cost of living and being parents in a culture where controls were very different from those in Africa. For the first time in our lives we were in debt with a car loan, mortgage, credit cards and no home help. In Africa we had become used to entertaining, having our floor and furniture polished, using cloth napkins, making meals from fresh ingredients, ironing clothes, having students round for chats, people dropping by, quiet evenings reading, eating on our veranda at a set hour, listening to the BBC, taking the children to the swimming club or beach without it being a great effort and knowing everyone on a small campus.

Los Angeles was the biggest culture shock we ever experienced. The university was overwhelming; we hated the bureaucracy and the phoney greetings without any real contact, but somehow we survived. The first few years were particularly rough because our assets were tied up in houses in Uganda and Cambridge and half the personal effects we shipped from Ghana had suffered water damage, thus robbing us of precious photographs, books and keepsakes. Although the girls quickly adapted to the different educational system, life was again hardest for Eunice who had to retrain by taking courses at California State and Pepperdine universities. She eventually settled down to an unreliable routine as a substitute teacher. It was work that did not bring friendships and she often went to five different schools in a week. She sometimes went for days without getting called, even though she had got up early in the hope of receiving a summons from a school. She also felt isolated from African affairs and few people seemed interested in, or called upon, her African expertise. Slowly, in time, she became wrapped up in domestic activities, particularly in gardening and cooking; she also learnt to use a computer.

In 1992 I began to sense a change in Eunice. At first I put it down to ageing. She had less self-confidence and seemed unsure of what she wanted to do. She became more dependent, less willing to make commitments and preferred me to come along when she shopped. She began to lose things; at first I thought it was accidental. She lost her camera when we went to Jamaica and forgot where she had left a new raincoat I had bought her in London. She forgot ingredients from simple recipes she knew out of the top of her head and began to burn food, particularly rice, through failing to adjust the gas or check on her cooking. For a short time I thought she might have a major hearing problem. From childhood she had been deaf in one ear but coped remarkably well. If our youngest daughter, Helen, who lived at home during the 1993–94 school year, told Eunice she would be out for dinner, Eunice would forget and grumble about her not being there for the meal. She had her hearing checked but nothing was amiss. In 1993 I finally realized that it was more than just absent-mindedness or deafness.

We were invited to participate in a National Endowment for the Humanities Summer Institute for schoolteachers in Casper, Wyoming. I was to talk about the history and geography of Africa and Eunice about the more practical aspects of teaching about Africa, and we were to be paid handsomely. Eunice was excited; it was recognition, a chance to do what she wanted. She planned carefully. She would talk about personal names, festivals, foods, art symbols like *adinkra* designs from Ghana, proverbs and show the teachers how to make and play the board game *oware*. She busied herself with her dolls to make sure that she had good examples of both Ugandan and Ghanaian clothes. She was also going to tell the teachers about her life, about teaching in Africa and the changes taking place in the status of women there. Eunice knew a lot about all these matters but when it came to the classes she became confused. She forgot what she had planned the night before and could not remember the teachers' names. In the end I joined her during her presentations, prompted her and generally gave her back her confidence.

Casper is situated at over 5000 feet. When we casually discovered at a local pharmacy that Eunice's blood pressure was extremely high, I put her confusion down to a combination of altitude and hyper-tension, but the following year her symptoms became more obvious. She began to lose her way on routes to schools she knew extremely well. Often she would write and rewrite simple letters and bank checks. She began to hide things, scattering her jewellery among different purses. She hid her keys and was constantly searching for them. She was called on fewer days to serve as a substitute teacher as she would lose her way to schools she had visited scores of times. She would bring back keys she should have left at school and preparing for classes and grading became more and more time-consuming. Suspecting she might be in the early stage of Alzheimer's I arranged to see her doctor at the Kaiser Hospital.[21] At that time they had no Alzheimer's unit and in common with many medical professionals they seemed to have neither knowledge nor interest in early onset memory loss in an otherwise fit woman in her sixties.

In August 1994 I went to Ghana as director of the University of California Education Abroad Programme. Because there was an accommodation problem and I was to go to a conference in Benin during the first month, it was agreed that Eunice should follow me after a month. She also wanted to visit friends and relatives in London. Though her brother met her at the airport, she had difficulty making it to the house of friends, who instantly realized she was very confused. She had packed strange things in a strange way and was unsure about how to visit her family. We had many anxious telephone calls to straighten matters out and on arriving in Ghana she had a terrible time at the airport until I rescued her, but by then aggressive Ghanaian porters had importuned her to give away quite a bit of her English money. She was constantly repeating the same questions. She had quite forgotten that she had been in Ghana five years earlier, but had less difficulty remembering that we had lived there 20 years before.

She never learnt the names of the students with whom she associated on an almost daily basis and became more and more paranoid, hiding her keys and her handbag, and locking doors and windows. She kept accusing the maid of stealing her personal items and ultimately reduced her to tears; in the end we had to employ our old maid Barbara who was less well organized, less efficient and lived far away, but at least Eunice knew her. Eunice would go walking every day at 6.30 a.m., normally with the university librarian Christine Kisiedu, but could never remember when the time or place for the meeting was altered. She also lost many more items when we went on trips so I had to pack and check her bags all the time. We both enjoyed our time in Ghana; we were close, spent a lot of time together, loved our garden, and appreciated the friendship of the students who often came to the house for tea, to use my telephone or just to chill out. She found it difficult to organize herself for leaving and became confused by the extra activities.

On our return we went back to the hospital where Eunice had a standard test to evaluate her short-term memory. Her score was poor; she was unable to remember three simple words that had been told to her a few minutes before, even though she was still agile in spelling words backwards and similar exercises. Over the next few years her score slowly declined until 1999 when it proved futile to ask her any simple questions. In September 1995 her driver's licence was rescinded on her doctor's recommendation. It was a bitter blow to her.

It took away her sense of independence and made her realize that something really was wrong. I remained in denial for several more years. She had a battery of tests, cat scans, MRIs, thyroid tests, spinal punctures and electro readings of her brain function. Many of them were uncomfortable. The only way to diagnose Alzheimer's was to eliminate other diseases and disabilities that could cause memory loss, such as minor strokes or a thyroid condition.

I kept hoping they would discover a small brain tumor, remove it miraculously with keyhole surgery and restore my wife to me so that we could enjoy the promise of our retirement and do all the wonderful things we had dreamed of, particularly travelling, improving our garden, dressing and marketing dolls in African dress and enjoying our family. It was not to be. We transferred our medical insurance to UCLA in early 1996 so that we could benefit from their Alzheimer's research expertise. New drugs, first Cognex and later Aricept, were being tried with a view to slowing the symptoms. We greedily devoured advice about other remedies like Vitamin E, Ibuprofen and Ginko Buloba, but her memory slowly disappeared. By late 1995 she began to lose her sense of direction. Going to hotels proved difficult because she would wander around if I were not there. Several times when she was not with me other people had to guide her back to her room. I stopped leaving her for even a short time on her own at a conference or meeting. I began to wait for her outside ladies toilets when shopping or at airports, for otherwise she did not know where to go when she came out.

Before her cognitive abilities disintegrated too much we decided to take a trip to England and Uganda so that she could see her friends and family. Eunice was very brave and realistic. She knew she had Alzheimer's and wanted to let everyone know that this would be her last chance to see them while she could still remember their faces and names, and have a normal conversation. We planned our journey for September to November when the transatlantic traffic would have lessened. We also partly built it around attending the Poznan meeting of the Society for Africanist Archaeology in Poland. We were in high spirits though we experienced further health setbacks. In January I began to have some jaw and arm pain. On visiting the hospital and undergoing a treadmill test it was discovered that I had a heart problem. I was kept in hospital and an angiogram determined that I required a triple bypass operation. In many ways my anxiety about caring for Eunice helped me to get well quickly. I depended on Eunice who took me walking each day until April when I had to give a lecture in Florida. By then we were walking more than two miles a day.

In May 1996 Eunice had her first seizure. It was frightening; she thrashed around, bit the inside of her mouth and tongue, rolled her eyes and remained unconscious for over half an hour. After a second attack we rushed her to hospital. She was subject to frequent attacks until a caring practitioner, Dr Meltzer, following frequent minor adjustments and changes of medication, managed to dose her correctly with a mixture of medicines so that by 2000 her seizures were small and manageable. In 1998 the attacks had been almost monthly; after each she was left with less mental ability and was handicapped for a few days with extreme tiredness, incontinence and immobility. By 1999 we had to use a wheelchair for a few days after every episode and built ramps from the house into the garden.

When we left for England in September 1996 most of that was still in the future. Though Eunice's appearance had not changed her behaviour had. She repeatedly asked the same questions and I had to help her with her clothes; she could no longer pack or unpack her case and she was reluctant to be left with people she could not remember. In conversations she remained silent, unsure of herself or of what the conversation was about. Her dependence on me meant that we spent a lot of time together. She became physically more loving. She had been a shy person, not wanting many people to touch her and embarrassed if I held her too affectionately in public. Her disease seemed to loosen her inhibitions and led her to welcome closer physical contact. I told her frequently how much she was loved; we hugged often and enjoyed the closeness that increased with the passing of time. A friend's wife would walk with her when I was in a meeting, but Eunice did not remember her name from one day to the next. She began to have increasing difficulty reading and I bought her a watch with big figures so she could at least tell the time, which she had begun to find difficult on a small watch.

In Uganda, though she enjoyed seeing her relatives, particularly her youngest sister Faith who was dying of cancer, everything became a blur. When I went to India for two weeks, leaving her in her sister Margaret's care, she lost the confidence to ask for what she wanted. All the things she had planned to do – attend Namirembe cathedral dressed in her best *busuti*, visit her old school at Ndejje, go to the palace where her old friend Lady Sarah, the Kabaka's mother, had lived, eat long remembered childhood foods – were left undone and she mainly accompanied Margaret on her daily rounds rather than fulfill her own wishes. On my return from India we did a few things on her wish list, but on our return home, she remained sad, occasionally bitterly resentful, about the things she had not done.

Her last trip to Africa was in January 1997 when we visited South Africa, a country she had always wanted to see since our aborted attempt in 1961. She wanted to see Mandela, or at least where he lived. I was on a United States Information Agency (USIA) mission in South Africa to see archaeological sites, advise on cultural conservation and give lectures in three cities. My old friend Bob LaGamma, whom I had known from my Togo trip in 1979, had arranged the trip and we were due to spend several days with him in Pretoria. When I travelled north, Eunice was to stay in Johannesburg with Violaine Junod, an old friend from Makerere days in the 1960s. Unfortunately, Violaine was unable to fetch Eunice from Pretoria, so a driver did and this got her off to a bad start. Initially, she forgot who Violaine was. Violaine had to leave her in the house for a short while and, on her return, found Eunice waiting with her bag at the front door wanting to 'go home'. Violaine quickly reassured her and never again left her side until I came back from the north four days later. Violaine bought picture postcards for her to send to family and friends and tried to help her write them, but she failed to complete a single card. It was her last attempt to write a letter apart from a brief love note to me in 1998 thanking me for caring for her.

Shortly after this trip her behavioural problems became more pronounced. She began to forget where she lived, could no longer remember phone numbers and got confused when she went into the garden. She would take sharp knives into the garden, presumably to cut up vegetation for compost. Three were lost, but gardeners clearing vegetation found one two years later. She kept leaving taps on, would absent-mindedly fill the bathtub or claim she had not had a bath only an hour after she had had one. She did strange things like putting grapefruit in the oven and ferreting away her possessions in strange places. Slowly, items of jewellery were misplaced or lost and some I have not yet found; a bunch of keys went missing; she was always looking for her purse. I began to put away her better jewellery and take away the purses. She began to pick up leaves, twigs and small stones and bring them into the house. She would nibble on dry cat and dog food as if they were snacks. A few times she wandered away, once while I was in the kitchen cooking and she was in the bedroom.

Fortunately, because of her Medicalert bracelet someone called the number and finally the police were alerted who called me to say where I could pick her up. The neighbours were good at looking out for her and making sure she did not stray. By late 1999 I had to lock the front door and back gate constantly.

In retrospect, I should have kept a log of her changes. It might have helped others in much the same way as Sir John Bayley's book about Iris Murdoch[22] helped me realize that millions of others, both patients and carers, go through the same travails. I learnt a lot from attending a carers' group for three years. The meetings could be depressing because they made one realize what huge problems some carers, many of whom are old or infirm, face with loved ones who are aggressive, afflicted with additional ailments like Parkinson's or a stroke, or have financial problems and unsupportive families. I was impressed by their fortitude and sense of devotion and I began to count my blessings. I enjoyed our support group pot-luck meals and felt assured that I could make it through difficult times blessed as I was with a loving family and an ability to research Alzheimer's through books, organizations and medical personnel at UCLA.

As her Alzheimer's progressed Eunice became much more affectionate and began to lose her Kiganda inhibitions. The Baganda are not demonstrative people and Eunice rarely hugged or kissed me or the children. Baganda women of her generation did not even pierce their ears; after the older two girls were born and I bought them earrings in Israel in 1967 they had their ears pierced, but Eunice waited until she got to Ghana, where babies have their ears pierced at birth, before she took the plunge. Though her memory was fading her love grew stronger. In any marriage there is competitiveness, especially if both partners work. It can be a stimulus to succeed, to prove oneself, but sometimes it brings tension. With our close interdependence that tension disappeared and I can honestly say that Eunice and I had our most loving relationship in the early years of her dementia. I think this love enabled me to face the more difficult years that developed after 2000.

What is remarkable about Eunice is the long time she had Alzheimer's. Her illness can be divided into three periods. In the early stage, which lasted from 1993 to 1997, she was mobile, could dress herself and converse, though increasingly in a confused fashion. During the middle stage she was still mobile but began to lose the ability to dress or wash herself and slowly became incontinent. She progressed from pads for the occasional accident, to padded pull-ups, to bulky wrap-around adult nappies. She became incontinent at night in 1998 and by the time we withdrew her from the adult day care centre in late 2000 she was fully incontinent and we were ordering nappies, bed protectors and all sorts of supplies through a mail order firm. From 1999 we had to use a wheelchair from time to time, particularly after a seizure. During this period her weight increased from under 130 to over 160 lbs. During this period her hand began to shake and we had to start feeding her; we bought her a lightweight plastic cup for drinking.

This middle period was when I felt most frazzled and in need of assistance. I was lucky. I noticed that the carer of an old man at the day care centre was East African and when I spoke to him I immediately realized from his accent that he was from Uganda. I asked him if he knew a Ugandan woman who might come to our house occasionally to sit with Eunice while I went shopping or did some writing. He said he had a sister and would bring her to our house. This is how we met Christine Nalubega who spent more than four years with us, first on Saturdays and from 8 p.m. each weekday. Before that our wonderful housekeeper from Guatemala, Margarita Perez, or her friend Rosalia, would help me as needed, but we felt that a Luganda speaker would be the most appropriate helper before Eunice lost all her language. Christine would take Eunice and Simcha our dog for a daily walk along our street; they became a familiar feature and people asked after Eunice when she did not appear.

The middle phase lasted until late 2001, though by September that year Eunice had to be supported on her walk, tired quickly and increasingly often was taken in the wheelchair. During the middle phase she became unable to sit in a bath, which meant adapting one of our bathrooms with grab rails and a walk-in shower with a bench. Changes were gradual but the deterioration was inexorable and by early 2002 she was clearly in the third stage of the disease. She had to have a hospital bed, with electric controls that enabled one to sit her up and bath her. We acquired a mechanical hoist (Hoyer lift) to lift her from the bed first into a wheelchair and later into a reclining 'geri' chair. Slowly her breathing became more difficult at night and oxygen was brought in. With lying in bed she developed pressure sores and an air mattress was ordered. With the help of the special mattress and constant vigilance we became skilful at obviating the dreaded bedsores that afflict so many people in Eunice's condition.

Many patients get sent to homes in the third stage where they can become depressed or refuse to eat. We tried to keep Eunice involved by playing classical music, which seemed to soothe her; occasionally, I could hear her trying to hum. I held her hand a lot or stroked her head and, particularly in the evening, would talk to her. Being with her was also relaxing for me. Her room, a lean-to on the wooden deck outside our bedroom, had been built in 1992. It had lots of windows and was intended as a place in which Eunice could exercise or sew; it also housed an extra closet and bookshelves. Shaded as it was by a big magnolia tree, Eunice called it the magnolia room. Though under-utilized in the early years, it was ideal for Eunice once she became bedridden, for it looked onto the garden she loved and in which she had laboured so diligently. We had fitted wooden blinds and other amenities, but in time the oxygen machine, humidifier and other items designed for Eunice's wellbeing overwhelmed the space. I believe Eunice liked that room because it protruded into the garden. On good days we would wheel her onto the deck for lunch where Tessa had fitted a misting devise that made even the hottest days bearable.

In early 2003 her condition slowly, almost imperceptibly, deteriorated. She stopped humming and words came only occasionally, often first thing in the morning as if she had practised them in her head during the night. One day she said 'I know you do' when I was telling her how much I loved her and at other times she would say 'thank you very much' when I bent down to kiss her or give her something. She lost the ability to say any names but occasionally called out to her mother or father. She slept more and more and had difficulty keeping her head from lolling to one or another side. Feeding became more difficult as she lost interest in food, though she was always delighted when chocolate ice cream appeared and her mouth would open without any urging. Her weight increased. I probably gave her too much to eat. It is often said that food can be a substitute for unrequited love but perhaps it was just my Jewish upbringing in which love means giving, sharing and nurturing and food is an essential component in that concern.

The very last phase of Eunice's life started in late August 2003 when she became even more detached and stopped eating food. We could give her a little soup and for a time, minced her meals and gave her baby food, but to no avail. She might take a little soothing sorbet or ice cream once a day, or for a time an occasional *matoke*, a cooking banana Christine brought, but by the end of September it was down to an occasional spoonful. As the hospice book predicted, the telltale sign of her passing was when she stopped drinking and, with the nurses, we counted down the weeks, days and finally hours. She developed a fever and her breathing became laboured; she could not focus her eyes and did not acknowledge my, or anyone else's, presence. Finally, she passed away peacefully on 4 October 2004, fortunately during the day so that I was at her side. It was if she had not died but was just in an altered state and I could hardly believe it.

Guided by the hospice chaplain, we decided on a memorial service and celebration of her life at St Marks Episcopal Church two weeks after her death. We chose that church because it is where they conduct a weekly service in Luganda and Eunice had remained true to the Church of Uganda, namely the Anglican or Episcopal Church transplanted to her homeland. It was a beautiful, uplifting occasion. The Kabaka of Buganda, HRH Ronald Mutebi II and her close friend Joyce Mpanga, former minister and member of parliament, sent messages to be read out at the service. More than 200 of her friends, fellow Ugandans, some of my former students, past colleagues and friends of our children and relatives shared in our sorrow and joy, including her brother Iga and niece Esther from England. For weeks letters arrived from all over the world speaking of her dignity, her smile, her welcoming hospitality and her achievements in Uganda, including a testimony from the speaker of the Uganda parliament who had been one of her students at the Lubiri School.

Children and family life

The arrival of children, Sheba in 1962, Tessa in 1963 and Helen, sadly after two miscarriages and a stillbirth, created our family and gave unity and meaning to our marriage. By the mid-1960s I had to make a difficult decision. Did I want to spend more time on my career, closet myself away to write, spend more days away from home on excavations or visiting sites or was I going to make the family the fulcrum of my existence? I chose the latter and never regretted the choice, though at times I envied the scholastic productivity of some of my peers, the honours they amassed or the money they earned from their writing. On reflection, the enjoyment I obtained from family outings, holidays in wonderful places, creative birthday parties, dinners on special occasions and involvement in our children's growth and education would not have been fully possible had I made a different choice. Each is a logical decision. Mine was partly based on the unique nature of our family, mixed ethnically, culturally and in religion and living for most of our married life in places where neither of us had been brought up and where we lacked the buttressing support of immediate family or friends from school, college and religious institution.

Eunice and I often wondered if we would have been better staying in one place. Visiting England or Uganda and seeing friends' children growing up in extended families, often in the same house for 20 to 30 years, made us envious of their stability, of their retention of school friends who lived nearby, and of boxes in attics full of the memories we had had to discard along the way. Africa was, however, a wonderful place in which to raise children. Though we lived through several coups, endured curfews, university closures and economic hardships, we never felt more secure than in Uganda and Ghana. The children could test their sense of wonder. They searched for chameleons; we adopted hinged tortoises that had been destined for the cooking pot in Hani, two of which lived under a divan in the living room; they caught a monster scorpion, captured a four-foot monitor lizard, tried to raise several hedgehogs, climbed Legon hill, explored the campus on their bicycles and befriended a veritable rainbow of friends from the Ghana International School and from the children of campus faculty.

We made the most of our opportunities for travel. In Africa we travelled by road to neighbouring countries, experiencing cultural and physical diversity. Biennial leaves enabled us to go to places like Norway, Switzerland, Scotland, England and Wales, not to mention the countries we saw *en route* and the wonderful journeys by sea to and from Africa. We were beneficiaries of the colonial pay structure, which still applies to many expatriates working in the Third World. Even a modest salary allowed one to employ maids, cooks, child minders, gardeners or even drivers. Workers became friends, part of an extended family, enriching our lives and allowing us to engage in gracious and leisurely activities that can be difficult without help. Some people found this aspect of life a moral dilemma, but we accepted it as a reality we could not change. In fact, when Jomo Kenyatta became president of Kenya he urged everyone who earned more than about £50 a month at that time to help their less fortunate compatriots by offering them employment in their homes.

Chapter 2

Education: England and Uganda, a mind unfolding

I N MANY WAYS my life has been a continuum in education, for I have never stopped feeling like a student. Even in retirement I need to engage in some scholarly activity. It took me a long time to allow myself to read fiction or magazines when not on holiday or travelling.

My schooling began at Church Road elementary school in Bolton, which was within walking distance of my home. After the first form all the classrooms contained 25 double desks in five rows, so every class had 50 pupils, but bad behaviour was not a problem. Our desks had inkwells and by the second class we were using scratchy pens; by the time we went upstairs to the last three classes we were using joined up writing. The school, which was typical of early twentieth-century schools, was built of shiny red Accrington brick with windows and other architectural features picked out in yellow brick. We were given a little bottle of milk every morning for mid break.

When I started school in 1936 the depression was at its height and some children were without socks or with only torn ones. Our hair was periodically inspected for head lice, or nits as we termed them. Other than the headmaster, who also taught, there were no administrators and, apart from him, all the teachers were women. We had no library and the playground was asphalt. For sport we were occasionally taken to the nearby park. A lot of the teaching was by rote, reciting times tables until they were second nature and learning poems by heart. Awarding stars to children who performed well fostered achievement. In winter we clustered around the radiators to keep warm and often developed chilblains on our toes. We did a lot of cutting out to make scrapbooks of bible characters and of world events, which introduced us to magazines and contemporary news.

I only remember one teacher well, Annie Heap who told us about great people from the past like Joan of Arc, Christopher Wren and

Francis of Assisi, people who had made a difference. Consequently, history became my favourite subject. Special events punctuated the year. On 11 November, Armistice Day, we bought red paper poppies at school and stood in the school yard for an interminable two-minute silence while a bugler sounded the last post on a trumpet. As Christmas approached we made decorations out of coloured paper. At one season there was a school play. I once had a small part in it and felt very proud when my picture appeared in the *Bolton Evening News*. Empire Day, 24 May, again meant standing to attention in the school yard, but I cannot remember much about it other than feeling proud of the British Empire, which stretched across the globe in red, and hearing heart-rending stories of heroes who had created it. I certainly believed the British superior to any other nation, particularly in war; we stuck by the rules and were magnanimous in victory. The films I watched like *Gunga Din* of a poor oppressed Indian fighting to save his officers reinforced these opinions.

In our last year we sat for scholarship exams, later known as the Eleven Plus, when our fate was sealed. Were we to go to grammar school or to a continuation school that lasted three years and led to technical or commercial school? There were three grammar schools, Bolton School, the most prestigious, which my brother Leonard attended, the Church Institute, an independent coeducational school linked to the Church of England, and the Municipal Secondary School, which my sister Freda attended. I had interviews for the first two and got a scholarship to the Church Institute. I was proud to be accepted. A new stage had begun in my education.

The Church Institute was close by the parish church in a rather old Gothic-style Victorian building full of character. An Anglican clergyman, the Revd A. D. Clark, was principal. We had uniforms, which we wore proudly, and school caps. In my last year I was a prefect, so a red ring replaced the blue ring on my cap; I felt like an angel. A remarkable history teacher, Marjorie Wood, who was also deputy head, shaped my career; 20 years later she would surely have been the principal. I was always called Posnansky and not Merrick, but girls were called by their first names. Marjorie Wood continued to call me Posnansky until I was in my forties and we had become good friends, and I found it difficult to call her Marjorie. She was a superb teacher. She had bright blue eyes and red hair. She looked like how I imagined Queen Elizabeth I to be. As soon as she entered a classroom she gazed around and everyone stopped talking.

We learnt Latin from our first year, which I hated. I was either badly taught or just had no ear for languages, much as I had no ear for music. The top 15 in the class went on to learn Greek, while the others were taught French and German. Greek Testament, the New Testament in Greek, was standard fare in religious studies, from which I was allowed to opt out. A new Education Act introduced after the war rapidly swept away this classical tradition. One of the biggest prizes in the school was called Latin Declarations for which I competed in my final year; before the full assembly we recited from memory some passage in Latin that excited us. I thought I did well with my piece from Julius Caesar's writings, but alas that year the judges decided that no student met the required standard; what a waste of effort it all seemed. The best part of the classical tradition was learning Greek and Roman history in our first year. Every child was assigned to a house, the three houses being Romans, Spartans and Trojans. The school anthem sung to the tune of 'Marching through Georgia' was 'Romans, Spartans, Trojans marching hand in hand', which was something they never did. I was a Roman and our sports colour was red.

Grammar school subtly weakened my family and community ties, particularly towards the end of my stay. The war was on and for a time my close friend Kenneth Potter, who later became a BOAC (British Overseas Airways Corporation) captain, and I joined the Air Force cadets. We learnt about planes, were taught how to handle antiquated Lee Enfield rifles and were introduced to a community of boys very different from those I met at Hebrew classes. I went on several school camps, first when I was 14 to North Wales where we did forestry work and lived in a round bell tent and the following year to Worcestershire where we picked plums for two weeks. I learnt about sex, not that we had any opportunity to practise it, from the other boys. I realized how different I was being Jewish in that I had difficulty finding enough to eat. I was also the only boy who did not own or know how to ride a bike, so I either had to ride back from the orchard perched on the flimsy carrier at the back of Johnnie Orrell's saddle or walk. I began to explore the countryside. Visiting Gloucester cathedral and other churches helped me understand English history and opened my eyes to the cultural landscape.

My chief scholarly interests at school were focused on history, geography and art. Besides Miss Wood, a new principal, Mr E. L. King, taught us from the fourth form and introduced us to learning about the past from historical novels. He particularly liked Conan Doyle's historical romances, which spurred me to read contemporary novels by Rider Haggard and his hero in African exploration and adventure, Allan Quatermain. Miss Wood encouraged us to look at the economic and social as well as political dimensions of history, thus stimulating my geographical interests. In my final year at school I had a superb geography teacher, Kenneth Briggs, who was probably the best teacher I ever encountered. He really helped me appreciate the landscape. On a four-day field trip he encouraged us to keep field notebooks, to observe and read the physical and human landscape and to look at contemporary problems like race in America and white settlement in Africa in geographical terms. We also learnt about Japan and South America.

I took art history as an option and studied classical architecture with Miss Wood, which I never regretted. My art teacher thought that my paintings resembled those of Henri Rousseau, though I did not know his work at the time. Life became more intense in the sixth form. Before then I had been introverted, involved in hobbies like making model aeroplanes out of balsa wood and collecting coins and stamps. Collecting things ultimately led me to a life of scholarship. I joined the Lancashire Numismatic Society, which met in Manchester, and wrote a paper on the coinage of Solon, some of the earliest Greek coins. I researched and later gave a paper on English pennies, which forced me into classificatory systems. I thought I would like to be a numismatist and attended a lecture by a Mr Mattingley, the keeper of coins at the British Museum. He told me that there was only one such job in England and he held it, but he encouraged me to think about museum work in general.

I had little interest in sport, largely because I had no role model. My father knew of Babe Ruth from his American Yiddish newspaper, but he never played ball with us, even on holiday. We did not listen to sport on the radio. This lack of exposure was a disadvantage at elementary school where many children had good coordination from playing games with their siblings. At secondary school the ball never came my way in football and I never seemed to get a chance to bat in cricket. Also, a rather critical gym teacher, Mr Johnson, turned me off physical activity. In spring there was swimming at the municipal swimming pool on Saturdays, but I went to synagogue then, so could not attend. Mr Johnson once beat me with a tennis shoe on my behind for not coming to swimming class. I never went to a pool for another

16 years and it jaundiced my attitude to physical education. Things became rather better in the fifth form as we were encouraged to engage in cross-country running in which there was a chance to chat while jogging and I could always stay the course. I ran the mile for my house in the school sports day and it was good to hear my peers urging me on. As an individual I felt proud of my team as well as of myself in a way that had not affected me in the team sports I had been forced to play before.

In the sixth form we had small class sizes, intimate contact with our mentors, and the chance to discuss animatedly among ourselves sexuality in Thomas Hardy's *The Woodlanders*, the historical dimensions of the Middle East and our chances of playing a part in shaping the postwar world. In most of my classes there were only one to three boys to six or seven girls. It was the first time that my hormones kicked in as a stimulant to excel and, though we talked a lot about girl–boy relations, we were very reserved with one another. We were encouraged to read and I must have read nearly 20 books on Stuart history alone. I did an individual project on American colonial history and spent a lot of time in the Bolton reference library where I first encountered the light blue volumes of the Hakluyt Society and their tales of bygone exploration. At the end of the year I received a special prize for my work. The teachers seemed surprised when I won open scholarships to Nottingham and Hull universities and got the top marks in geography for the whole Oxford exam board in the Higher School Certificate. The school had not put me in for Oxford or Cambridge, but when the results came out the principal approached me to see if I wanted to go to Oxford where he felt he could get me in at the last minute. I often wonder whether I was right to have turned down the offer, but it was reassuring to be approached. I knew little about Oxbridge and had no one to consult, but was in any case happy to be following in the footsteps of Marjorie Wood, who had graduated from Nottingham.

I was the first member of my family to go to university and was glad I chose Nottingham. I loved its park-like setting, the lake, the neoclassical Portland stone buildings and the fact that it was trying to break out of the pack of newer universities, which 50 years later it has brilliantly accomplished. Nottingham was far enough to be well away from home yet near enough to be accessible by rail and bus. Though my open scholarship was in ancient history I quickly changed to medieval and modern history and geography when I realized that ancient history required a lot of reading in Latin and Greek, which I had hoped I could drop. I enjoyed Nottingham. Our classes were never more than 30–40 and I got to know the teachers well, though relations were less close than they were to be in Africa and the USA. I was only invited to the professor's house once and I remember it being an ordeal. One thing I disliked in our first year was that we all had to write essays on the same topics, resulting in a mad scramble for books in the library. Fortunately, unlike in America, students could only take out two books at a time for a limited period. The library was not too large and I learnt to appreciate the art of browsing, which is fast dying out because modern students surf the web and only look for specific books. Many of my best discoveries resulted from serendipitous finds.

I combined history with geography, which I never regretted. I particularly enjoyed learning to draw maps in geography lab classes and surveying the university grounds in spring with chains, plane tables and levels. I treasured this experience, which I tried to introduce into the teaching syllabus for archaeologists at the University of Ghana. In America students are expected to pick up these skills when they attend a field school, but all too often they have to be picked up too quickly and many students ultimately rely on informal training learnt over many years and rarely critically assessed. Historical geography ultimately led me into archaeology. Our professor, K. C. Edwards, used some very readable books by Peake and Fleure on cultural evolution and history from the beginnings of humans, which was how I learnt that the first people probably originated in Africa. We went on geographical field trips to observe and appreciate the environment, draw what we saw and make valid interpretations about the physical and cultural history of the landscape. In summer 1950 I joined a geographical field group that went to Norway and, in my second year, though not doing geography honours, I read an extra class on historical geography and went on a week's field trip to Sussex.

In history we had some fine teachers. John Holt, an assistant lecturer whom at first I thought was a student, taught medieval history; he was interested in King John and later went on to write books on him and on Robin Hood. His teaching took us into the economic and cultural life of the times and away from the old emphasis on political events, religion and law. He inspired me to consider how archaeology might supplement documentary sources by teaching us about lifestyles and I began to read about medieval

Christian missions as economic communities. The most influential teacher was probably Jim Fryer, who taught British history and whose career was cut short by the war when he joined the armed forces. He had no doctorate or book, but was one of the finest lecturers I have known with a superb sense of timing. He rarely consulted a note and paced up and down in front of the class, rolling his own cigarettes and chain smoking. He always ended his lectures on a cliff-hanging note that made one want to get to the next one to know what happened. His lectures on the rise of European socialism and nineteenth-century political thought influenced me politically and made me realize how much people had struggled for civil and labour rights, equity and justice. He was interested in grand themes and in how personalities affected or were affected by events. He introduced me to a tutorial with a single teacher, for he had us come in to read our essays and hear his comments. A study of Austen Chamberlain exposed the multifaceted aspects of imperialism, so exciting in Britain yet often disastrous in Africa or Asia. Fryer was instrumental in making me think about causality and how things may have turned out differently with other actors. I recall a heated discussion about Randolph Churchill's personal failures.

In the early 1950s Nottingham had a dynamic and youthful vice chancellor, Bertram Leslie Hallward, who had great vision; the university was growing fast, with new buildings, new programmes and a sense of future possibilities. It was small enough to meet students from other disciplines, usually in the Portland or main building at the bottom of which there was a large common room with pigeon holes for one's mail. Most students ate their lunch and dinner, as well as their mid-morning or mid-afternoon snacks, in the cafeteria-style refectory. Only when I went to the United States did I come across students eating breakfast out. Notice boards for the numerous student societies were in a long corridor and if one wanted to attract student attention it was necessary to put a lot of effort into painting attractive signs in an era before copiers. Walking up and down this corridor was a good way to meet people. The library was adjacent. A terrace facing the lake on which the sun shone in the spring, lawns and flowering trees provided a refreshing contrast for those of us from the dirty, gloomy industrial towns of the era before restrictions on coal fires were introduced in the 1960s.

More students played than watched sports, particularly on Wednesdays and Saturdays when there were no classes, and for a time

I ran cross-country. Shows put on by student groups were more popular than at American universities and for the first time I learnt to appreciate Gilbert and Sullivan. There were Saturday night hops, but the highlight of the student academic year was the union ball. It was only at college that I owned and wore a dinner jacket, for in my professional life I have always managed to avoid black tie events. I took part in the Rag, when students raise money for charity by dressing up, behaving crazily in the city and singing the university song about its wooden mascot chickaroo with gusto. In 1951 we walked through the city carrying a model of the skylon tower, the symbol of the Festival of Britain, and erected it in the town centre.

We were staunchly loyal to our hall of residence, Wortley Hall, and I was one of its first occupants. It consisted of five single-storey prefabs around a grassy courtyard, some beautiful grounds and an old house where the warden Mr and Mrs Arthur Radford lived on the upper floor with a dining and common room downstairs. The buildings had been hurriedly erected as temporary quarters for London students evacuated to Nottingham during the war, I believe from Goldsmiths College. The rooms were small but single, which for me was a great boon. Each room had a small bed, easy chair, desk, chest of drawers and bookcase. We shared a bathroom at the end of the corridor as well as an electric kettle, an essential feature of English college life in which tea drinking was habitual and hospitality involved offering tea rather than anything stronger. If we wanted to phone, which rarely happened because telephones were few and expensive, even in the 1950s, we had to go to the main house. Like most other students I had a radio (or wireless as we called it then), which I bought secondhand. At meals we sat where there was space at long tables and in time got to know most of the people in the hall pretty well. Only one student (there were 51 of us) had a car; about a quarter were a few years older than me, having been in the forces before coming to college. My closest friendships at college were made in Wortley with Brian Fletcher, who later became a geologist, and Dennis Mills another geographer. We often had tea together, or the occasional sherry, confided in each other about our romances, or lack thereof, and in some instances got up to trouble. For example, after one of our hall dances, we removed the glass globes protecting the outside lights of our rival, Hugh Stewart Hall. Unfortunately, it rained, thus short-circuiting our rival's electric system and plunging the whole hall into darkness. Even after 50 years we still have periodic get-togethers. In fact, I attended one in 1997 and it was as if time had stood still. After a few moments we were young men again.

Though I enjoyed my time at university I remember few of the people who studied with me. I recently read Christopher Isherwood's *Lions and shadows: an education in the twenties* and was astounded by the detail he could provide, the names and personalities remembered. I can recall the highs, have fortunately cast aside the lows, even though they seemed overwhelming at the time, but faces have become quite blurred. In 1971 I attended a Nottingham University gathering and, though I had only left 15 years earlier, I recalled few faces or names; I was surprised when people came up to me and recounted numerous anecdotes in which I figured but had totally forgotten. Dialogue was particularly difficult to resurrect, but I have never been any good at remembering quotations. I was awe struck when Mortimer Wheeler, in his seventies, quoted whole passages he remembered from his school days. I think memories persist in different ways; for me places rather than words remain.

Though while in the sixth form in 1947 or 1948 I had taken part in an archaeological excavation on river gravels near Bolton looking for Mesolithic finds, practical field work only became a key focus in my career plans when I went to university. For my second summer vacation I took part in an excavation that Frank Willett of the Manchester Museum directed near Burnley, about 15 miles from Bolton. He was excavating what he believed were a series of small long barrows or mounds. We ultimately discovered that they were probably potato clumps[1] that had never been dug up because of nineteenth-century blight. At the end of my second year at university I finally learnt to ride a bicycle for the first time and went on a cycling holiday to visit medieval cathedrals like Wells, Winchester and Salisbury, Roman sites like St Albans and prehistoric sites like Stonehenge and Avebury. At that time such sites were without surrounding fences and very accessible. I stayed in youth hostels and small bed and breakfast houses that I spotted by looking for vacancy signs in windows. It was a wonderful way to get fit and at the same time see the countryside. On a bike one can think and relax in a way that is much more difficult in a motorcar.

At the end of the journey I joined my first archaeological field school on a Roman villa excavation Ralegh Radford ran at Somerton in Somerset. It was a glorious occasion; I learned a lot, had wonderful excursions and it clearly helped me decide that archaeology would be my life's pursuit. I also felt useful. They had no professional surveyor, so my geographical training stood me in good stead. I was put in charge of levelling and helped with plane table work and taught various other people how to survey. I had the good fortune to share a room with Ronald Tylecote, a remarkable man with a great future in front of him working on the origins and early development of iron working. He was a self-effacing man and I only learnt he had a prosthetic leg when he went to bed. His handicap was certainly no handicap to him. I also gained experience in Roman ceramics, particularly *terra sigillata* or Samian ware, the most popular workshop-produced ceramics in the second century AD. This shiny red slipped ware was made in various forms clearly identifiable from site to site from northern England to southern India. I discovered that the classification had been worked out on an East Midland excavation at Margidunum and the type collection was housed in a small museum at the University of Nottingham.

On my return to Nottingham I touched base with the curator of the Margidunum Museum, Professor H. H. Swinnerton, a retired professor of geology of great distinction. I helped him in the museum and that contact further helped shape my future. In my second year, site clearance for new university buildings revealed a medieval industrial site on the university grounds. Masses of twisted ceramics, ash layers and burnt furnace structures indicated a medieval tile and pottery kiln. Though it was winter and the trenches were wet, and the clay soil sticky and heavy, we excavated. It was my first experience of directing an excavation; I had to survey the site, encourage a crew, keep records and try to interpret everything. Professor Swinnerton, then in his late seventies, was unable to help in the field, but he painstakingly pieced together our finds and found the association of the kiln with a Cistercian monastic property that had existed in the area where the university was now expanding. We worked at weekends, in the rain and in failing light trying to finish the job before the trenches were filled in and construction begun. This pressure and the comradeship of working together, often in miserable conditions, was an attraction of archaeology. We felt we had something to contribute to the university and to history.

As a result of this interest a few of us, during my final year, started an archaeological society of which I was elected president. For a provincial university this was a great initiative. We invited a different speaker each month. We were brash; we had no money to give to our speakers, except for fares, but nevertheless invited the professor of archaeology in Cambridge, Graham Clark, as our first speaker. Later speakers included the head of the archaeological division of the Ordnance Survey, Mr C. W. Phillips, renowned as the excavator of Sutton Hoo. Other speakers were equally prestigious. I chaired the meetings and entered the world of archaeology through the meals we had with the speakers. I also learnt important lessons about how to give a public lecture. I was aghast at how many distinguished speakers failed to prepare their talks, pitched them at the wrong audience or brought too many irrelevant slides. Graham Clark changed my life by asking what I was going to do when I finished my studies at Nottingham. I told him I hoped to take an MA in history in which I would research the medieval cartulary (collection of records) of a Lincolnshire Cistercian abbey and try to excavate the site at the same time so that I could use both sources to reconstruct the social and economic life of the monastic community. He suggested instead that I should get a credential in archaeology and invited me to apply to his college, Peterhouse. I was encouraged in this by Nottingham's vice chancellor, at one time the youngest fellow of Peterhouse who died in 2003 aged 102 as the oldest fellow emeritus. I was accepted.

My government scholarship was extended and, after excavating in France on a cave site with rock art in Burgundy, directed by Leroi-Gourhan, and earning some spending money by working for the Bolton Corporation as a gardener on housing estates, I went off to Cambridge, excited because I realized I had at last got a clear career objective. The work for the corporation was useful for more than the money I received, which was £1 (then the equivalent of $2.70) a day, because it taught me so much. I worked with two men who had been in menial jobs all their lives and were twice my age. One supplemented his meagre pay packet by running a fish and chip shop six nights a week. I learnt about the pride of the working poor, who did not regard themselves as poor even though they had never had very much. They had pride in their work, knew how to pace themselves and were first-rate colleagues who listened to the radio and knew a lot more about the world around them than I had imagined. It was if I were making my own trip to Wigan Pier, but unlike George Orwell, perhaps because I was local to the area or because the war had changed social conditions, improved expectations, provided job security and a firmer social welfare base, I did not find the harsh rawness of class difference. These men were my mates; we looked out for each other. We sat on our haunches to have our simple sandwich lunches and discussed many things, but not trivia. The outdoor life was good and I began to appreciate the values and hard work of a social group other than my own.

Cambridge in many ways was a wonderland. First, I never got over the beauty of the colleges, their setting along the green banks of the River Cam or along old, narrow winding lanes. I do not think that even after years of witnessing the majesty of Africa, of seeing the Taj Mahal at dawn, the Grand Canyon at dusk, Victoria Falls by moonlight or the golden glow of Jerusalem, I will ever forget King's College chapel set against a multi-hued sky in early evening with the light glittering in its stained glass windows and its stone tracery so perfect and fragile. Founded in 1284, Peterhouse is the oldest of the colleges and at the time its junior common room was known as the sex club, denoting more than the passage of 600 years. One of its many attractions was its size. In 1952 there were only 206 students. We dined at one sitting, unlike other colleges, under the watchful eyes of the portraits of famous former students, most of whom were household names to any English historian. We sat at long tables on backless benches, polished by hundreds of years of use and care. We were given tankards of pewter and silver and could order beer if we wished. Silver candelabra lit the tables. Peterhouse had a reputation for fine food, the legacy of some bequest from ages ago. I told the kitchen I could not eat meat or seafood and was given really fantastic food during my stay.

I lived out of college on St Peter's Terrace, a block away on Trumpington Road beyond the Fitzwilliam Museum. It was a pleasant walk through Peterhouse gardens and past the croquet lawns that claimed too much of my time in the spring term. Rationing still existed in 1952 so we had to take our butter, jam and sugar to table every breakfast. My room had a gas fire and my greatest joy was toasting crumpets. At Cambridge one had an academic tutor or director of studies, in my case Graham Clark, and supervisors for whom one prepared weekly essays. Mine were Charles McBurney for Stone Age archaeology, Glyn Daniel for the history of archaeology, and a senior doctoral student, Mike Thompson, for Mesolithic archaeology. On arrival at their suite of college rooms one was always offered sherry and a comfortable seat. Only McBurney saw two of us together. My companion was Gill Duckett, the only woman in the Tripos (Part II). Like me she was not from public school. She was irreverent, asked personal questions that enlivened our sessions, introduced me to many people I would never have met, and invited me to Newnham, the women's hall I would otherwise probably not have visited. She eventually married John G. Hurst, the medieval archaeologist who opened my eyes to the future of historical archaeology.

Students still wore gowns to classes and in the evenings if we wanted to be out after 10.00 p.m. we had to get permission from the senior tutor. Being out after midnight was forbidden except for key events like a May Ball. After 10.00 p.m. two college fellows would walk the streets in cap and gown, each accompanied by two college porters in black and known as bulldogs whose duty was to apprehend students out after hours. Enterprising students learnt to outwit the bulldogs by climbing into college by secret ways even though the gates were locked and ground-floor windows barred.

I find it difficult to realize that I was only at Cambridge as a full-time student for 32 weeks. In that time I became an archaeologist, learnt to play croquet and squash, went on several excavations, played ice hockey during the terrible winter of 1952–53 when all the Fens and ponds froze over, read a great deal and made friends with many academics and students with whom I still correspond. I even had time to visit friends in Oxford, London and other places, to see plays, join societies and attend lectures and seminars, my favourite being the Quaternary Research Group meetings, which stood me in good stead later in Africa. Life was intense and I enjoyed it fully; there was a gracefulness I had not witnessed at Nottingham and the sense of history of the place overawed me. Cambridge is a town one can master on a bicycle and everyone rode – great flocks of students with swirling gowns like giant crows racing from place to place. I loved the university library with its wealth of books and working in the Anderson Room seated on lush red leather seats. In the spring I punted on the Cam and invited friends to Cambridge to share the pleasures and show off my skill on the river.

All good things come to an end and before I graduated I applied for and received the prestigious Gertrude Cropper graduate fellowship at the University of Nottingham to do research. Where to put me was a problem. There was then no department of archaeology and history had little space, so I finally became a graduate student in the department of geology with Professor Swinnerton as my supervisor. I had thought of writing my thesis on the Bronze Age burial barrows on the moors above Bolton but decided against that idea as there was no suitable supervisor. Finally I settled on a regional survey of the Pleistocene chronology and prehistoric archaeology of part of the East Midlands. I was assigned a long narrow room in the geological research laboratory located in an old house near Wortley Hall. Being in geology was great for me.

There were several other graduate students with whom I got on well. They taught me a lot, particularly about the significance of student to student training as opposed to the formal coursework then being endured by many students in the United States before being allowed to undertake research on their own. At lunch we all met in the lab of the chief technician, Mr Ron Hendry, to discuss the world, sports, particularly cricket, and the university, as well as play a quick game of darts. I learnt a lot of geology from the other students, how to identify rocks with a hand lens, how to use a geological microscope and how to understand the landscape in a new way. Most were working on foraminifera, tiny, microscopic molluscs used in identifying geological strata. Much of the knowledge was useful in determining geological age. I even at times helped with lab classes in the geology department and doubt if any of the students realized that the instructor had never taken a single geology class; I knew the talk and was learning a little of the walk. My walk led me to gravel pits where I looked for flint, quartz and quartzite debitage, the evidence of early human stone working and for fossils. The latter were scarce and all I found were mammoth teeth and the humera of prehistoric bovids known as *Bos primigenius*. Most of my time was spent collecting mounds of stones from the gravels and then trying to find out from where they came in an effort to sort out the direction of flow of former glaciers that had scooped up the stones in their relentless path of etching out great wide valleys. The difficult rocks I brought back to the department so that the real geologists could provide the identifications.

I saw Professor Swinnerton on only three occasions in a formal capacity to review my work so had to rely on self-discipline to keep up with my research, which was hard at first. There were then no special funds for field work so my travel in the East Midlands came from own pocket, but I did get a little help with my two principal excavations at Lockington in 1953 and at Swarkestone in 1954. I learnt how to borrow equipment, transport and bulldozers for back-filling, and how to enlist the support of the many students who became my crew and the various specialists who bolstered my academic deficiencies. This was probably the most social period of my life. I ate many of my meals, particularly dinners, at the faculty club behind the university where I would play snooker in the winter and croquet in summer. Geoff Mosley, a geography research student who later became a lecturer in Newcastle, Australia, often accompanied me. It was then the period of double summer time when it stayed light until 11.00 p.m. and Geoff introduced me to hill climbing in Derbyshire on our motorcycles and afterwards we would drive through winding roads near Ashbourne in the Dove Valley.

On such forays into the countryside I came to know the burial mounds, standing stones and other reminders of the area's prehistoric inhabitants. My LE Velocette, sometimes called 'silver ghost' because it was so quiet, was my favourite vehicle. It was radically innovative in that it had a shaft drive instead of chain one, a hand gear change instead of a foot one, was water cooled and had four cylinders instead of the then normal two, so I could avoid having to premix petrol and oil. It had shin guards, side panniers and a Perspex windshield, features later adapted by the Japanese bikes and Italian scooters that swept in the later 1950s and put an end to the British motorcycle industry. At that time traffic was still light and the LE enabled me to visit my mother in Bolton or sister in Stoke quite easily and facilitated my visiting all the museums and collections in the area I covered as well as appreciating monuments within their environmental contexts. Though I enjoyed my Land Rover in Africa nothing gave one as much ease with an area as a motorbike. I was fortunate never to have had a spill though I came close on an icy road by the women's hall of residence in Nottingham in 1954.

At Nottingham I began serious field archaeology. Until then I had largely assisted on digs, building up my skills, learning what I could or could not do. I had taken part in 11 digs ranging from palaeolithic to historic. As part of my doctorate I excavated several Bronze Age barrows. My first was at Lockington just over the Leicestershire border. The field was flat but I had identified a barrow from crop marks on an aerial photograph. I could not afford labour so had to attract helpers by advertising in a useful British archaeology calendar that listed excavations open for volunteers. All my helpers became friends. We sat and talked during the September rains huddled around a cast iron stove. A crew of four to six students removed a great amount of earth. We found the original ground surface with its burial, but inconveniently during the three days I was away at the September meeting of the Prehistoric Society in Scotland. My helpers, none with prior archaeological experience, knew enough to call in the Leicester Museum to help them and I returned to assist the encasement and cutting away of the grave block that was taken to Leicester for slow careful excavation and parallel conservation within their laboratory. I organized the dig as a training school and teaching archaeology helped me come to grips with the purpose of what I was doing. I learnt much from my colleagues, one of whom, David Stronach, had been on the Hoxne dig in Cambridge for a few days a year before. He later went on to become one of the archaeological greats of my generation with his work in Iran and later Turkey. Lockington fired me up to plan a formal field school at Swarkestone the following year.

Before that took place I managed to persuade the university extra mural department, now called continuing education, then housed in the old university college buildings on downtown Shakespeare Street, to allow me to direct some classes. I was to teach in several locations, including Derby and Loughborough. I was normally the youngest person there. The mature students brought with them so many skills, great but often uncoordinated knowledge about British history and prehistory and a willingness to challenge my still nascent views about the past.

I suppose chutzpah drove me, but at that time I was a strange mixture of gauche shyness and ambition. In Nottingham, as a member of the stuffy Thoroton Society founded in the nineteenth century to further antiquarian research, I wrote several memoranda suggesting that archaeology be placed on a more modern footing. I wanted to encourage learning about archaeology and to organize group activities rather than consider the search for the unwritten past as an arcane pursuit for the elderly. I was persistent, my views were discussed and some of my ideas slowly adopted, but by that time I had moved on. Wherever I was at the time I was always an enthusiast. In 1954 there were no classes in British archaeology anywhere in the Midlands and I saw extra mural studies as a possibility to build up interest. This was before the Open University and popular TV shows about the past existed, when many people yearned for further education. Workers' education institutes were still popular, but with courses on economics, civics and English expression they were mainly designed to rectify educational deficiencies.

Cultural activities were largely the province of university extra mural departments. At that time Nottingham had a regional tutor,

Maurice Barley, with considerable knowledge of English vernacular architecture who had been conducting field classes in local archaeology. He was based away from Nottingham, in Newark, so there was scope for classes in Nottingham. There was an initial reluctance to let me teach; I was thought too diffident but several people must have spoken up on my behalf. Fortunately, my first class went well. I had learnt a lot at Cambridge and my students appreciated my breadth and my slides. From the start I was keen to use slides, then large glass-bound three-and-a-quarter-inch square black and white transparencies. I also made good use of coloured chalks to create blackboard maps, charts and diagrams.

The success of my first class gave me status and led to courses in Loughborough and Derby. Going to Loughborough in winter was hard as the roads were often icy and there was a lot of fog at that time. I would get home cold and wet, but it was useful experience that allowed me to read more widely than I would have done. I increased the weekly classes to twice a week in the evenings and then organized a spring field class in which I took students in a bus to see some of the Trent Valley monuments in their context. We tramped over gravel terraces, viewed Bronze Age burial mounds, stone circles, menhirs and later Iron Age hill forts and ended up with Norman churches, medieval architecture and finally my own particular interest, windmills of different kinds and vestiges of the industrial revolution – factories, canals and mill buildings, including fascinating three-storeyed lace making cottages with large casement windows to bring light to tired eyes. My last venture during the summer before I left Nottingham was a two-week residential class on British archaeology at Buxton in the Derbyshire highlands; in the afternoons I would take the students to the many sites I had explored on previous weekend field excursions. I made a Sri Lankan (then known as Sinhalese) friend called Raja, who worked for the antiquities department in Colombo, but I have forgotten his full name. He had a friend from Uganda, Ibrahim Mugenyi, to whom he wrote about my imminent departure for East Africa. I contacted Ibrahim when I got to Kenya and he introduced me to the Africa that was so essential to my future existence.

Though I enjoyed my doctoral research, as I assembled data, interpreted objects found in museums and searched for collections that remained in private hands I often felt rudderless. If I had an archaeological philosophy at the time it was based on environmental determinism, for Cyril Fox's *The Personality of Britain* had influenced

4. Excavating at the Hoxne Stone Age site, 1953. Left to right
John Mulvaney, Merrick and Richard West.

me.[2] I made distribution maps, and related the distributions to routes, resources, soils and presumed original vegetation. I placed the East Midlands in a broader context of British prehistory.

My thesis was in three sections – an evaluation of the geological background of the Stone Age sites and finds I had discovered; a description of the Stone Age finds; and a section on later prehistory looking at archaeological material to the end of the Iron Age. The first two sections were published.[3]

Looking back I now realize it lacked a clear theoretical focus, but it was typical of a time when British archaeology was substantive and descriptive. Kenneth Oakley from the British Museum was my external examiner. After completing the writing and having it typed up with three carbon copies, my internal examiner Professor Swinnerton and I showed up at the British Museum for my oral examination. The event turned out to be a gentlemanly chat. I was advised about some minor corrections to be undertaken before handing in a bound copy to the university library and told that I 'could sleep well', by which I understood that my doctorate would be approved, which it duly was. I left for Kenya before hearing the outcome; when it came it was an anti-climax because no one around me seemed interested and I had no one with whom to celebrate. It was so different from what I have grown accustomed to in the USA where rites of passage are valued, where children graduating even from primary school, and certainly from junior high school, wear gowns, or at least pretty clothes, and have a special ceremony and plenty of speeches. I often regret that I have no photograph of myself graduating at either the BA or Ph.D. level.

Though I taught for Makerere's extra-mural division in Kenya, I did not become directly involved in university education until I got to Uganda. There I quickly gravitated to Makerere and its circle of academics, its library and promise for the future. Shortly after I arrived, the dean of arts, Kees Welter, asked me to give a series of evening talks on Africa's past. These were useful, for they directed my reading and helped me explain what archaeologists were trying to do in Africa. I was appointed a fellow of Northcote Hall and invited to Makerere teachers' homes. In 1962 I was asked to give the first full course on African archaeology. I had six students and they all became senior academics. This was an exciting period when new syllabi were being dreamed up and adopted, and when Africa became a core subject area for social scientists and humanists.

Before I joined the college in 1964 I was invited to be an outside member of the African Studies Committee designed to find ways of Africanizing the syllabus. From the start it was felt that the key to new development had to be in graduate studies. It would be from the expanded ranks of graduate students that new senior teaching personnel could be selected either for overseas training or immediate appointment to Makerere. At that time, fewer than 30 per cent of the university teachers were African, and they were mostly at the assistant lecturer level. Many did not have doctoral degrees. It was also felt that too many subjects, including African literature, African religions and African music, art and archaeology, were not represented at Makerere and that there should be a crash programme to introduce them through graduate training. It was strongly felt that African studies had to be taught on an interdisciplinary basis and that all students must take three different aspects of African studies before embarking on a second-year MA thesis. It was a tough regime. Colin Leys, a dynamic young Canadian political scientist, pulled ideas together and obtained three-year funding from the Rockefeller Foundation. Jim Coleman, the foundation's representative who was based at Makerere for three years as a visiting professor of political science, significantly helped the idea along. In 1964 a handful of students, all expatriates, was accepted in religious studies, agricultural botany and archaeology. In December 1964 I became the first substantive director. The next three years were perhaps the most action filled, dynamic ones of my life.

In the mid-1960s Makerere University College was at its peak. There was change all around, new buildings going up, student numbers increasing and numerous foreign visitors passing through. I got to know the key African studies people in the United States. In the 1960s America had money to invest in African education and in education about Africa. US universities were actively recruiting faculty, many of them British, who had taught in African universities or served in research posts in Africa. Everyone was keen to see African universities retain African intellectuals rather than let them take government posts. This led to some rapid promotions, for example Ali Mazrui taking the chair in political science on his return from Manchester. Crash training programmes for teachers for the numerous new secondary schools being established was another exciting development. In Kenya, Tom Mboya organized air lifts of Kenyan students to the USA while in Uganda 150 enthusiastic British and American students arrived for a one-year course at Makerere before fanning out all over East Africa to teach.

The programme involved Makerere faculty, including me, introducing them to the African component of their disciplines. Through living in the halls of residence and mixing with African students they were introduced to some of the major issues facing young Africans. Their *esprit de corps* was remarkable and many went on to work for long periods in Africa. This was also when the Peace Corps was becoming effective, with many of its volunteers stimulating education in remote districts neglected by East Africans because of difficult work conditions. Within a few years the Peace Corps volunteers, their British Voluntary Service Overseas counterparts, and doctoral students funded by Ford and Rockefeller programmes had brought about an infectious liberalization of research.

University teachers in the 1960s were creating new approaches to Africa. In 1964 I became a lecturer in history at Makerere and taught classes covering the whole of African history from the origins of humanity dating back several million years until the period of independence in 1961. The few general books that attempted to cover the period either left out certain areas, like North Africa, or gave scant notice to what had happened in Africa before the rise of Egyptian civilization. As far as I know these were the first university classes in Africa to cover the whole of human history. I tried as far as possible to personalize the classes by showing slides of places only vaguely mentioned in textbooks or missed out altogether. Although I moved to the graduate programme in African studies in my second year at Makerere, I continued to teach the early part of the first-year syllabus until I left for Ghana. I always felt that teaching newcomers to university was the most important job for a university teacher. It allows the instructor to help those most in need, to spot outstanding students and to boost enthusiasm for one's own discipline.

The students in my Makerere graduate class were highly motivated and very bright; they were mostly from overseas and some had knowledge of Africa from classes in their home university. My class was just as instructional for me as it was for them as I introduced them to the multidisciplinary aspect of studying Africa's past. We discovered together the rich oral literature, engaged in an exciting search for botanical, medical and zoological evidence of human variation and susceptibility to disease, looked at crop history and animal domestication. Interdisciplinary studies were in vogue in African history at that time and everyone was learning from each other. We were at last moving away from diffusionist ideas on the origins of kingship, the use of stone in building and similarities in material culture. In a newly emerging Africa scholars felt it was a putdown to credit ancient Egypt or Ethiopia with all the major social and cultural developments.

At Makerere at that time we were blessed with visits by leading scholars from Britain, the United States, South Africa, Nigeria and areas where vigorous debates were in progress. Many of my later colleagues at UCLA visited Makerere in those days, including John Povey, the Kupers, Ned Alpers, Chris Ehret, Dick Sklar, Mike Lofchie as well as luminaries in global African studies like Lucy Mair, Colin Turnbull, Basil Davidson and Victor Turner. We were able to go into the field that lay on our doorstep to appreciate preindustrial technology, African art and the environmental backdrop. Students lived on campus, had no other commitments and were happy to participate in numerous seminars.

In 1966–67, when the African studies programme was in the last of its initially planned three-year existence, a lively debate was initiated about the future of African studies. Some lecturers, including me, felt that our contribution had proved itself, that a lively African studies programme attracted foreign students, funds from abroad and helped to develop a vigorous multidisciplinary graduate experience bringing together students trained in different departments. I also felt that Makerere students should experience a multidisciplinary programme away from the constraints of the department from which they had just graduated. Being in such a programme would help them develop an institutional *esprit de corps* that may not have been possible in a department in which they were the only graduate student. From my time in England I realized that it could be difficult to make the break from undergraduate to graduate. I also believed that the injunction to take three subjects for two years at the graduate level would broaden a student's Africanist experience and help build up cross-faculty contacts or what we now know as networking.

On the opposing side, strongly represented by the sociology professor Raymond Apthorpe, was the idea that the departments needed to be built up by concentrating research at the departmental level. This would enhance the status of the department and graduate researchers could serve as teaching assistants for the undergraduates. There would thus be regular feedback from research into the under-graduate curriculum. Foreign students, and their fees in foreign exchange, could still be attracted. These were all solid arguments and the programme, as it had been planned, was phased out. This meant that my salary as director would go. The principal, Yusuf Lule, offered me an administrative position, but by then I had already received and accepted an invitation to take up the chair in archaeology in Ghana.

Looking back, I feel that the African studies programme at Makerere had served its purpose but that, at a time when Ibadan and the University of Ghana had active African studies programmes, the plug was pulled too quickly on the Makerere experiment. Both the Ibadan and Ghana programmes were designed as research institutes with libraries, fellows and attached professorships. Training students was only part of their activities and there was a vested interest at both the national and university level in developing their institutional strength, an interest that did not exist at Makerere where the programme flourished on outside funds that many in the university would have liked to have seen going to help existing departments.

Chapter 3

Education: Ghana and the United States

I N GHANA I REALLY learnt what it meant to be a university professor. In Uganda I had been an interdisciplinary advocate and archaeologist. I did not have to deal with a staff and the needs of a department, but in Ghana I was the head of a department. Very rapidly as expatriates left I became the senior chair in both the faculties of arts and social sciences and at different times acting dean of both social studies, as social sciences were termed at Legon, and dean of graduate studies, when those deans were away from campus. In many ways my mind became much more focused on the role and needs of the university in a developing country. The year 1967 was a good time to arrive at the University of Ghana; the campus was still fairly new;[1] the gardens were well maintained and the trees mature without being overgrown. The tensions and shortages that marked the end of the Nkrumah era had abated and there was a positive sense of movement.

I felt that the first two years of my time in Ghana, under the National Liberation Council, were the most open. The general standard of life was improving; the *Legon Observer*, the university's independent news magazine, was at its critical best; there was an ongoing debate about the future; the economy, ever so slowly, was improving; and there was an excitement about the anticipated return to a civilian government and open democracy in 1969. Coming from Uganda we found the army to be a refreshing eye-opener. Instead of being afraid of the soldiers we found they were well groomed with polished boots, smart uniforms and friends of the people. Army camps were open to casual visitors and army vehicles did not force other vehicles off the road. It was a time of university expansion, the numbers of staff vacancies were going down as academics returned to Ghana and because of new agreements with foreign universities, particularly Canadian and British, short-term foreign academics were arriving. Though I was only at the university for nine years, I spent a term there as a visiting professor in 1983, a year on a Fulbright in 1988–89 and a semester in 1994–95, so was able to see many changes in 30 years.

Although teaching at the university began at 7.30 a.m. and went on throughout the day, life was lived at a leisurely pace in 1967, for the ratio of academics to students was relatively small. One had the luxury of overseeing the same students from entry to graduation and getting to know a good many more through the many activities on campus and the fact that every teaching staff member was also a member of one of the halls of residence. Being on campus, students occasionally came round to our house and my wife and I enjoyed seeing them in this impromptu atmosphere. Legon was very different from Makerere. First, it was huge, two miles across, and eight miles from the centre of town, in fact in the countryside. By the late 1990s, however, Accra had virtually enveloped Legon and there was a 24-hour petrol station and convenience store across from the main gate, an unimagined luxury in the 1960s and 1970s.

Campus life was modelled on achieving the quiet dignity and integrity of an Oxford or Cambridge college. There were masters of halls, terms called Michaelmas, Hilary and Trinity, a general supply store called Manciple's, a grocery called the Buttery and each hall with a bursar. We wore gowns for academic board meetings. There was a large comprehensive bookshop and banks, which Makerere did not have.[2] Legon followed the great British tradition of asking a new professor to present a public inaugural lecture. I gave mine in 1969 wearing my red doctoral gown with the vice chancellor serving as chairman. Legon had more departments than Makerere, with classics, archaeology and different languages all considered important. The newest and largest department on campus was the school of administration, which Makerere did not have until much later. Sports were more formalized, with cricket played in halls and on a university basis. Key events marked the calendar – matriculation for incoming students at the beginning of the year, when the vice-chancellor gave a keynote address, and congregation for graduation at the end of the year at which the chancellor or head of state spoke and everybody dressed up. This was held in the administration building courtyard with the clock tower as a backdrop. American visitors often found this degree of formality strange, but it ensured a strong feeling of tradition and blended in well with Ghanaians' respect for ceremony.

5. With senior staff and advanced students, Department of Archaeology, University of Ghana, 1975.

Most departments, including archaeology, had their own lecture rooms. Like Makerere, instruction was based on a modified British model. Faculty approved courses the Academic Board later confirmed, and examinations were set in consultation with external examiners who came out at the end of each academic year. Standards were high and promotions for academic staff slow; at one time most departments in both social studies and the arts were headed by acting heads who were still senior lecturers. All students read three subjects in their first year. After taking the first-year examination they then took two subjects in their second year and in some cases could specialize in one subject in their final year. In most cases, instead of picking their own subjects to read in college they were assigned to departments. Only the top 30–40 per cent could be sure of getting the subjects for which they had applied.

Since law and business administration could be taken at the undergraduate level, the brighter, or better prepared, students from urban boarding schools in the south of the country had a better chance of getting onto these courses. Law tended to attract bright women students whose families saw it as socially advantageous. Such courses were chosen more as gateways to secure jobs and higher starting salaries than out of interest in the subject matter. This ultimately starved other disciplines, including the sciences, of the brightest students. Many students were assigned ancient history, religious studies, philosophy and archaeology, even though they may have initially chosen history, economics and political science. Once locked into these departments they could not change their subjects except to drop the one they liked the least after their first year.

In 1970 the professor of political science Victor Levine and I lobbied the faculties for a more flexible course system. We lost out to the conservatism of Ghanaian academics wary of change, particularly change based on an American system about which they knew little and of which they were inherently suspicious. Though in the early 1990s a modified course system and semesters, instead of 11–13 week terms, were introduced, students were still locked into subjects they had not chosen. The only advantage of this modified course system was that they had a greater choice of electives and courses were examined as they went along, making their final degrees cumulative rather than depending on a make or break examination at the end of their degree programme.

University life was very attractive in the 1960s. We had housing, health services and everything we needed on campus. There were funds for research and the university library's collection was equal to any and far better than most in African studies. Designated officers assisted faculty with their overseas leave bookings and cleared items like cars through the ports, a not inconsiderable benefit. There were regular concerts and from time to time the Institute for African Studies' drama division put on plays. I still remember *Soul Brother*, written by a lecturer in the English department, as being one of the most enjoyable productions I have attended in any country. We were able to get fresh milk and eggs from the university farm, veterinary attention for our cats and dog, Christmas trees in December and fresh bread from the hall kitchens. When the Ford Foundation opened a guest house there was a restaurant serving meals at very modest prices and the hall senior common rooms sold wine by the bottle. For a time the British Council helped the senior common rooms acquire British newspapers. It was a real treat to read the recent newspapers over a pot of tea. We did not realize quite how good life was until things began to change after 1972–73.

As the economic situation deteriorated and student allowances were curtailed, it became increasingly difficult to buy textbooks, especially after 1975 when prices reflected world rather than Ghanaian price structures. In the mid-1970s the British and Dutch governments began to phase out their supplementation schemes aimed at retaining irreplaceable staff. Various foundations that had supplemented US faculty were also phased out. Meanwhile, the Ghanaian cedi plunged precipitously, making it virtually impossible for expatriate staff to remain on Ghanaian salaries. Between 1967 and the mid-1980s expatriate faculty membership fell from 48 to 8 per cent, with many foreign faculty now coming from Egypt, eastern Europe or the Indian subcontinent where salaries were also low. Many Ghanaian senior staff either left Legon, resulting in a major brain drain, or found it imperative to take on second or third jobs to supplement their meagre stipends, thus spending less time on research or mentoring students. By the 1980s some were running their cars as taxis and growing food on their compounds. In the early 1970s a professorial salary was worth the equivalent of $5000–6000 with allowances, which included health care, a car allowance and housing. The average university lecturer could afford to buy books, have house help and pay school fees.

By the 1980s a professorial salary, with allowances, had slipped to the equivalent of less than $200 a month, namely less than 5 per cent of what could be earned in Europe or the United States. At the same time the prices of cars, domestic appliances and books had risen, in some instances more than 20 times, making the purchase of a new car virtually impossible. The only way to earn a little extra money was to apply for long-term study leave to work in Nigeria, which was an option in the 1970s, take further employment in Ghana and hope for a contract from a foreign corporation or foundation, or even take non-academic work overseas. All these problems heavily impacted on teaching. Departments had to manage with the few lecturers who remained, often those unable to obtain jobs elsewhere, and the few graduate students who helped teach classes. Research suffered, class sizes grew, library holdings became strained and students were unable to buy their own textbooks.

The decline in educational standards took place against a backdrop of spluttering and worsening services like electricity and water. When a terrible drought hit West Africa in the 1980s, the Akosombo dam level dropped below critical limits and electricity had to be rationed; sometimes whole urban areas received no power for a whole day. Without electricity the water supply also became intermittent. Copper telegraph lines were stolen, drains were dug into to divert water for fields, transformers broke down and many services collapsed. With the growth in student numbers, those without hall space would 'perch' or illegally squat in overcrowded rooms; once proud halls could no longer serve food and students had to fend for themselves on single electric burners or wick stoves. The senior common rooms also deteriorated. In fact, the university had to some extent become irrelevant and commanded little national respect. With the gardens no longer maintained, the grass not cut and trees not trimmed, the campus lost its former beauty. Women sold nuts in paper cones, oranges and roasted corn or fried yams by the sidewalk for students who no longer went to eat in their halls.

The decline in university standards was paralleled in the schools where wages were too low to attract good teachers; in fact, many schools were forced to ask students to provide basic items like chairs and desks. With the change of government in 1981, the National Resistance Movement was anxious to expand educational opportunities, but this meant putting even more strain on resources. All this was in the future when I started in Ghana, but every problem has its roots and the beginnings of such problems were already appearing while I was at Legon.

I gave several public lectures about the crisis in higher education in Africa in the late 1980s in which I stressed that if the excellence of the 1960s, which some see as the golden age in African higher education, was to be resurrected then drastic changes had to be introduced. First, the size of the older universities needed to be reduced to make them centres of excellence and national relevance. It seemed crazy that developing countries were paying to train their best and brightest youth but failing to take advantage of their skills. Africa was producing doctors, scientists and educators, yet had gross medical, environmental and educational problems. In the 1960s, when state controls were stronger, most African countries required people they trained to sign agreements to work for the state upon graduation, but such agreements had virtually no effect.

Since some top brains had to be retained in Africa to tackle Africa's problems, I suggested that key universities have think tanks where key scholars can write and serve the government on paid contracts rather than African governments depending on short-term advisers from abroad. Foreign aid should be spent on subsidized medicine and equipment rather than on fees and perquisites for foreign consultants who know less about Africa than Africans resident in African university think tanks. I also felt that students should be required to have internship training during their studies to equip them for the realities of life. To offset the reduced size of universities, more provision needs to be made at the lower end of tertiary education for institutes of technology, craft and industrial skills training centres, agricultural colleges, as well as business and computer schools. In Africa one of the sad legacies of colonialism was the gross discrepancy in salaries and community respect between universities and colleges where practical skills were taught.

Though my views attracted large audiences and broad interest, and my talks were summarized in the Ghana press, change has been glacial. Population growth and the expansion of schools and universities has made the situation worse; most African capitals are awash with frustrated graduates who cannot get jobs and who float from one new industry to another hoping to catch the new wave before it collapses. First it was alternative technologies, later new crops for export, then travel and tourism, and recently the expanded internet and mobile phone industry, but each new avenue presents limited opportunities with ultimate success measured in profits and productivity based on recruiting fewer rather than more graduates.

There were, however, many excellent features about university education in Ghana. When I first taught in African universities in the 1960s they were idealistic institutions representing national aspirations. There was lively debate in most African universities about how to make students aware of and proud of their African culture and identity. At Ghana, all first year students were required to take a course in African studies that covered everything from the distant past to present day arts. Because the class was large, between 600 and 700 students, it was not always popular and it was difficult for lecturers to get their information across, particularly at a time when there were few audiovisual aids. Still, it had an impact and I was surprised when Ghanaians recounted to me remembered bits of what I had told them in my two presentations at the beginning of the course. In 1967 students had not yet joined the rat race to pay their fees – in fact as late as the early 1970s they had all their expenses paid, plus free meals in hall, a book allowance and a small personal allowance. Students in the 1960s and 1970s engaged in lively conversations about the world around them. They were, and still are, better informed than American students about developments in the USA, Western Europe or the wider world in general. They are keenly interested in philosophical and economic theory and know all about the IMF and World Bank.

It was no accident that many budding African novelists with something to say came from African universities. The hall system at Legon, with common rooms, high table dinners and faculty living close together on a beautiful campus, promoted interdisciplinary discourse we did not fully appreciate until it was too late. Seminars at the University of Ghana were more stimulating than in America; they attracted a more diverse and interdisciplinary audience, normally with a pre-circulated paper and free-for-all discussion. A community post and mail office where people met, a service station where petrol was sold at a controlled price, and for many years carol singing and other activities also brought people together and fostered a sense of community. The campus provided a beautiful and safe environment in which children could ride their bikes freely. It was like a large village, with its own hospital and clergy. Students lived on campus and could drop by to see their teachers. There was a sense of intellectual identity that I have never felt in America, though possibly would have done had I taught at a liberal arts college, which basically the University of Ghana was at that time.

The university was a key national asset with its teachers commanding respect and its professors consulted on national affairs. Unlike American universities, every department normally had a large number of junior staff to help with clerical, cleaning, library and other functions. In archaeology we had eight and yet most of the time we only had four or five senior members, as academic staff were called. At the time of my appointment the professor was head of department on a long-term basis. Professors were given entertainment allowances and some of this money was spent on organizing a staff Christmas party at which junior staff brought their families to meet senior staff members. My wife worked hard to make such parties a success. Rites of passage, particularly births and deaths, were accorded special attention. What I particularly enjoyed in Ghana was that on arriving at the department people went round greeting their colleagues, shaking hands and reinforcing bonds.

Going from this to a large American university was a shock to the system. For quite a long time I felt disappointed that no one shook one's hand in the morning, that I could walk across campus and not see a single person I recognized, that no one else in my neighbourhood worked at the university, that it took me nearly an hour to get to work and that I never saw any students on a casual basis. Students took one's courses in the same way as they snacked while walking around the campus. Courses were chosen to suit their timetables as much as their academic needs. They seemed acutely aware of which courses were likely to yield higher grades. Courses were taken by students from different years whereas in Ghana or at Makerere there were first-year courses that could only be taken by entering students. An African syllabus was preplanned, the courses discussed in detail and the exams set long before they were taken. In the USA one basically wrote out what one would teach, circulated a course outline and got on with the job on one's own without consulting any colleagues. Examinations were often set the night before and the scripts marked without any review of the results; the individual instructor had the power without deferring to anyone else and there was a direct relationship between teacher and student.

In 13 years of teaching in Africa no students ever questioned their marks. Had they done so, the matter would have been put before an exam board. If a student could not attend an exam it was impossible casually to arrange an alternative date. The student would need to appeal to an examinations board and might be allowed to take the exam later in the year or during the next academic session. In my first class in the USA students wanted an explanation of how marks were assigned. The whole marking system was different and still puzzles me. In Britain and Africa a pass mark, or C, is above 40 per cent, a B from 50–70 per cent and an A above 70 per cent. In America it was possible to have marks in the 90s and a C was in the 60s or 70s. I never quite knew why the lower numbers were never fully used. There was a definite grade inflation that increased in the 1970s and 1980s. In Ghana first-class degrees were a rarity, no one in archaeology had ever got a first or an A overall. When I arrived at UCLA about a third of the students regularly got A grades in their courses, Cs and Ds were rare and Fs were most unusual. This difference in grading meant that some very fine students from Africa with upper second-class degrees, meaning an average of B+ or more, failed to receive scholarships, whereas had they been in the States their degrees would have been solid A grades.

The big difference between the American and African system was in some ways a reflection of the two ways of life. In Africa, a department was a unit controlled by its head or chief. The department and university, of which it was part, were examined from outside and held to a standard comparable with that of the examining body. In America the individual faculty member was subject to evaluation. If he or she was found wanting by failing to measure up to peer norms, then that individual was denied tenure or advancement. Departmental strength ultimately depends on the combined strength of its individuals. Relatively few American chairholders make radical differences to their departments during their three or four years of tenure, but some exceptional leaders do. In the history department at UCLA the tenures of Professors Mellor and Ruiz (1997–2005), though coinciding with a drop in university funding, were exceptional in that they gained greater visibility for the department, support from community sponsors and a sense of cohesion in a rather diverse faculty. Chairpersons act as advocates of the interests of the departments they serve and in this respect the American university is a very democratic institution.

I suppose it was the sheer size difference that most overawed me when I arrived. The history department in 1967 had, if I remember rightly, 64 tenured faculty members arranged in regional fields and a part-time head of department who changed every three to five years. We were scattered on different floors and even after ten years I sometimes still had difficulty putting faces and names together. There was never a sense of a department. One felt loyalty to one's regional field, in my case Africa where there were five of us, but not to history as a whole. I did not recognize the existence of a specific UCLA history tradition or school. There were faculty seminars but these were largely attended by history faculty. Interdisciplinary interaction came at the organized research unit level, in my case African studies and archaeology, but even then faculty from disciplines with no Africa or archaeology experience rarely attended the sessions. Seminars in these instances were less friendly or collegial than they had been in Ghana. To some extent there was a paradox – more freedom in America, some members of the department seldom came into their offices, but on the other hand also more formal.

When I first arrived I would wear sandals and colourful African shirts to work and felt relaxed. When I was invited out in the evenings I would put on my suit with a shirt and tie and look more formal. I quickly found that this was atypical. On one occasion, in a rather reproving way, a jacketed colleague said he wished he could dress like me. Slowly my suits began to atrophy as I stopped wearing them. They were too formal for teaching and unacceptable for going out to dinner. As I went to few funerals or weddings in those days, my suits were left to grow old, or at least outdated, in the closet.

The biggest attraction of an American university is the strength of the graduate programmes. Graduates at UCLA, and at other major US universities, comprise between 30 and 50 per cent of student numbers. Graduate training lasts longer there than in the UK or Africa, with the average graduate spending four to six years over their degrees compared with an average of three in Europe or Africa. From the second year they normally serve as readers, helping professors grade their courses, or as teaching assistants, running tutorial classes that can involve up to 20 or 25 students at a time. For lower division classes in which the numbers are high, they are essential. One big difference in the US system is that entry-level classes are often taught by junior faculty coordinating numerous teaching assistants, whereas in Europe and Africa it is more commonplace for older, more seasoned academics to teach the larger first-year classes. Miles Burkitt, who taught Stone Age archaeology at Cambridge for more than 30 years, filled this assignment remarkably and generations of students remembered him with affection. Older, tenured, faculty members in America prefer to teach small graduate seminars that allow them to deal with their own research interest. Graduates also serve as research assistants, so universities with strong graduate programmes have stronger research records. Graduate seminars can be planned to explore a specific topic from various angles and thus supply the professor with the data required for a new synthesis.

The greater democracy of the American system is also reflected in research. Though researchers at African universities can apply for research grants individually, they are expected to work through their departments when applying for money outside the university. The department will frame a research programme and then apply to the university to support it; the funding will then come back via the department rather than directly to the individual. In the United States, while a departmental chair may support the efforts of his or her colleagues, it is up to individuals to frame their own research proposals. This of course may lead to inequalities in research funding, but it is unquestioned and reflects the recognition of individual ability or the relative market forces within the discipline.

Organized research units bring together scholars who are interested in a particular approach, geographical area or time period not covered by a single department. Unlike departments they are more ephemeral and often depend on strong leadership to give them shape and identity. Being smaller than departments they can be more attentive to their members' needs. The African Studies Center had extra strength because of federal funding. It offered less than other centres in terms of course work and its MA was based on offerings from cooperating departments. A centre's strength is that it can bring together like-minded scholars working for common aims. For the African Studies Center, this was to strengthen African studies as a whole by keeping up the pressure on departments and the central university administration to appoint more Africanists. In America much of the success of centres and institutes depends on their success in attracting funds for fellowships, endowments for conferences and chairs from interested local philanthropists. In recent years the Institute of Archaeology, named after a major benefactor Lloyd Cotsen, has gained considerable success because of the energy of its successive directors.

On first encountering an American university one is struck by how parochial many of its students are. American universities, unlike African ones, have no national mandate. It surprised me that there was no survey course on American archaeology at UCLA. Though the US media is rich in press, radio and TV resources, the average American student has little knowledge of the wider world. When I took school teachers, all graduates, from Wyoming to Africa in 1995 I was surprised that two-thirds had never been outside the country and had no passport and that a third had never travelled east of the Mississippi. US students have avenues for enhancing their knowledge of the outside world. Through agencies like the Peace Corps they can visit a Third World country to work alongside young nationals for a couple of years, or they can apply to commerce or state departments for attachments to US embassies, normally for the summer vacation. However, there are relatively few such internships, or even Peace Corps appointments. One good way of learning about the world is to study abroad for an academic year, term or semester.

The University of California has a relatively large programme covering more than 30 countries and often, as in England, France and China, several institutions in the same country. Unfortunately, excellent though the programme is, it is not compulsory and only 2–3 per cent of the eligible student population[3] participates; and more than three-quarters of those are women.[4] Programmes in places like Israel, Japan and Korea are attractive to Jewish or second-generation Asian students seeking to discover their roots.

The University of California's African programme began with Ghana and Kenya in 1969. The Ghana option was abandoned because

6. Director, UCLA African Studies Center, 1989.

of political and economic problems in 1977 and the Kenya one because of political instability in 1982.

The Ghana one was revived in 1988 and, for a time (1981–92), a programme was run in Togo. There is also a programme with the American University in Cairo and with several colleges in Natal in South Africa. The University of California programme is one of the best in Africa;[5] it gives students an awareness of another culture and normally offers opportunities to travel to other African countries as well. Many participants go on to study Africa at the graduate level or become interested in working overseas for a time in development studies. One weakness of the programme is that it is restricted to sub-Saharan Africa and to English-speaking countries. Efforts to begin programmes in Francophone Africa have so far failed.

At different times I initiated or ran education abroad programmes in Ghana and Togo. I wanted to encourage students to take on assignments that would teach them how to become researchers and something about the country in which they lived. In Togo, students helped on a market survey and had to find out about a particular activity in which the people they were studying engaged. I insisted on some students from the host university working with them to enhance their experience and help with communication. When first considering Africa many of the students had lofty goals that embraced large fields of study, such as looking at religious beliefs, which would only have been possible through knowledge of the local language. Once they got to the country they began to realize that it would be easier to study practice rather than belief, or topics related to education, farming, crafts and everyday life. Education abroad programmes provided me with an excellent way of interacting with students, which was impossible on campus. Though sometimes on duty for 24 hours, consoling sick or homesick students, encouraging their research and helping them to cope with different cultures, I found the experience really rewarding, as did my wife who accompanied me on the Ghana programme. We looked back with great pleasure at such occasions as our Thanksgiving and Christmas Day dinners. We loved to see students beginning to appreciate and love Ghana as much as we did.

Chapter 4

Religion and race on three continents

I N MANY WAYS I HAVE always seen myself as an outsider looking in, which is perhaps the penalty for being an expatriate without a specific community. I used to see it as the destiny of a diasporan Jew, but coming to America made me realize that Jews in the United States have a strong sense of community. I suppose the feeling of detachment can be traced back to my roots in Bolton where there were never more than about 30 Jewish families when I was a child, though the number rose to 40–45 towards the end of the Second World War. With peace and the greater use of motorcars, families gravitated to Manchester, a larger urban centre 12 miles away, and by the late 1960s the Bolton Hebrew congregation, like so many other small English Jewish communities, had ceased to exist as a viable unit.

Europe

We were a large family; my father had 11 children and when I was born we had 18 immediate relatives in Bolton; in Manchester there were another dozen or so cousins, second cousins and my mother's half brothers and sisters and their families. My father was close to his brother Morris who lived in Hanley, now part of Stoke on Trent, which, though it seemed far away and involved two train changes, was only 45 miles to the south. The two families would get together for the many festivals and often for our single week's summer holiday in Llandudno in North Wales. Including *landsleit*, people who came from my father's home country or with whom he was related in even the vaguest way, we had our own smaller Jewish family community, insulated in many ways from the broader English society. Religion and cultural tradition separated us from the people around whom we thought of as *goyim*, different and, to my young mind at the time, inferior. *Goyim* ate different food and were suspicious of us. As the sleeping partner to Messrs Hackney & Garnet, my father had an interest in a business selling clothes on hire purchase. Though we had always known the Hackneys, my parents never called them by their personal names; when they occasionally came for a meal it was a rather stiff, formal occasion. Mother retained a link with Mrs Hackney after Mr Hackney's death and it took us a long time to realize that her name was Annie.

Though we never consciously learnt Yiddish[1] – it was father's native tongue but mother always used English at home – we nevertheless picked up words to do with foods, parts of the body or simple activities like *schlep*. I only distinguished which words were Yiddish when I was in secondary school and being introduced to a broader world through books. We used Yiddish words for parts of the chicken like *bailik* (breast) and *fligl* (wings), as well as *lokshen* for soup noodles. Many words had a more homely, earthy and realistic feel in Yiddish, like *meshugge* or *shmateh*, and at the time seemed untranslatable. I never really knew which words were Hebrew and which were Yiddish. All I knew was that Yiddish was an expressive, emotional language, in contrast with English, which seemed colder and more formal.

Religion shaped the pattern of our lives. There was a weekly and annual cycle of activity. The sabbath, referred to as *Shabbos*, was the high point of the weekly cycle. The table was laid with a clean white cloth and father came back from work earlier than usual. We would never even contemplate going out on that night. The *Shabbos* candles were placed in brass candlesticks, which, unlike my own, were polished weekly. We often had our weekly bath on Friday night in preparation for the *Shabbos* meal. Father said *Kiddush* and passed around the silver goblet of wine in descending order of age.

Our meal was either cold fried chopped fish in cutlet form or chopped boiled gefilte fish. Mother would make a large batch of fish on Fridays, as well as prepare the *Shabbos* lunch, always homemade chicken soup with butter beans, carrots and *lokshen* followed by roast chicken, roast potatoes, sometimes a *chelzel* (dumpling stitched up in chicken skin) and usually a rather overcooked vegetable. Our desserts varied, but we certainly ate a lot of stewed dried fruit (*kompot*), particularly prunes, apricots and raisins and sometimes a *lokshen kugel*, my favourite dessert. After the evening meal we often had fresh fruit and chocolates were passed round. The fruit was always seasonal and we looked forward to the winter when little tangerines from

North Africa were available. There were also dates in wooden boxes and dried figs, which I disliked.

Except during the war and for a few years after, Bolton was unable to support a regular Friday night service. Men worked hard and late. *Shabbos* morning, however, was a different matter. Dressed in our suits, we walked to *schul,* as we called the synagogue or temple, through a relatively impoverished working-class neighbourhood. We were probably conspicuous because at that time Saturday morning was still part of the working week. The route is still fresh in my mind, though I have forgotten the names of the streets. I remember passing through Chadwick Park with a museum at the centre containing Egyptian mummies and sarcophagi. The park walls and buildings were of millstone grit discoloured to dark grey and black from the pollution of the mill stacks. We normally arrived at *schul* just before 10.00 a.m. by which time the morning service had begun.

As one of the older members of the congregation father had a seat in front. The *schul* was a converted three-storey house. On the ground floor were rooms for meetings and for Hebrew school or *chada,* which we attended until at least aged 13 on Sundays and on three or four weekdays after our regular school. The second and third floors formed the *schul.* Only part of the third floor was intact and was used as the balcony where women sat during High Holidays. The *bimah,* where the cantor or minister conducted the service and where the scrolls of the law (*sepher torim*) were brought, was in the centre and raised a good foot from the floor surface. An ark at the eastern end with a thick blue velvet curtain decorated with a gold *Magen David,* Shield of David, covering its door, contained the *sepher torim.* We had no elaborate stained glass windows, the carpeting was threadbare and scant, and with only an occasional inefficient electric space heater, we were cold in winter. Our service normally lasted a good two hours. We were an orthodox community so only the prayer in honour of the royal family was in English.

There was a sort of controlled confusion; people came and went, chatted, prayed, or davenned gently swaying at different speeds, but there was warmth of communal togetherness. We sang the responses with gusto and the final songs like *Adown Awlom* (Lord of the Universe) and the *Hatikvah,* our song of hope that later became the Israeli national anthem, in rapturous discordance, for we all knew the words and were quite glad to be leaving. For a brief time during the early war years when the congregation was at its height, our minister the Revd Isaac Richards[2] formed a choir from the senior *chada* male pupils to try to induce a little harmony. Being a small community in a working-class town, many of the men were shopkeepers and could not afford the luxury of closing their businesses, so they would return to their shops in the afternoon.

On *Shabbos* children could not work, do homework, shop, or even listen to the radio. Mother often visited other Jewish women in the afternoon within walking distance of our home. They kept their hats on and addressed each other formally. We sometimes accompanied her and benefited from the women competing to provide the best teas. No food was prepared that day. Though there were few Bolton Jewish families they always had access to kosher food. Our minister was the *shochet* (ritual slaughterer of animals) and, as we did not have a Jewish butcher, the community arranged to get kosher meat through a gentile one. At times we would buy live chickens and take them to the minister's house to be slaughtered on a Thursday night. We were always aware that our food was different from that of other people, that our dietary laws protected us from bad food and that we ate better than our neighbours. This was undoubtedly the case because great reliance was placed on food and the stereotype of a Jewish mother over indulging her children was very true.

We never ate out or brought in cooked foods in case the fats used were suet from cows or lard from pigs. When we were young we did not know anyone with a fridge so pickling delicacies such as tongue conserved our meat supply. We kept meat that had been salted and washed in the kashering process cold on the cellar steps. Fish was a great standby during the week with *finnan* (smoked) haddock on a Monday as the fresh fish took time to reach Bolton from the Irish Sea through ports like Fleetwood. We had a healthy fear of what we could not eat, *traif*, which included all meats, foods with uncertain fats and most foods to which we had never been introduced. This fear helped keep us separate. We did not eat out and in any case Bolton had few restaurants apart from its 700 fish-and-chip shops and the largest number of tripe and pig trotter shops in the whole of England. Occasionally, as a great treat, Auntie Annie would bring smoked salmon, salami or sausages from Manchester and even on occasion bagels and black (rye) bread. Though our food was rich in fats, the range of spices and vegetables we ate was limited. I had to wait until I got to Africa to experience a wider range of greens, peppers, artichokes, asparagus and avocados.

The seasonal cycle revolved around the Jewish holidays. *Rosh Hashanah*, the New Year, was a time for new clothes and silver candlesticks; it was when even mother came to *schul* and father stopped working. It was when we attended evening and sometimes afternoon services and ate too much. The minister or cantor, and occasionally we had both, would dress in white and many of the men wore white *yarmulkes*, or in father's case a soft flat-topped hat. Many men used *talesim* (prayer shawls) and the *schul* was filled to capacity with people we never saw during the year. Everybody wore their best clothes and the women looked splendid in their new outfits, hats and jewellery. The service lasted upwards of four hours and on the last day of the festival there was always *yiskor*, a prayer for dead relatives. As children, we were sent out for that and would wonder what was happening inside and why everyone was so anxious to be there. There was also the blowing of the *shofar*, the ceremonial ram's horn, a skill no member of the community possessed but which Mr Samuel Isaacson, who owned a small furniture shop and served as cantor, got better at each year. After the service there was wine and sponge cake downstairs. No special allowance was made for children so from an early age we learnt to imbibe small quantities of sweet kosher red wine or occasional golden muscatel.

After lots of greetings and catching up, we finally wended our way slowly home. Mother and the girls normally left before the end of the morning service to get the food ready, but father, my brother Leonard and I came back either via my sister Ray's house or my brother Barney's. We again had wine, cake and hard biscuits, *kichels*, which we always pronounced the best we had ever tasted. We invariably arrived home late and no sooner had we had our leisurely lunch, which we called dinner, than it was time to turn round and go back to the *schul* for the *Mincha* or afternoon service.

Yom Kippur, the Day of Atonement, was a special time. We had to have an early meal to be ready for the fast before it got dark. The sombre *Kol Nidrei* service, at which we prayed to cleanse ourselves of sins, was probably the best attended event of the year in Bolton and its symbolism had a big effect on me as a child. The following day my father would set out very early for the service, at which most of the older men wore special slippers to stop their feet hurting, and we followed later. The men spent the whole day there and rested and chatted in the *schul* between the *mussaf* and *mincha* services. People grew tired and emotional as the day wore on. The *schul* got hot and stuffy as people remembered their lost relatives and we longed to escape. It was difficult to stand still for so long and to be chided for talking. I remember roaming the streets, window shopping, even visiting the central library and museum, which was clearly forbidden. Children under 13 would break their fast with lunch, but after our barmitzvah we had to last until the evening when we broke our fast downstairs with wine and snacks the women of the congregation had brought. That, however, was just to fortify us for our walk home and the great feast that awaited us with delicacies like chopped liver, soup, chicken and other goodies. Succoth, the Feast of Tabernacles or harvest festival, followed soon after. Being in the rainy part of England few in the community bothered to build the flimsy little structures in their back yards where one is supposed to eat, sit and rejoice in the bounty of the land.

We were very conscious of our religion at school where prayers were said first thing in the morning and from which we, as Jews, were excused. Unfortunately, because prayers offered one of the few occasions for a general assembly, this often meant missing important announcements. We missed seven or eight days of school because of Jewish holidays, which we found especially difficult at the beginning of the school year when pupils were bonding into their new classes. There were also classes in religious knowledge, which we sat out. The school made much of the build up to Christmas with carols being learnt, decorations made and parties anticipated, and we all had to bring something for the end of term gathering. Mother always made cup cakes, but there were many things at the party we were warned against eating, particularly mince pies. At first I believed they contained minced meat and only later learnt that they were made of dried fruit and what we could not eat was the suet they contained. While Christmas was cheerful with the town decorated and illuminations lending a fairyland atmosphere, we focused on our own festival of Chanukah. However, we sang many of the carols because they were joyous songs and it was difficult to avoid them.

Until I went to secondary school Easter was a difficult time for me, for kids often shouted taunts like 'Who killed Jesus?' My school was known as the Church Institute when I started, but was later renamed the Canon Slade Grammar School after the far-sighted vicar who had founded it in 1874 as England's first coeducational day grammar school. Each week began with a service in the nearby parish church. Though run on Christian principles – both headmasters were Anglican clergymen – I probably got more respect as a Jewish child than I would have received elsewhere. There was a genuine interest in religion and I was often invited to talk about my religious practices. Though I learnt a lot about Christianity in an osmotic sort of way, on looking back I am sorry I did not learn more about it. Canon Slade taught me religious tolerance, to understand and respect other religions. Posters about missionary work in Africa and collection boxes for the Society for the Propagation of the Gospel, which were displayed in the parish church where we went for singing practice until I was thrown out for my inability to sing harmoniously, were curiously my first glimpses of Africa and of the goodness that was intended for folk very different from ourselves. At home we had a blue and white *pushke* (collection box) for Jews in Palestine. Every now and then bearded Chassidic Jews, who would not even accept a cup of tea in our family's kosher home, would come to empty the box. They believed in the messiah but not in the political Zionism to which I was already aspiring.

Growing up during the war was fundamental to my belief system. I assiduously followed current affairs through *Picture Post* photographs, many of which I cut out and placed in scrapbooks. From these pictures I have vivid memories going back to 1937–38 of the Spanish Civil War, the exile of Emperor Haile Selassie of Abyssinia, the imprisonment of Gandhi and the rape of Nanking – all frightening images that played havoc with my imagination and gave me a sense of a world with big problems. I quickly realized from my *chada* classes that Jews were a people long subject to oppression and I began to identify with all people outside the fully accepted fold. In our congregation, we talked during the war about what we had read in the *Jewish Chronicle* about the destruction of the Jews in Europe. Newsreels in the cinema of the horrors the Allied troops found in the concentration camps they freed from German control in 1944 and 1945, especially Bergen-Belsen, struck home. A Penguin special my brother Leonard bought about these revelations, which contained horrifying pictures, strengthened my Zionist leanings.

The aftermath of the war and the struggle for Jewish autonomy in Palestine strengthened our small Jewish community. Getting together in a time of austerity was one of the few things we could easily do. On Thursday nights we would meet in the Hebrew schoolroom to sing Hebrew songs and exchange news, hopes and aspirations for a Jewish homeland. A branch of the *Habonim* youth movement and later of the

Bnei Akiva (Children of the Rabbi Akiva) briefly flourished. Leonard was active and gave reviews of books by Arthur Koestler. I painted posters advertising forthcoming events to *schul* attendees. When Israel came into being in 1948 the momentum lapsed; we were too small a group to maintain a varied programme and the lure of Manchester's larger Jewish community was too great. This was a time of tension in England. British troops were trying to maintain a fragile peace in Palestine and were subject to terrorist attacks by Jewish militants, including blowing up the King David Hotel in Jerusalem and hanging seven young British intelligence officers, all conscripts. My friend John Hurst, the eminent medieval archaeologist, was fortunately spared. In Bolton and Manchester stones were thrown at Jewish businesses. We were easy targets.

Around this time I attended summer schools organized by Jewish youth study groups in Switzerland (1947) and Ireland (1948). There were about 60 young men and women in each group, mostly from larger Jewish urban centres like Leeds, Manchester and London. Every day we had classes in modern Hebrew and sang Israeli songs. We studied the Bible and Jewish history, but mainly communicated among ourselves. Going to Switzerland was the first time I had been abroad. The whole summer school had cost only £16, including fares and accommodation, but at that time this was the equivalent of at least three times the average weekly working wage in Britain. I had around £2 to spend and it was a dream to be able to buy cream cakes and Swiss chocolate, for in Britain chocolate was rationed and rather plain and ice cream still unavailable. We prayed on the train wearing our *tephilin* and felt blessed at having lived in Britain and been spared the horrors of our European counterparts. We delighted in the majesty of the Alps, the beauty of Geneva and the efficiency of Swiss electric trams and trains.

The Dublin trip had the virtue of being directed by Immanuel Jakobovits, a lively and charismatic young Dublin chief rabbi who later became the chief rabbi of the whole of Britain and eventually landed up in the House of Lords. The Jewish youth study groups gave me a feeling of confidence about being Jewish, a good basic knowledge of Judaism and an appreciation of Hebrew song, which I still enjoy if hardly ever practice. I still, however, felt conscious of coming from a tiny Jewish community without the networks most of the others possessed and saw Jews from big urban centres as socially more confident. With my restricted social life in Bolton, the sum total of my dating experience before going to university was having taken a female school friend out once to afternoon tea.

University was a wakening experience on a social level, as I suppose it is for most young people. Initially, I was accommodated in digs with seven other students and felt instantly aware of my Jewishness because the High Holidays and *Succoth* came in rapid succession and I had to get to *schul*. When I asked the landlady, who provided breakfast and dinner, for meals without meat, lard or other *traif* food, she became resentful of my presence, not without reason. I was homesick and remember a turning point being when Uncle David, a commercial traveller, came to town and invited me out to a very fine meal with some of the finest fish I had ever tasted. I found the Nottingham Hebrew congregation welcoming and was invited home for lunch from *schul* by the Knobils, a German refugee family with whom I was to enjoy many wonderful repasts complete with a well-sung grace after meals. The *schul* also had a detached Hebrew school and hall for social activities where I met most of the women friends I was to make in Nottingham during my undergraduate years, for in 1949 English universities were still male dominated.

There were only two women in my history group of 30 to 40 students, of whom one was engaged and the other was a nun. To get to know the other sex one had to be socially adventurous, attend Saturday night hops, which I was too shy to do on my own. Though Jewish women were more emancipated than non-Jewish women at that time, Jewish men outnumbered Jewish women by three to one at provincial universities and by nearly six to one at Oxford and Cambridge. I met the very few girlfriends I had during my first four years at university by socializing at the social centre of the Nottingham Hebrew congregation. I was also conscious at that time of my mother's advice not to bother with women until one was sufficiently affluent to consider marriage, and the marriage age for professional men was regarded as older than 25. After one term of eating very little because I was still keeping kosher and surviving on tomatoes, beans or spaghetti on toast, normally eaten at a fast-food style cafeteria, I moved to Jewish digs on Redcliffe Road where I stayed for a year. Though I ate better, it was probably not very good for me socially because I would come home to eat and work, and so became rather reclusive. My Jewish landlady seemed mystified that a Jewish boy could be studying history and not something more appropriate like law or medicine. She also did not consider me to be working if I were reading, only if I were sitting at a desk and writing.

My school career, university and the horror of the war all pushed me towards Universalist ideas. I believe that the major message to be gained from religion is 'Love thy neighbour as you love yourself'. This is the message of Jesus and of Rabbis Hillel and Akiba based on the injunction in Leviticus 19. It is a message of equality, tolerance and love, the antithesis of beliefs in the righteousness of a particular religion or set of beliefs; it is antithetical to war, to unbounded personal accumulation of wealth and, in the final analysis, to capitalist theory and practice. I believe that wealth has ultimately to be used to protect people from the degradation of poverty, disease and hunger. When I went to university in 1949 I joined the world government movement in which Lord Boyd Orr was prominent, as well as the Liberal Party, which steadily went down in national popularity until the 1980s, and was optimistic about the future and promise of the United Nations. We had the high ideals of so many other groups that have come and gone since then, fighting human inhumanity, environmental degradation, genocide and bigotry. The selflessness of such high idealism sows the seeds of its own inadequacy. Ultimately, the laws of evolution, of the survival of the strong, the need for personal and group achievement prevail with success and progress measured in material and measured ways. This particularly applies in America where one's position in society, one's possessions, one's associations and one's impact on a community in terms of the munificence of one's surroundings or the totality of one's generosity, count for more than one's good intentions or personal beliefs.

I joined the Jewish Society at the University of Nottingham and became its most prominent member, serving as secretary and later as president of the small group of about 20 students. We managed to challenge, and of course lose to, the much larger Catholic Society in field hockey and cricket. We had virtually no funds, but had the chutzpah to invite eminent speakers to address us, including the Jewish historian Dr Cecil Roth and social worker Basil Henriques, one of my first indirect contacts with Jamaica. I remember Basil telling us about a group of down-and-out delinquent youth he once took on a field trip from the slums of London. One boy, whom he discovered was Jewish by birth but who had no Hebrew school training and certainly no barmitzvah, said at the end of a long walk that the sandwiches contained bacon and that he could not eat them even though he was hungry. He had lost everything in his background apart from the prohibition against pork. As I look back on my life, in many ways I feel a bit like that small boy. I no longer attend *schul*; I do not belong to a Jewish community; I do not observe the Sabbath or fast on Yom Kippur but I still will not eat pork or shrimp and persist in eating matzos over the Passover. And this is at a time when many of the more pukka Jews I see around me have no compunctions whatsoever about eating shrimp or lobster, or enjoying leavened bread over the Passover. It is funny what traditions persist!

In January 1951 I attended a Jewish religious student conference in Haarlem in the Netherlands composed of representatives from Jewish societies at British universities and their Dutch counterparts. Many of the British students had been associated with Jewish youth study groups. We spent five days in conference and religious study and five days with Dutch families in Amsterdam. It was a memorable experience. Most of our counterparts had tattooed numbers on their forearms, courtesy of their time as teenagers in Nazi concentration camps. We were all seeking a braver, better world and it was exciting to be alive. It was a hard winter and we skated on the canals. We prayed in the inspiring but then very chilly seventeenth-century great synagogue and the glory of the sunlight filtering through the large windows was unforgettable. My Judaism, my Zionism and my faith in humanity and world justice were all affirmed by that most memorable of winter breaks; I still remember practically everything we did day by day.

At the Jewish Society we had many earnest discussions about the future of world Jewry. Would it persist? Would it disappear in our generation with assimilation? Would another horror like the Holocaust arise and how would we react? We looked at the state of Israel and I remember a discussion we had in October 1950 based on an article in the *Observer* newspaper by the eminent historian Philip Toynbee who prophesied that:

> In 100 years' time there will be no 'Jews' anywhere. There will be, with good fortune, the state of Israel, with its own distinctive but non Jewish contribution to make; and there will be citizens of other countries with Jewish blood in their veins but without Jewish thoughts and feelings in their head.

How wrong he was! England at that time, or at least the towns in which I lived, was drab and conventional. We had few immigrants;

our university had hardly any foreign students. Only once did race play a fleeting role in my life. It was at a Jewish charity dance in Nottingham where there was a live band with a black female vocalist. For much of the time her services were not called upon and she sat on her own looking increasingly lonely. I was with students in their early twenties and suggested we ask her to join us, but no one was interested and several admitted it was because she was black. I was and still am the world's lousiest dancer but I got up and asked her to dance and she seemed pleased to be noticed, but my companions were amused by what I had done. This incident made me realize that my own people still kept their prejudices even after the horrors of the recent war and it sensitized me to black–white relations. Later, on a geography field trip, I shared a room with a Ugandan called John Kiwanuka, who afterwards became minister of education in Uganda, and through him began to acquire some knowledge of Africa. These small contacts made me aware of various news items on Africa. I remember the buzz surrounding Seretse Khama of Bechuanaland's marriage to a white secretary, and the wedding of the daughter of a former British chancellor of the exchequer, Sir Stafford Cripps, to a Ghanaian lawyer Joe Appiah in 1954. I later became great friends with the Appiahs.

As a research student, first at Cambridge and later at Nottingham, I became engrossed in my work and religious thought and practice took a back seat in my life, but this was to change in my last year in England. I had led a sheltered social life. I dated very little until late 1954 and when I did it was platonic, which explains, I now realize, why the relationships never lasted. On excavations I began to develop closer associations and, in turn, fell in love with three remarkable, beautiful women with compatible interests who were not Jewish. It was an agonizing time of my life, for my Judaism was inflexible. I could not perceive of marrying a non-Jewish woman, yet my basic philosophy was to accept the beliefs of others. I had been brought up to believe that one should not even think of commitment until one was comfortable and could support a wife. I was busy trying to finish my doctoral thesis, apply for career positions and eventually prepare for the move to Africa. It was all too much. I became engaged for a month to Amy who could not see why a wife needed to follow her husband's faith and, for the only time in my life, I had a form of mental and physical breakdown; I was laid low for over a week when I could least afford it. I suppose one could say that Judaism, and a basic timidity, were just too strong and I went to Kenya in October 1956 full of personal doubts and confusion.

Africa

Africa was less of a culture shock to me than it seems to have been to my students going out there 45–50 years later when it was far more developed. Curiously, perhaps because the Kenya to which I was bound was still very British in 1956, I found going to America in 1977 a greater shock. I had already learnt that there was a Jewish community in Nairobi and was favourably surprised on my first journey along the main road, then the Queen Elizabeth Highway, to see a new *schul* and community centre. On the first Friday night possible I attended services and was warmly welcomed. At that time the emergency was still in force and getting to know the Jewish community provided an excellent entrée into Kenya life. Although there were many highly placed Jews in Kenya, they were still excluded from the two main European clubs, the Muthaiga Club and the Nairobi Club, which played an important role in British official life. Jews were nonetheless very influential. The Bloch family owned the main hotels, the Norfolk and New Stanley, the largest transport company and many urban properties were Jewish owned and Israel Somen, the mayor of Nairobi, was Jewish. There were Jews in the Royal Technical College that Princess Margaret had recently opened and that formed the foundation for the university.

Among the Jews I got to know were Nat Kofsky, the director of the Conservatoire of Music, Arthur Haller, chairman of the Maize Marketing Board, Maurice Rogoff, the police pathologist, and many others who were either retired or owned businesses in the city. The 'winds of change', as British Prime Minister Harold Macmillan termed them, were blowing through Africa, but few in the community seemed to have felt them. The Jewish community was cut off from Kenyan Africans and tended to know them only as house servants. Their *memsahibs*, as the wives of expatriate Europeans were often termed, walked around with keys to stop them getting at the sugar or other petty household supplies. The servants lived in boys' quarters, tiny airless single rooms at the back of the house, mostly without electricity and with inadequate sanitation. Few Jewish people bothered to have serious conversations with them and I was horrified to find that they held the same stereotyped views of Africa and Africans as the rest of the white population. I remember heated arguments over Sabbath dinner, very rude I suppose for a guest, about independence, which I believed could come within five years, whereas the prevailing view was that it would take 50. They claimed that Kenyan Africans were like children, were incapable of learning, had poor judgement and were corrupt. A constant theme I heard throughout Africa from European settlers was that no one understood Africans as they did, so newcomers or outsiders had no right to pass judgement or offer advice. The chief flaw with this argument was that it was usually made by people who had seen Africans all their lives but had never taken the opportunity to get to know them as equals capable of the same human emotions as they were.

One heard that all Africans looked alike, that it was impossible to tell their age and that they did not have the same feelings as white people. How could they if they sang and played drums at funerals? Other stupid ideas were that they had less regard for human life and because they had children like rabbits were less upset when a child died, often because of the limited medical services. Africans were provided with few educational opportunities – only two government secondary schools accepted African boys in the Nairobi area in 1956 – yet their lack of education was regarded as their fault. For the few white children there were two excellent secondary schools just for boys.[3] Mission trained Africans were regarded as untrustworthy and my boss Louis Leakey seemed to think that the only good Africans came from rural areas. He claimed that one could trust traditional chiefs but not African intellectuals who had gone away for training and lost their traditional values. He, like most Kenya whites, was against universal suffrage. Tom Mboya, the up-and-coming trade-union leader and politician, was regarded with great suspicion.

Pay scales, stratified along racial lines with Europeans on top, Asians in the middle and Africans at the bottom, militated against equality and one heard outrageous remarks from people who did not even regard themselves as racists. I went out a few times with the daughter of a Jewish businessman who had abandoned her degree course at Edinburgh because she could not abide British social relationships and was horrified that white women at the university went out with Kenyan men. How could they do that if they knew how they lived in Kenya? The white owner of a farm near Nakuru, where I excavated a site in 1957, said he could not stay in a London hotel because of the possibility that Africans had used the bath or slept in the beds. He would never, he claimed, visit London again.

At my field station at Olorgesailie, 46 miles from Nairobi, I had to get a permit (*kipande*) from the district office to take any Kikuyu from one area to another and half my workers were Kikuyu. One, Mr Kanyugi who spoke English, taught me a lot but mostly to respect Africans. Another, Mr Kanunga, an older Mukamba man of 46 from an area southeast of Nairobi, did not speak English and was technically illiterate, but I came to depend on his wisdom in so many ways and rapidly learnt Swahili. He was a wonderful, self-reliant worker with heaps of initiative and, like my other staff, paid a minimum wage. The men willingly worked long hours in one of the hottest areas of the Rift Valley without ever seeming to count the hours. I became hot and often wanted to rest, but they shamed me by their responsible behaviour. Kanunga could build houses, make fire, twist rope from bark strips and whittle wood into all sorts of shapes. He had no front teeth, so carved himself a realistic set from ivory or bone. I was reminded of them when I visited George Washington's estate at Mount Vernon outside Washington DC in 1985 and saw the founding president's wooden teeth. Mr Kanunga's were much more realistic. I made one memorable trip to Kaumoni where Kanunga's family lived and he introduced me to his extended family. Here among his people (whom he only got to see for a few weeks once a year) he was highly respected, loved by the whole community and regarded as extremely intelligent and versatile, yet back in Nairobi he was seen as an illiterate African and accorded no respect at all. The inability of rulers to look beyond their ingrained stereotyped impressions has been one of the enduring tragedies of colonialism whether in apartheid South Africa, pre-civil rights United States, or occupied Palestine.

I met very few African intellectuals; there were none at the Coryndon Museum, which I visited each week on my return from my base at Olorgesailie. There was a handful at the Royal College, several of whom were married to white women they had met on overseas study. The main opportunity to meet educated Africans was through my contacts with Makerere College extra mural programmes run by Ieuan Hughes, a gifted and energetic Welshman. He and his wife Kate, who became lifelong friends, often gave parties at their house for students and extension instructors, but even there one seldom met Kenyan African women. Their husbands were reluctant to take them to European parties because their English was often poor and their dress sense rather unsophisticated.

One could also meet African intellectuals through an urban

Anglican Christian mission that performed pastoral work in the townships on the outskirts of Nairobi. The minister in charge had heard about my lectures on biblical history and archaeology at the Jewish cultural centre and persuaded me to write a series of articles for their newspaper, *The Rock*. White Kenyans regarded these Kenyan Africans as unsavoury radicals at best or latent communists at worst. Most, however, seemed to hold politically liberal views and aspired towards a just society in which *Uhuru* (independence) would come sooner rather than later. It was from such gatherings that I learnt about African writers, still largely from West Africa, who were beginning to make a stir with their novels about a changing Africa. It irked African intellectuals that, even with a foreign degree, their pay scales were different from those of their European counterparts, many of whom spoke no vernacular language and had little knowledge of the culture and environment of Kenya. I found the social climate of Kenya very disturbing.

In March 1957 the Gold Coast achieved independence as Ghana. This was big news in Kenya; everyone spoke about it and letters were written to the *East African Standard*. The general consensus was that Africans would be unable to cope, would introduce untold corruption and that an African government anywhere on the continent would give other Africans uppity ideas. Independence took place and the sky never fell, but it occurred in a charged atmosphere. Though colonialism was bad in Kenya, at least there was some preparation; there were a few secondary schools; many Kenyans were returning from overseas with degrees and Kenyans were teaching at Makerere College. There was discussion about the future in both Kenya and Britain where many politicians realized that the colonies had to go. In the prevailing spirit of Prime Minister Harold Macmillan's slogan that Britons had 'never had it so good' and the escalating move away from the austerity of the early 1950s and the failed policies of Suez and the east of Suez disengagement, most people believed that political change should occur sooner rather than later. In France, de Gaulle was pulling out of Algeria and planning to create a regional union of independent Francophone states that were economically dependent on France.

A research visit to Uganda in June 1957 turned into a challenging and enriching experience. I was to help Professor Richard Foster Flint from Yale, who was engaged in writing *Pleistocene and Glacial Geology*, look at geological sites. I would spend four weeks in Uganda with my old friend Bill Bishop, and then another two weeks helping Professor Flint in Kenya. Uganda was an eye opener. It was beautiful, green and had no white settlers, only civil servants, teachers, missionaries and commercial people. The different ethnic groups mixed easily, especially at Makerere University College, then the only full centre of university education between Khartoum and Johannesburg. A student I had taught on an extension course in England had given me an introduction to a Ugandan, Ibrahim Mugenyi, son of the Omukama (King of Bunyoro). Ibrahim's close friend John Kaboha was at that time an assistant district officer in Uganda and I stayed with him in Mbale on my way back to Kenya. He took me to his friends John and Faith Barlow and there, nine months after arriving in Africa, I experienced my first real African meal. We stayed up talking until very late and I became convinced then that I wanted to work in the freer social atmosphere of Uganda. Fortunately, there was a vacancy for a curator of the Uganda Museum and, with the departure of Peter Shinnie, an opportunity to be the director for archaeology. By May 1958 I was in Uganda.

In Kampala I frequently met Africans of my own social, educational and economic status. Unlike in Kenya, there were educated African women who accompanied their husbands to social gatherings and engaged in lively political discourse. The Uganda Society, founded in the 1930s, put on monthly lectures on all manner of topics relating to Uganda. I became an eager member, served on the committee, was president in 1964 and a joint editor of the *Uganda Journal* from 1962 to 1967. I addressed the society on seven occasions and led four very lively excursions to craft and historical sites.

The Uganda Club, founded in Kampala by the far-sighted and effective British governor Sir Andrew Cohen, was open to Africans and Jews and critically situated near the city centre. It brought people together for lunch and tea and provided a convenient place to meet and read newspapers. I was soon elected to the committee and, as its youngest member, was assigned the job of arranging a monthly Saturday night dance, which was designed to attract younger members. Many young people regarded the club as stuffy and I had to work hard to attract new members. I must admit, though, that if one wanted a lively night out it was probably better to go to Top Life, the popular dance hall in nearby Mengo where the music was less frumpy and there were many more women. We did, nevertheless, attract a large number of diplomats who were at that time setting up consulates in anticipation of independence, and I met my future wife, Eunice Lubega, at the April 1959 dance. Eunice was quite a celebrity at the time, for she had been the first African woman to graduate in Africa, which she had done from Makerere in 1955 before going to Oxford for a year.[4] At future dances I made up my own groups, which included Eunice and friends from the administration, like my future best man Michael Harlow, an assistant district commissioner in Jinja, as well as from the private sector.

I was conscious and proud of my religion in Uganda. I wanted to date Jewish women, but the Jewish community was small and the only eligible ones were the school-age daughters of friends. Itinerant traders formed the roots of the community in the early twentieth century, but few stayed long judging from the inscriptions on the tombstones in the small Jewish section of the Kampala cemetery. In the late 1950s we could occasionally raise a *minyan* of ten men for an informal service, but did not hold regular services. We met infrequently, as when there was an Israeli visitor, or held abbreviated services in congregants' houses on the High Holidays. Among the few Jews I remember were an accountant, two contractors, a couple of shopkeepers, several university lecturers, and a large family of Bombay Indians (*Bnei Israel*), the Solomons from Entebbe.

Mr Solomon ran the water pumping station near Entebbe, had nine children and seemed to be as Asian as I was British. The government, which grouped its employees in the civil list by race, certainly regarded him as such. He had more daughters than sons, which was difficult in Uganda because he wanted them to have Jewish husbands. His eldest daughter Ruby became a friend and joined Eunice and me on several outings. Many members of the small Jewish community in Uganda held the same views about Africans as their more established counterparts. With Ugandan Independence Day and Yom Kippur coinciding on 9 October 1962, we knew there would be visitors and arranged a *Kol Nidrei* service in someone's apartment. We let the incipient diplomatic delegations know about the arrangements and I was asked to conduct the service. Although I was nervous and conscious of my poor singing voice, it went off well. Israel's representative, a minister called Yigal Allon, was present, as were the French ambassador and Professor Melville Herskovits, the doyen of American African studies.

Straight after independence the community disintegrated. Former civil servants took their golden retirement handshakes and returned to

Britain; people in the commercial world felt worried about the economic future and left for Kenya or Britain; and some, including the Solomons, went to Israel. I met Mr Solomon and some of his children in Israel in 1967, but he had failed to find a job, felt nervous about learning Hebrew in his fifties and generally seemed unsettled.

The focus of the community after 1962 became the Israeli embassy, particularly in the mid-1960s when Uri Lubrani was ambassador and Arye Oded first secretary. Both had very close relationships with Africans. Arye took a degree in his spare time at Makerere and conducted research on the Bayudea, a disaffected Baganda group who took up Judaism in the early twentieth century and were petitioning Israeli help. The Israeli embassy organized communal Seder meals for the expanding Israeli community.[5] I remember one particularly large Seder held in Jinja around 1965 at which there were more than 50 celebrants. The occasional religious services that had meant so much to us as isolated colonial Jews evaporated because the more secular Israelis preferred to regard the Holy Days as holidays from their normal routine and take advantage of days off for sight seeing.

My Judaism and interests in race relations were tested in the early 1960s when I began dating Eunice. She worked for the Church Missionary Society (CMS) as a teacher at a girls' boarding school at Gayaza, 11 miles north of Kampala. We fell in love. It was a logistically difficult courtship. She had house responsibilities and was expected to be in by 10.00 p.m. most nights and on Sunday evenings had to attend a communal meal presided over by their formidable head teacher Joan Cox. Despite late nights limited to Saturday and stay-overs being impossible, we persevered. Our relationship was quite open. Because I was trying to gain visibility for the museum, I was well known in Kampala and often in the newspaper. I had early on given a lecture to senior girls in the school, so her students knew who I was. Though the racial atmosphere was considerably more relaxed than in Kenya there were no highly placed mixed couples at that time. People had liaisons, but they were discreet, rather shady sexual relationships rather than the coupling of intellectual equals.

Several high-ranking officials, including the head of the Uganda Electricity Board, who was also honorary treasurer of the museum, had unofficial African wives, but they were never formally acknowledged and never joined their partners at social gatherings. There were mixed families, like the Bells and Wilsons, who had quite a bit of standing in society because their British progenitors had been high-ranking British officials who ensured they were looked after when they left Uganda, but many were landless urban workers navigating a precarious existence between different social and ethnic worlds. Eunice and I were determined to protect our children from such a situation. In November 1960 we became engaged and talked to many people about our plans. American friends, knowing the social situation at the time in the United States, were solicitous but apprehensive. The Archbishop of Uganda who invited us to dinner was discouraging, basically saying that we should heed the word of God. Many CMS officials wanted to see Eunice appointed deputy headmistress of Gayaza on her way to becoming its first African head. Her colleagues at the school were supportive, despite possibly disapproving of her marriage. The Nairobi Jewish rabbi, Julius Carlebach, a sociologist before becoming a rabbi and very conversant with East African social conditions, basically told us that marriage at the best of times was difficult but that if we felt we were personally compatible then the rest would fall in place. He was right.

We had a beautiful wedding on 10 February 1961 in the Uganda Club where we had met. The British Resident for Kampala, the equivalent of the district commissioner elsewhere in Uganda, had had his offices beautifully decorated with local flowers and what we feared would be a sterile affair turned out to be a moving experience. The reception was blessed with the attendance of so many missionaries whom Eunice knew and friends of different ethnic groups. It was a joyous occasion and though none of my family attended, telegrams from family were read out and my sister Freda sent us a record of Jewish melodies popular at Jewish weddings in England. I enjoyed the occasion more than any wedding I have ever attended, as well I should. The only minor regret was that Eunice's father did not attend. He had been put out because his daughter, who had gone so much further educationally than any of his other nine children, was not marrying a member of the Church of England.[6] My religion was more of a problem to him than my race, but in time he became reconciled to our marriage. He was right to believe that religious difference was a more difficult hurdle to overcome than differences in colour, ethnicity or native language. Ours was the first mixed marriage to be featured pictorially on the front page of the *Uganda Argus*. Our example inspired other couples to take the plunge and within a few years several European lecturers at Makerere, including Ian Livingstone and Peter Rigby, had followed suit.

7. Eunice and Merrick on their wedding day, Kampala, 1961.

We took our honeymoon in two parts – a long weekend at the Kaptagat Arms Hotel in Kenya and, two months later, a longer bus-man's holiday drive to a museums conference in Livingstone, Northern Rhodesia, looking at sites and meeting colleagues *en route*. The Kaptagat Arms had been a country club restricted to Europeans, but we heard it had recently changed hands and adopted an open policy. We booked, but on our way grew nervous when we passed a sign saying it was for 'Europeans only'. When we got there Major Towers and his staff treated us royally, for Eunice was the first African guest to stay there and we the first mixed couple. Guests stay in little cottages, each with a wood-burning fire because at over 8000 feet there is a nip in the air. The African staff regarded Eunice as special, for it gave them a sense of pride and dignity to serve an African guest as the equal of a white one. Curiously, Mr and Mrs Flockhart, who had taught me at elementary school, were there; they were nearing retirement and now teaching at a nearby mission school. Given that many hotels did not admit black or Asian guests until Kenya's independence in late 1963, Kapatagat became our special place for holidays.

We planned our trip to Livingstone very carefully because we knew that many white establishments *en route* would be unwelcoming. Initially, we had intended going as far south as Pretoria so that I could visit the famous Australopithicene sites, but were advised that if we attempted to enter South Africa we would, as a mixed couple, be refused entry. Our first problem came when we crossed from Tanganyika into Northern Rhodesia. We had booked ahead to stay at the only hotel in Mpika, but when we arrived they claimed they had no room in the main hotel so had to put us in the annex, basically a shed next to their cleaning supplies. Not wanting to rock the boat, we ate in a frosty atmosphere with people staring at us. The African hotel workers told us there was room in the hotel but that the proprietor did not want trouble from the other guests.

In Lusaka we had to stay at the most expensive hotel, for it was 'international', meaning it could accept African guests. It was not difficult to see why the Central African Federation was breaking up. It was white run and the small white population of Northern Rhodesia and Nyasaland was finding it difficult to hold onto an untenable racial policy at a time when much of Africa was rapidly moving to independence.

When we moved on to Livingstone where I was chairing a Museums Association of Middle Africa conference, we faced instant difficulty because several of our participants were Africans from Nigeria, Niger and Ghana and the UNESCO representative was an American of Japanese descent. None of the hotels would accept them as guests. Finally, with the help of the director of the Rhodes–Livingstone Museum, Dr Desmond Clark, the Livingstone township agreed to accommodate everybody in the residential quarters meant for short-term and single white employees. Eunice was the first African ever to stay there. One of the museum curators assumed that Eunice was a Muganda princess and kept telling us how our Africans were different from theirs. It was meant as a compliment. On one occasion when Eunice was buying an ice cream a woman told her to stand up straight and not lean against the counter; on another someone took a photo of her driving our rather stylish Citroen ID19 car. We attended a Seder night at Livingstone and encountered views that were the same as those of the long-term Jewish settlers in Kenya – suspicion of Africans and an apocalyptic vision of the future if and when white people left. Two years later, at a conference in Lusaka with Professor Terence Ranger of Dar es Salaam University, we were thrown out of a bar for daring to bring with us some East African students from the nascent university being established in the capital. And this was only a few months before independence!

From Livingstone we drove to Southern Rhodesia, where again we had to stay in an international hotel, this time the Jamieson in Salisbury. We visited the rabbi in Salisbury only to find that he lived in a flat with a lift for whites only, so we broke the law. We had booked in at the lodge in Great Zimbabwe, but on arrival found we were unable to stay in the main lodge, even though we had booked through the director of monuments. In the end we were accommodated in Queen's House, built especially for the visit of Queen Elizabeth, all because Eunice was an unacceptable presence. When visiting the Inyanga ruins in the eastern part of the country near Umtali, we had to split up for the night because our host lived at the Anglican mission in Penhalonga, which was a men's only institution. The following night we stayed illegally in town where Africans were not allowed after dark. While I was busy with archaeology, the Anglican vicar's wife who took Eunice around told her that she was the first black woman to sit in the front of her car. People often adopted this kind of patronizing attitude towards Eunice without even realizing that they were biased.

Looking back it seems remarkable that political and social change ever took place. I do not think that attitudes changed, but that metropolitan colonial administrators realized that the writing was on the wall and decided to cut their losses. In September 1959 I attended the Pan African Prehistory Congress in Leopoldville. Although there had been serious riots there and independence was less than a year away, Leopoldville, with its broad well-kept boulevards, smart boutiques and good restaurants had everything for the Belgians but nothing was being done to prepare Africans for self-rule. There were only six African graduates, and secondary education and basic social services for Africans were abysmal, yet the Congo National Parks catering for resident Europeans and tourists were the finest in Africa. While driving through the eastern area of Kivu province I was taken aback to see people being carried for miles in wicker stretchers to dispersed medical facilities.

It was no surprise that in July 1960, a week after independence, the Congo erupted. The army mutinied and, in their tens of thousands, refugees fled to Uganda. They came with graphic tales of rape, mutilation, destruction and terrible mayhem. They came in all the vehicles they could find, leaving their African employees without resources or pay. The people of Kampala, both African and white, were charitable and cared for them; they collected money and clothes, brought food and provided shelter. It was only later that we learnt that most of the refugees had panicked and that very few of their stories were true. The few cases of attack had been magnified and rumours spread like wild fire among a population prepared for the worst. Novels like Robert Ruark's *Uhuru* (1962) inflamed a similar climate in Kenya, but the quiet assurance of Kenyatta, like that of Mandela 30 years later, quietened things down but not before the economy had been weakened. Many Europeans feared the worst and could hardly credit that Africans would not try to seek a payback for the years of abuse they had endured.

With marriage came decisions about our religious future. Both of us were religious, enjoyed the community of worship, blessed our food and tried to lead good moral lives, yet we were also modern liberals who believed in equality of opportunity. We never argued about it, but perhaps should have because neither of us was willing to embrace the other's religion. We were not particularly social in the sense of wanting to belong to clubs or sporting associations, and in the absence of a strong local Jewish community I was quite happy just to drift. Eunice, once she left Gayaza, moved into a very different world. She had her social activities in the choral society and her life was wrapped up in educational activism and in belonging to organizations like the Uganda Association of University Women. She had secular, interracial and interdenominational contacts. In fact, our friends were mostly nonconformist in the broadest sense.

For a brief time we toyed with the idea of joining a third religion. At that time Bahai was strong in Uganda and they were building their Africa temple on an imposing hill on the northern outskirts of Kampala. We liked the idea of a many sided temple and appreciated their sense of beauty, the splendid gardens without and wonderful rugs within. Their prayer books, with the wisdom of the prophets of all religions from Moses through Jesus and Mohammed, appealed to our universalistic ideals. Many members of the community, who liked the idea of attracting mixed couples into the fold, entertained us royally and I still salivate at the thought of some of the wonderful Persian dinners we ate. Since then I have never been afraid of mixing strange and sweet spices into my savoury cooking. What convinced us not to join were suspicion of the unknown and the presence of the Bahai prophet, Baha Ullah. We wanted our contact with the divine to be direct rather than through an intermediary.

I visited Israel in 1960 and again in 1962. At the back of my mind was the idea that I would find my true identity as a Jew. I had been told that going to Israel was like going home. In 1953 the Israel Antiquities Board had offered me a job and I often wondered if I should have taken it rather than go on to do my doctorate at the University of Nottingham. In 1960 it did not feel like going home. Israelis seemed very different from me and their lack of interest in people other than Jews in Israel surprised me. My host, Moshe Stekelis, was a professor of German origin who taught prehistory, but his colleagues at the Institute of Archaeology seemed little interested in the Stone Age, which predated the Bronze Age early Jewish immigrants. I lectured at the institute and its director, Dr Yigael Yadin, invited me to write a paper on East African prehistory for *Qadmoniot*, their popular archaeology journal in Hebrew. Visiting Israel did not make me feel more Jewish. On the contrary, it made me feel more of an expatriate, like a world citizen not quite at home except possibly in Africa where I was happiest. With marriage I began to wonder whether Israel might be a wonderful place to settle down as it had absorbed people from so many different societies.

Eunice, baby Sheba and I visited for a week in March 1962. We had an enjoyable time, but I felt no more attracted to Israel then than I had in 1960. It again struck me as parochial, even though many people were trying to make it a major player in African development issues. Many Africans were fascinated with the Jewish miracle, with how refugees from an urban Europe could turn deserts into farmland and begin so many profitable and successful enterprises. We were to spend our first weekend in Kibbutz Daliya near Haifa, but for Eunice everything got off on a wrong footing, at least with respect to religion. Visiting the Holy Land for the first time, Eunice expected the Sabbath to be a magical event and give her a feeling for the essence of Judaism. To please me she had tried to make Friday evenings special in our home, particularly after my mother's visit to Uganda for two months just before we left for Israel. We had even arranged to have kosher meat sent by rail each week from Nairobi and lit candles on the *Shabbos* eve. Imagine her surprise when none of the kibbutzniks even changed clothes for Friday night, there was no service and ham was on the menu! She could not reconcile this with what I had been telling her about Judaism. In Israel she had expected more not less observance of the Sabbath. The final straw came when we travelled to England from Israel and at my sister's house she was offered coffee after dinner. She knew that having milk with a meat meal was not kosher, so took black coffee even though she preferred it with milk.

When my sister and her husband had their coffees white she realized that anything could go in Jewish practice and became less interested in its observance.

Though Eunice did not feel like making a Jewish home and preferred to keep her own beliefs, we nevertheless observed many Jewish traditional holidays such as Pesach (Passover) and Chanukah, with their focus on the home and family. We attended several communal Seders but preferred our own. Chanukah was also a family occasion. The children rapidly learnt, and still remember, the words of *Hanerot Halolu* and *Maour Szur* and the ritual of passing the candle and wondering whose candle would last the longest. From early on in our marriage we also enjoyed the secular aspects of Christmas – the decorated Christmas tree and Christmas pudding with brandy butter – and chocolate Easter eggs at Easter. We kept in touch with friends through Jewish New Year and Christmas cards, though tended to stress peace on ours. Our symbiotic approach to religion never felt hypocritical. Both religions have their beauty, their traditions and a belief in human brotherhood and sisterhood as well as a superior and unknowable life force. Religion has an instinctive optimism in the future. In recent years I have observed that people are distinguishing between being spiritual and being religious, but I believe one can be both.

Even when we began thinking of our children's education the problem of having a family religion never arose because they went to Mrs Brice's nursery school. Auntie Brice was Jewish, born in Israel and married to Uncle Ernie, an ex-British Palestine policeman. All manner of children attended her kindergarten from the son of the then Colonel Amin to children from different ethnicities and religions.

In our early married life race was not really an issue. Many of our friends were liberal and often had equally mixed marriages. The early 1960s were an exciting period in Uganda and *Transition*, published in Kampala, voiced much of the excitement. Many scholars who visited Makerere were accepting of mixed marriage. In Uganda at the time we were excited by developments in the United States where John Kennedy was our hero. People welcomed the Peace Corps as well as the huge influx of idealistic American and British students the teachers for Africa programme brought in for teacher training at Makerere to staff the expansion of the school system. We were shocked by the plight of black Americans and thrilled by the successes of the civil rights movement. The teenage daughter of one Makerere colleague went over from Uganda to take part in the bus rides through the South. There were even collections being made to send food and clothes to those suffering in the United States. I was very excited when I was invited to go for the first time to the United States as a visiting professor at UCLA in 1966.

I arrived in New York and stayed in a charming Georgian building, the King's Head, which was the faculty club for Columbia University where I gave a lecture. On entering the dining room I felt I had hardly left Africa because all the serving staff was black, though the diners were more white than at similar faculty gatherings in Africa. I was given all sorts of dire warnings about the dangers of going to Harlem, Morningside or onto the subway, yet all the learned academics I came across were bemoaning the wars in Africa.

I got to Los Angeles just after the Watts riots. We had expected to see horrible urban slums, but the houses were as good as we knew in middle-class sections of African towns. What did stand out, however, was the difference in appearance between the houses there and those we saw on the Westside and in Beverley Hills. They were different worlds, yet so close together. Our friend Violaine Junod, who had worked in the UCLA African Studies Center, suggested we rent a flat in Malibu. We were excited about living by the sea and my sister Dora offered to find somewhere for us. She contacted six places in our price range, all of them unlet. Dora inspected them, but before leaving would mention that her sister-in-law came from Africa. In each instance the manager assured her that there was no problem about that, but later would call to say that the apartment had been let. Finally, we stayed in Westwood near the university. During our six-month stay Eunice found that many African Americans, who were still called Negroes or blacks at the time, were less welcoming than she expected. Their distance was no doubt due to ignorance, possibly fear of Africa. They had been taught that Africa was backward, films perpetuated stereotypes and even though activists were proclaiming the 'Black is Beautiful' slogan, there was still hesitancy about it among most people, one of the saddest legacies of being disparaged during and after slavery.

In 1967 we moved to Ghana where we spent the happiest nine years of our lives. For various historical reasons Ghana has the most trouble free race relations of any country in which we have lived. The Portuguese arrived off the coast of what became the Gold Coast in 1471. The Dutch, the English, Danes, Swedes and Germans followed them. For Europeans the Gold Coast was 'the white man's grave' and, until the advent of quinine in the mid-nineteenth century, few lasted longer than 12 months. European women and children did not accompany their menfolk, so there were many liaisons resulting in whole dynasties of mulattoes, including the early nineteenth-century Wulffs, the staff of Accra's Christianborg.Castle.[7] As a result, all along the coast there are Ghanaians with Portuguese names like Nunoo, Dutch names like de Graf and de Graf Johnson, Irish names like Swanzy, Danish names like Hansen and English names like Dickson and Brown. Many were the products of mixtures going back for centuries, so there were numerous gradations of skin colour and, unlike in East Africa, these mixtures were respected. Probably only in Ghana could the child of a Scottish father and Ghanaian mother, like Flight Lieutenant Gerry Rawlings, be accepted as head of state. Nowhere did we meet so many mixed couples.

At the university we knew at least six Jewish–Ghanaian married couples. All their marriages lasted and several took part in some of the wonderful Seders we conducted outdoors under coloured lights. Until 1973 there was a vigorous Israeli community that ran a Jewish school; some Israeli children also attended the Ghana International School and Mrs Quist's dance academy, where they mixed freely with Lebanese children. Israelis were involved in ventures such as Dzizengoff, an agency for Westinghouse and Jeeps, Tahal, planning a water and sewer system for Accra, as well as several agricultural ventures. There were also several families of black Hebrews, African Americans who had settled for a time in Israel and then moved on to Ghana. Even after Ghana broke diplomatic relations with Israel, many Israelis stayed on in their various ventures and their embassy buildings were not vandalized or taken over.

With Ghanaians being so tolerant and good humoured, we never thought much about either race or religion at that time; we just felt accepted and respected. Our older daughters began to go to boarding school in England from 1973. We looked for progressive, gender mixed schools and finally settled on Abbotsholme in Derbyshire. Its principal David Snell, one of the finest human beings I ever met, had been the headmaster of the Ibadan international school in Nigeria and accepted children from many different backgrounds. Though the school had a chapel and followed a Christian religious routine it was interdenominational. Our girls enjoyed the beauty of the practice without feeling they had to accept a particular doctrine. Tessa learnt to decorate the chapel, a skill she has honed over time. I visited the school several times while on sabbatical in Cambridge. I stayed with the Snells and appreciated the way in which they nurtured the children without trying to induce conformity. In 1974 I was invited to apply for a faculty position at UCLA, which I eventually accepted in 1975. I took up the job in 1977. With the new post our life changed more than we could have imagined.

America

A week after I arrived in Los Angeles, a multipart series on *Roots*, focusing attention on race relations and the legacy of slavery, had its TV première. Many interesting discussions took place, not least among my extended family in Los Angeles. Most Americans knew very little about the Atlantic slave trade or understood its American legacy. Although lynchings in the American South were less than a generation away there was a sense of complacency among many white Americans who felt that enough had been done to help disadvantaged African Americans and other minorities. There was a strong feeling in the university that too much was being done to hire minorities. One former graduate student in history wrote a piece in the *Los Angeles Times* claiming that he had not been appointed to a teaching position in African history because he was white. Few white people had really put themselves in the shoes of their less privileged neighbours. Though the *Roots* series raised some people's understanding about race in America, it made some Jewish people wary of African victimhood in case it drew sympathy away from Holocaust studies and their own sense of victimhood. It was no coincidence that a TV series on the Holocaust followed shortly afterwards.

I have never been in a country as focused on race as the USA, where people's origins and what they do assume so much importance. Although it is considered rude to ask personal questions about race, sex or age, they still occupy many people's attention. Whenever someone moves the neighbours say an Armenian, Iranian or Jewish person is buying the house. 'Jewish' has a national or ethnic rather than religious basis. In Africa, most white people were lumped together as Europeans – or *Wazungu* in East Africa, *Obruni* in Ghana or *Yovo* in Togo. Religion was not important, but being foreign was, much to the chagrin of African Americans whom locals perceive as *Wazungu* because their American identity is more evident than their African one. When we first arrived we received abundant unsolicited advice on where we should live. We really wanted to live near the campus but wanted a house with four bedrooms so that each daughter, for the first time in their lives, could have their own room and I wanted a room for a study. Coming from Africa where salaries were low we did not have the accumulated capital for much of a down payment and house prices in west Los Angeles were just too high. My sister Dora suggested the 'valley' where we would be able to get a larger house at a lower price, where parking was less congested and shopping was easy in large malls. Many people advised us against looking there on the grounds that minorities were not welcome, that I would be subjecting our family to harassment at worst and prejudice at best. The few mixed couples to whom we spoke were more reassuring and in the end we bought a largish house in Northridge. As a family we never encountered real prejudice. In some ways we were more of a novelty being British and from Africa rather than a white–black couple.

This was a time when bussing was a hot topic. To achieve some sort of racial parity in schools and prevent segregation it was decided that black children from poor neighbourhoods, where schools were over crowded, facilities inadequate and teaching less than rigorous, should be bussed into white neighbourhoods which were better endowed, had less school crime and better teaching habits. That was the theory, but the opposition was intense. People in white neighbourhoods feared integration in the public schools and many decided to move out of Los Angeles County to Ventura County to the west, or to places like Thousand Oaks and Simi Valley where they could maintain their white 'disciplined' standards. It was all a bit like Ian Smith's defence of civilization in Rhodesia when, in a Canutish attempt to hold back inevitable events, he declared unilateral independence in 1965. Though our youngest daughter was classified as black and we lived 100 yards from a neighbourhood school, she was nevertheless bussed as were other children of her age. It was all a bit disastrous. Eunice taught some of these pupils who arrived tired after up to 90 minutes on a bus, the children kept to their own groups and a lot of resentment was built up.

It would have been better to have put more money into inner city schools to improve their facilities, to pay teachers incentives, reduce class sizes and give parents more say in school development. But we had arrived at a time of shrinking budgets and any question of spending more on social services was taboo. In 1978 Proposition 13 was passed overwhelmingly in California. This froze or reduced existing property taxes and decreed that new taxes should not exceed 1 per cent of the property value. The tax base was instantly shrunk and social services were sadly affected.

Eunice had a job with the Los Angeles library board. The last hired, often minorities, became the first fired and she was out of work. She decided to go back into teaching but the Los Angeles Unified School District (LAUSD) would not accept her credentials of a London BA and a University of Oxford teaching diploma. She had to go to the local state university to earn new credentials. I often wondered whether she would have had the same problems had she been white and come from Europe. She tried to become a resource teacher for Africa, but the interest was not there in the LAUSD, even among black pupils who were often rude to her as a substitute teacher. Our two youngest children spent part of their school careers in Los Angeles public schools. Both found them large, impersonal and racist. In Africa they had been used to being international, but in America it seemed socially important to identify with a specific racial group. It was impossible to move freely between groups and at times our daughters were regarded as *Oreos*, black on the outside and white on the inside after a popular biscuit of that name. They never fully took part in school activities and did not even participate in that most American of activities, the prom dance at the end of their school careers. When our youngest daughter got accepted to Berkeley, other girls at the Granada Hills High School assumed it was because of her colour. In fact, her grade averages and scholastic achievement test scores were above the minimum set by the University of California.

Though for the first time in my life I could have joined and participated in a neighbourhood temple, I did not. In Africa I had been more observant as a Jew, perhaps because I felt the need to preserve my Jewish sense of identity. Here in the United States other people were doing it for me. We attended a few *simchas,* like barmitzvahs, but the melodies were different, even the Hebrew was different. Also, I did not sense any family support for formally moving into a Jewish life and I did not want my family exposed to anti-black feeling. I had my worst experience of open racism among Jewish rather than white folk.

I was deeply interested in African–Israeli relations and the coziness between Israel and South Africa disturbed me. The South African government used Israeli arms to control its African citizens and to conduct wars in Angola and Namibia. The arms and exchange of intelligence were also used to engage in strikes against perceived threats from African nationalist refugees in neighbouring independent states like Lesotho, Mozambique or even as far north as Zambia. Many African Americans voiced their opposition to Israel's links with South Africa. As somewhat pariah states, Israel and South Africa felt the need for mutual reinforcement.

In this climate of tension in South Africa and in the heat of the run-up to the US elections of 1980, in late 1979 I gave a talk at the UCLA faculty centre on 'Africa, Israel and the Jews'. I traced the development of Jewish communities in Africa and emphasized that Africans had always had good feelings towards individual Jews, whom they identified with the Bible rather than with the stereotypes developed by prewar Europeans. Africans understood Israel's struggle for independence after the Holocaust and admired the strides it had made in building up a modern state. They appreciated the technical aid Israel gave to Africa in helping to promote better agriculture and communal development. I stressed that most African states felt proud of being African, that though the Organization of African Unity (OAU) was under funded, had an inadequate staff and poor logistic ability, there was still strong support for the organization and for different United Nations agencies like UNESCO and the ILO, which were doing good work in Africa.[8] I concluded that for African states loyalty to the OAU and to fellow African states was strong and that while they appreciated Israel's friendship, their African brotherhood with Egypt was stronger. Consequently, as soon as Israel invaded Egypt in 1973, a fellow African state, most African states felt an obligation to break off diplomatic relations.

I further commented that the feelings African Americans had for Africa were similar to those that Jewish Americans had for Israel, so the concerns of African states over Israeli policy resonated with African Americans in the United States. These emotional affinities of the two groups meant that if there were a conflict in which Africans and Israelis were on different sides, it could not help but affect US Jewish–African-American relations. I asked my audience to put these emotional relationships into perspective when considering disagreements between African and Jewish Americans. My talk was well received and as a result I was invited to give a reprise at a Sunday brunch at the Stephen Wise Temple.

The Stephen Wise Temple, one of the largest Reform temples in Los

Angeles, is beautifully situated in Bel Air. I gave a short personal history to introduce myself mentioning that my European family had died in the Holocaust and that I was a committed Jew who had on several occasions visited Israel, where I had relatives. Nevertheless, after my talk I felt pilloried in a manner I had never previously experienced. Various questioners kept insisting that Africans were ungrateful to Israel and refused to accept stated African motives for the break – rich Arab countries must have seduced them with money and bribes. They said it was impossible to compare Jewish suffering with African-American suffering under slavery and contrasted Israel's progress with the failures of the new African nations. They discounted the amount of aid the USA had given to Israel compared with the meagre help given to Africa. They kept bringing up African-American hostility to Jews, citing Jesse Jackson's reference to New York as 'Hymietown'. In their questioning, which verged on barracking, one person kept referring to Africans as *Schwartzkopfs* (Yiddish for black heads) even though I had mentioned that my wife was African. They could not see that their remarks were as insulting to me as 'Hymietown' might be to them. One questioner failed to see that Idi Amin was not speaking for the whole of Africa and seemed to think that all African leaders were alike. After that experience I felt that if that audience represented a liberal cross section of Los Angeles Jews I did not want to be associated with them. I have given money from time to time to Hillel organizations at UCLA but that has been the limit of my formal association.

Since coming to the United States I have heard many wounding remarks from American Jews who were unaware of my African-Americans connections. From reading local newspapers like the *Jewish Journal*, I have come to realize how focused the Jewish community is on its own navel and how little concerned for countries outside the Near East. Many Jewish commentators express genuine humanitarian concern for Tibetans, East Timorese or Native Americans, but cannot see Israel's occupation, land acquisition and denial of human rights to Palestinians in the same light. I regard myself as a humanistic liberal Jew with an obligation to speak out if I do not agree with Israeli policy, but realize that others regard frankness about Israel as Jew hating. A dialogue is not welcomed, words like Third World are used as terms of abuse, and the United Nations seems only to be respected if the majority agrees with American viewpoints. One learns to keep quiet in the US on certain matters.

In 1991 religion and race again impinged on my life. Though I keep a modicum of dietary laws, I am not an observant Jew and associate with Jews, non-Jews and people of various ethnicities. In the long haul I suppose my best friends have often been my wife and children. In the academic years 1989–91 there was a great deal of tension on the UCLA campus between Jewish and black students, with petty insults hurled between the staffs of *Nommo*, the African-American student newspaper, and *Ha Am*, the Jewish student one. It all started when a county supervisor wanted public support withdrawn from the annual African marketplace because it allowed one of its stallholders to sell literature deemed anti-Semitic. I often visit the marketplace, which is colourful, full of fun places to eat, has lively entertainment and stalls selling African, Caribbean and African-American merchandise such as clothes, material, crafts and artwork. The stall in question was attracting very little custom and it would have been best to have ignored it. The market is put on by a group of volunteers who cannot be expected to vet each and every item put up for sale in every stall. Bringing the future of the African marketplace into public debate moved the discussion into murky waters of black–Jewish relations, which really have no place in what should be a celebration of African creativity. Emotions became inflamed and the extremist fringes on both sides seized the centre ground. Rabbi Chaim Seidler Feller, the director of UCLA Hillel, set up a black–Jewish faculty committee on which I served, but like many such problems on campus the whole question quietened down with the end of the academic year. However, it was in this climate that I faced my own professional crisis.

My first year as director of the James S. Coleman African Studies Center was spent on sabbatical in Ghana, where I initiated the new education abroad programme and served as a Fulbright professor. It was a productive and happy year but in my absence the teaching programme, the MA in African studies, became separated from the centre's activities. On my return I found a turf problem of considerable proportions. The administrative assistant, who worked half time on the programme but wanted to make it full time, petitioned for an assistant and control of more of the limited African studies space. I was sympathetic to the case she was making to expand the programme, but unfortunately there were neither precedents nor resources available to fulfil her ambitions. That year we had more MA students in African studies than at any other time. They were supportive of the administrative assistant's power play but the university administration was unwilling to expand our budget at a time of general budget cuts. Tension rose and as a result several students decided to take the whole question of African studies at UCLA to an open forum involving all students and faculty in the university.

Intemperate remarks were made in the *Daily Bruin* and the issue got entangled in the ongoing tension between African Americans and Jews on campus. A former African studies student, Kwaku Person Lynn, wrote a particularly virulent article in the *African Sentinel*,[9] the Los Angeles African-American newspaper, in which he claimed that the first Jews were black, that European Jews claim to be a race but are not, that the Holocaust was minor compared with the atrocities perpetrated against African people, and that Jews were the chief financiers of the Atlantic slave trade. He attacked Jewish involvement in UCLA where 'the director [of the African Studies Center] is a European Jew ... known to have endorsed colonialism in Afrika (*sic*)'. The diatribe went on to attack Jewish attempts to control curriculum development. In fact at UCLA, as in many US universities, from the time of Herskovits at Northwestern until the present, Jewish scholars have been at the forefront of fostering an interest in Africa. Some of the most distinguished Africanists were liberal South Africans like Hilda and Leo Kuper in anthropology and sociology; others have included Richard Sklar and Michael Lofchie in political science, Klaus Wachsmann in African musicology and Wolf Leslau in Ethiopian studies. None of them put their Jewish identity before their commitment to Africa; and few were even practising Jews.

I felt that my African academic integrity was discredited. The emotional and political climate these arguments generated on campus made it difficult for me to continue as director of the African Studies Center. Had I been younger I would have fought, but my health had deteriorated and I had less energy than before. Nevertheless, before I relinquished control I managed to obtain a No. 2 ranking for the UCLA African Studies Center, so I left with a clear conscience. My successor eventually won the battle I had started to restore the centre to a united programme linking research and public policy to the educational division.

After my retirement in 1994 I continued with two of my teaching assignments, the first, in which I have participated since the 1980s, being an honours class on genocide with some coverage of Africa. At first I concentrated on Uganda, which in the 1980s was undergoing a savage civil conflict. I felt it was important for students to realize that genocide was not confined to Native Americans, Australians, Cambodians, Armenians and Jews but also happened in Africa. Over the years my focus shifted to Burundi and later Rwanda. I now begin with imperialism in the Congo and the brutality of the Herero genocide in German South West Africa where more than 80 per cent of the population was killed between 1904 and 1907. The precedents of Belgian King Leopold's Congo in the 1890s and the destruction of the Herero had a lasting impact that continued the debasement of Africans begun with the depredations of the Atlantic slave trade. Colonialism accelerated the steady dehumanization of Africans and created the stereotypic viewpoints I encountered on first going to Africa at the beginning of my career. This dehumanization is characteristic of all genocidal episodes and I try to instill in students the universality of such processes. As a proud Jew I worry about the processes at work in the 'promised land' for which we all had such high hopes.

My other post-retirement activity is an honours collegium class in which we examine the legacy of slavery and imperialism. I encourage students to study literature and watch films that depict the effects of colonialism. George Orwell's 1934 classic, *Burmese Days*, for example, is a fine example of how a social structure can impose cruel attitudes on otherwise well-meaning individuals. Students are responsive to finding hidden meanings in films and novels, but most importantly they lose the parochial superiority that is so easily adopted in the United States in the absence of a comparative world and historical perspective. I try to indicate that many of today's inequalities, environmental disasters and political crises have deep historical roots.

A long-term ambition of mine has been to see a genocide museum and centre set up in Africa. I first proposed the idea in 1988 when our African Studies Center was exploring the possibility of a sponsored link between the United States Information Agency and Makerere University in Kampala; we hoped that genocide studies might provide a component for cooperation. I visited Luwero north of Kampala, the epicentre of Milton Obote's attempt in the early 1980s to depopulate an area to prevent Yoeri Museveni's resistance army being able to secure support from a peasantry opposed to his regime. It was ethnic cleansing on a vicious and thorough scale. In 1985, when Obote was overthrown, Ugandans collected the victims' skulls and piled them up in heaps similar to those of the Cambodian killing fields. Our idea was to hold courses on genocide, as well as build a museum so that the genocide would never be forgotten. The museum would do justice to the history of genocide in Africa and to the genocides that had taken place outside Africa. I proposed that the Luwero centre function as a memorial garden where an archive and research centre could be established. We were unable to come to an agreement.

Some of the Makerere faculty opposed the idea on the grounds that it over emphasized the suffering of the Baganda at the expense of other people who had suffered; others felt that Makerere should look forward, concentrate on development issues and forget the horrors of the past. I spoke to the president, Yoeri Museveni, and later to the future Kabaka of Buganda, Ronald Mutebi; both were sympathetic but could only offer moral support. I thought that the American Holocaust Museum in Washington might help, but it did not even answer my letters; the Los Angeles Museum of Tolerance sent a polite note wishing us good luck but no support. As a Jew I was disappointed, and my disappointment increased following the Rwanda genocide of 1994. If we are to understand genocide, to recognize the early warning signs that can alert us to future catastrophes, we need to put the Holocaust and other abuses of humanity into as broad a historical and geographical perspective as possible. Rwanda and Kosovo did not just occur spontaneously; the warning signs were there, but the informed prophecies went unheeded. 'Never again' turned to 'oops sorry' and commissions of inquiry, but courses, museums, healing centres and historical awareness were not established. The momentum that might have raised public awareness of the problem and suggested possible ways of subverting and alleviating the problems had been lost.

In the early twenty-first century, which one hoped would have seen an end to the genocide, ethnic cleansing, torture, indiscriminate bombing of civilians, group punishment and man-made famines that so stained the twentieth century, the problems still persist. Some flash points are large, like the possible break up of Indonesia, others are small and go unnoticed in places like Africa. In the brave new world I foresaw 50 years ago, there was going to be an international presence, cooperation between nations and morality, but alas moral standards seem to be relative. Nations judge nations on the values they deem important to their own parochial national interests; economic and political interests subvert humanitarian concerns – man's quest for property, water rights, oil profits and access to voting blocks in the Western 'democracies' mask the simplistic views of yesteryear.

Chapter 5

Career: preparations, excavations, museums and universities

A S AN ARCHAEOLOGIST it is often difficult to decide when one's career begins and when formal education ends. I suppose I could count my career as an archaeologist as beginning when I was paid for doing what I enjoyed most. As a student at Nottingham University I had directed excavations at the Lenton tile kiln and well sites, but was not paid for it. I did it because it had to be done and leapt at the opportunity to prove my metal; also, as someone who had been on a dig and knew what it was about, I had obligations to the archaeological society.

My first paid excavations began with salvage, later termed rescue archaeology, at Lamport in 1954 and at Ingleby in 1955 for the ancient monuments branch of the Ministry of Works. John Hurst, who had suggested my name, thought that Lamport, being what appeared to be a large Bronze Age barrow, would fit well into my academic research. It had to be removed to allow for the strip mining of the iron ore beneath. A huge drag-line excavator on tracks with an extendable 30–40 foot boom and two workmen were waiting to assist me and I was to stay in a nearby farmhouse. Some 26 large trees, mainly elm, several with trunks up to six feet in diameter, covered the five-foot high mound. We started by clearing the site, felling the trees and making a map. Within a few hours we discovered we were dealing with a windmill site, for all around the mound were large flat stones, in some cases up to 20 inches long set into the earth on their long axes radiating from the centre. Each stone, set 30 feet from the centre and 18 inches apart, projected a few inches above the ground with the greater part buried beneath. They were clearly designed to anchor the tail post used for turning a post mill into the wind. They allowed

8. Lamport Post mill, Northants, 1954, aerial view from the top of the drag-line excavator.

whoever was pushing the mill to get a firm hold on what would have been a slippery slope.

This was the day I became an historical archaeologist. I needed to go into the archives to look for old maps and to consult the *Victoria County History* and other guides to Northamptonshire to find out what I was doing. I also consulted Sir Gyles Isham, the local landowner at Lamport Hall whose library contained books and plans going back to the seventeenth century. Sir Gyles was a keen supporter of the project and invited me to stay at the hall when I revisited Lamport in 1960.

English local archaeological societies form the backbone of British archaeology and members of the Northamptonshire branch helped considerably by searching through the archives while I was at the site. Members of these bodies, which were mainly founded as antiquarian societies in the nineteenth century, often with their own libraries in elegant urban premises, work as volunteers on archaeological sites and become repositories of information that individual researchers could never acquire without living in the area. Volunteers from the Derbyshire, Northamptonshire and Leicestershire societies helped me during my graduate work and two of these societies helped fund my research; they all provided outlets for my first archaeological reports. I was overwhelmed by the enthusiasm of the Northampton volunteers.

A typical day at the site would begin at 6.30–7.00 a.m. I would go back to the farm for breakfast at 9.30 a.m. and snack on the site at around 12.30 p.m. When my paid labour left at 4.30 p.m. I would go back to the farm for dinner, then return to the site to greet and work with the volunteers who would stay until it got dark at around 10.30 p.m. I followed this routine for three weeks. On Saturdays and Sundays we only had volunteers, so started at 9.30 a.m. and ended at around 7.30–8.00 p.m. There were advantages to working with the Staveley Iron & Chemical Company, which mined the ore, for they had equipment I could borrow. They helped me remove stumps standing in the way of excavation and put me at the end a boom and extended it to 70 feet so that I could take aerial pictures. They even offered me a job if I decided I did not want to be an academic.

At Lamport we eventually found two mills – one seventeenth-century one on top of the mound, which documentary sources and artefacts including clay tobacco pipes confirmed, and a thirteenth-century one beneath the mound. The mill had stood atop two cross walls. Its thrust had caused structural weakness in the stone wall that was clearly visible and had led to the mounding against the walls to secure the integrity of the mill. It was possibly the only post mill of its kind in England.[1] We also found some flint tools and quite a bit of debitage belonging to the Bronze Age, so I eventually gained some material for my doctoral thesis.

Ingleby was a very different site, but again with mounds and in woodland. At Lamport I had learnt how to blow up tree stumps, which was very useful at Heath Wood in Ingleby. Ingleby, just south of the Trent in Derbyshire near Repton School, consisted of a group of pagan Danish mounds. Previous excavations had indicated their early ninth-century age. The site was at the interface of the Christian Anglo Saxon south of England and the pagan Danish/Norse north. We dug for four weeks and demonstrated that the small mounds were presumably pagan Danish cenotaph ones though in at least one instance there was clear indication of cremation activities and we found some pretty silver wire embroidery. I never thought much

9. Lamport Post mill showing cross walls.

about it as it did not tie in with my doctoral work, but as one of the few pagan Danish cemeteries in England the site was significant and 40 years later more extensive excavations validated my findings, which for an archaeologist is very reassuring.[2] These excavations and ones I helped on at places like Hoxne, dating from the middle Pleistocene, Arcy-sur-Cure, a series of Palaeolithic rock shelters in Burgundy where I worked in the summer of 1953, as well as the megalithic site of Barclodiad-y-Gawres in Anglesey and the Wharram Percy deserted medieval village in Yorkshire in 1952–53, meant that, having dug on sites ranging over the whole timespan of humanity in Britain, I was prepared for most eventualities.

My full-time career in archaeology began when I was appointed warden of prehistoric sites at the Royal National Parks of Kenya in 1956. My education was continuing but now at an informal level. I realized that to be an effective warden I had to pack in a great deal of reading about Africa, East Africa and archaeology. I also had to learn

how to communicate with visitors, staff and colleagues. Shortly after
arriving I met someone who made a huge difference to my life – Ieuan
Hughes, the coordinator for the Makerere University College extra
mural department in Nairobi. It was at his house that I first met black
African academics. I had left the completely white world with which I
was familiar and a little disillusioned. I taught several classes for Ieuan
in Nairobi, one on African prehistory and another on primitive art,
which was largely about African art.

As far as I am aware this was the first course on African art ever
attempted in eastern or central Africa. There was little to read on the
subject at the time though there were plenty of printed images to
which to refer. I was determined to demonstrate continuities between
the prehistoric past, as indicated in rock art, and the art pieces that
were by then attracting the attention of collectors. In the 1950s the
average student did not appreciate the context of the art, did not know
that wooden masks were parts of elaborate raffia costumes that
transformed an ordinary person into a mythical figure or animal. The
racial attitudes of many intelligent people who wanted to learn were
permeating their approach. African art was not part of their European
civilization; it was different and, to many, inferior. I met a lot of
resistance from one unexpected quarter.

Louis Leakey was upset when he heard of my class on African
prehistory. He said it would allow the wrong people to find prehistoric
sites, collect artefacts or somehow disturb the contexts in which the
artefacts were located. Although Louis regularly published popular
articles in British weeklies like the *Illustrated London News,* and even
gave broadcasts on his discoveries for the BBC, he never attempted to
educate the wider East African public. I wrote several articles for the
Nakuru-based *Farmer's Weekly*, and several about me appeared in the
East African Standard, then the main Kenyan newspaper along with its
new tabloid competitor *The Daily Nation.* My classes had a direct
impact on my practical work, for in 1957 I decided to appeal for
public volunteers for my digs at Olorgesailie and later at Lanet. I
wanted volunteers for two good reasons, first to provide intellectual
encouragement and company on my digs and second to help pay the
cost of what we were doing. These days it is called sponsor-
participation and it is the basis for such admirable organizations as
Earthwatch or our University of California University Research
Expeditions Programmes, which I would use in Ghana in the 1970s.
For the first time excavations were opened up to high-school students,

though unfortunately African students did not as yet join, partly because there were so few of them and in the Kenya of the 1950s Africans and Europeans did not really participate equally in such programmes. Archaeology was regarded as a rich man's pursuit.

In 1956 African archaeology[3] was slanted towards the study of early man and the Stone Age, what one might call the universal ancestors of humanity. When I arrived at Olorgesailie I was excited. I had never seen so many stone tools. Here was a site with literally thousands of beautifully fashioned hand axes and cleavers associated with a Pleistocene fauna on discrete patches of land surfaces within a sequence of lake levels. The nature of the lakes, presumably indicative of increased precipitation or trapped drainage, consisted of white coloured stratified diatomaceous silt deposits. As I quickly learnt from visiting other sites in the East African Rift Valley area, Olorgesailie was not unique. At Olduvai Gorge in Tanganyika, which I visited with Bill Bishop, Revel Mason and Louis Leakey, there was a much longer sequence of human activity laid out in up to 300 feet of lake deposits stretching back before the Pleistocene and encompassing the small microliths and blade tools so distinctive of hunting and gathering populations of thousands rather than hundreds of thousands of years ago. One problem at Olorgesailie was that there was no access to what research had been undertaken other than the occasional popular article and Leakey's anecdotal asides.

At that time accurate dating was difficult so archaeologists concentrated on classificatory methods. They measured every conceivable dimension of stone tools, worked out attributes and defined classification sequences. It was laborious and rather dull. I excavated one site away from the main fenced-in area at Olorgesailie where I found an old land surface within a sequence of lake deposits in which the key lithic components were tools, such as small scrapers, unlike the hand axes, cleavers and stone balls common on the main Olorgesailie sites. I had a small crew of volunteers and the area we opened up was relatively small but it was fascinating to find old lake surfaces with the polygonal shaped cracking reminiscent of modern dried up surfaces. From the nature of the tools I called it the Hope Fountain site, because the tools and the flakes were similar to a site of that name in South Africa. Now of course we would never resort to such 'cultural' ascriptions as even then I knew that there was little likelihood of any other affinity to a South African site. The tools probably reflected a particular activity rather than any cultural relationship.

10. Excavating Hopefountain site, Olorgesailie, 1957.

Stone Age archaeology was in a straitjacket at that time as our chronology was based on associations with a faunal and geomorphological sequence. With the discovery of potassium argon dating by the end of the decade we knew better and the alkaline rich volcanic deposits of East Africa transformed the discipline and freed archaeologists to begin to study human behaviour rather than classification systems. I published my findings in the *South African Archaeological Bulletin* in 1959, the first complete archaeological report from Olorgesailie ever to appear.[4]

Though I was to excavate at least five more Stone Age sites in East Africa,[5] my time at Olorgesailie convinced me that if I really wanted to understand the people I was studying, I would be better served working in more recent contexts, preferably ones with written, oral or other sources in addition to stones and bones. Though I excavated several small sites, there was no clear pattern to my work until I tackled the scenically stunning one at Lanet south of Nakuru. Leakey had devised a sequence of cultures from the Late Stone Age to the present. Following European terminology he classified most of the ceramic rich sites as Neolithic and had a sequence of Gumban A, B and C. As he had claimed a very early date for pottery use in East Africa he used his sequence to fill in the time slot from 8000 BC until the present millennium. He correctly associated pastoralism with these early cultures but also in his 1935 *Stone Age Races of Kenya*

Colony he assumed that the Neolithic sites represented a movement from the northeast of Caucasoid populations similar to those in northeast Africa. The Gumban sequence was well represented in the Nakuru area where Mary Leakey had dug Hyrax Hill.

Lanet was an earthwork, a bit like a hill fort, surrounded by hollows with banks around them. It overlooked Lake Nakuru, fringed with the pink of thousands of flamingoes, and, at over 6000 feet, was relatively cool. The area was undisturbed; there had been no deep ploughing and although the farmer was at first suspicious of our intentions, he eventually gave his permission. I called for volunteers and managed to get a bunch of enthusiastic school children. We sliced through the enclosure wall and excavated one of the hollows. We found a great deal of pottery, all of it characteristic of Gumban B, but we also found an iron hoe and other evidence that the site was Iron Age and not Stone Age. There were plenty of cattle bones and not much else, indicating that the population did not hunt or fish, even though game was abundant in the area. It was one of the first sites to be radio-carbon dated and again the dates were from the second millennium AD. This suggested we were dealing with a pastoral society similar to those moving into East Africa over the past 3000 years. There was nothing to suggest that the occupiers of Lanet came from northeast Africa. When we scraped down to the original rock surface in the interior of the enclosure we found parallel rows of hollows pecked out into the bedrock similar to countless others stretching across Africa, the ancestors of the popular board game known as *oware* in Ghana and *mankala* in Central Africa. Lanet firmly placed my research emphasis on the Iron Age and recent past.

The Makerere extra mural department in Nairobi was at that time my only link with higher education. There was a technical college in Nairobi, but it had few students and only a small faculty; curiously, it had a geology department, the idea being that it should provide departments that Makerere College in Uganda lacked. In 1957 my eyes were opened up to wider opportunities when I spent a month in Uganda working with Bill Bishop and helping Professor Richard Foster Flint from Yale, who was gathering data for his new book on Quaternary geology, tour Pleistocene sites. I visited Makerere, then a University of London college with a leafy, quiet dignity and cut off from the vulgar noise of the town below. I met several university lecturers and numerous African students, many still wearing short red gowns for academic occasions, including their meals in hall. On that

visit I learnt that there would be a vacancy for the curatorship of the
Uganda Museum and that the newly-installed director of the Uganda
antiquities department, Peter Shinnie, was advocating the dissolution
of his department because he felt that Uganda had insufficient
antiquities to warrant a special department.

I quickly let it be known that I was interested in moving to Uganda
and that I felt that the dissolution of antiquities was a retrograde step.
I advocated that the Uganda Museum subsume the department's
antiquities and that a budget be allocated to the museum for looking
after them. In due course the vacancy at the Uganda Museum was
advertised; the curator would direct all the museum's activities and
work with a board of trustees. My chief competitor was John Blacking,
who had made a name for himself in African music in South Africa.
The retiring curator, Klaus Wachsmann, had also been a musicologist.
With my experience of developing museum displays at Olorgesailie
and enthusiasm for expanding archaeology, I was considered the
better choice, particularly as I was single and only had to come from
Kenya. Though the physical assets of the antiquities department were
reallocated to the museum, only a token budget of £100 a year was
assigned.

I worked harder in my first year in the museum than I have ever
before or since. The museum had closed in 1957 because of structural
problems, but there were now excellent plans to complete a hall of
man that told the story of people in Uganda through their activities.
This was a new approach in museology. Previously, classification had
been by tribe or ethnic group, which was rather sterile; also, most
displays contained too much information without a running story that
a casual visitor could easily follow. In the museum we highlighted
activities like farming, fishing, crafts and music, moved on to social
systems, ritual and government, and then ended with agents of
change. Much had been accomplished by the time I arrived and the
displays were the most professional I had seen. I felt strongly that the
museum should not be static but should mount different exhibitions
at regular intervals. In January 1959 we reopened the museum with an
exhibition celebrating its 50 years of existence; a further exhibition
illustrated the geological and human history of the Western Rift.

We encouraged school children to come on visits to the museum
and expanded the number of concerts the attendants, all of whom had
musical ability, gave of Uganda traditional music; we also added a
dancer. By the end of the year our attendance figures equalled the

11. Uganda Museum, 1960.

population of the Kampala area, a feat few museums ever attain. The
Uganda Museum was wonderful. Unlike many African museums, its
collections had been assembled gradually and were comprehensive, as
Tribal Crafts of Uganda by my two predecessors Margaret Trowell and
Klaus Wachsmann, which is basically the museum catalogue, attests.
We were fortunate to have Valerie Vowles, probably the best ethnographer in Africa, maintain the collections immaculately. The store-
rooms had shelves on rails to maximize space, an innovation only
introduced to the United States 20 years later. She had developed a
system for periodic inspection of every item, refreshing accession
numbers as necessary and sealing artefacts in plastic bags to keep out
insects and dust. One role I took on in the museum was that of
photographer. We had an excellent darkroom but no air conditioning
so I worked at night to ensure that the developer and fixer were the
right temperature. Often I did not go home to my house at the side of
the museum until after midnight.

In 1960 we mounted an ambitious temporary exhibition on
Christian and Muslim missions in Uganda up to 1910. We had to
search out and photograph the old missions, contact the overseas
mission headquarters for material and make the exhibition relevant to
our main displays. I was pleased when we received requests to copy
our pictures for use in schools. That, as well as several art exhibits,
including one on oriental art and another on contemporary Nigerian

art, gave the museum a reputation for being dynamic. Our visitors
knew they could always count on something new. Eventually, we had
our attendants make and sell musical instruments.

I wanted the museum not only to be a resourceful research unit but
also, and especially, to be relevant, which is why, in conjunction with
the Makerere extra mural department, we eventually took to the road
and ran weekend courses on the land, resources and culture of
particular areas. We were most successful in Soroti in Teso where
participants brought in and talked about an item important in their
heritage that would form part of the projected folk museum. We ran
courses at Mbarara and Fort Portal and, in the two principal national
parks, set up museums on the geomorphological and human aspects
of the park areas. To showcase what we were doing we organized a
conference of museum curators in Kampala in 1959 at which we
established the Museums Association of Middle Africa (MAMA). We
set up a training programme for museums in the area and published
guides on museum conservation and other topics. All this was
accomplished because everyone in the museum cooperated; we had a
receptive public and managed everything on a shoestring budget. The
whole museum with four professional staff, six attendants, three
technicians, four groundsmen, but no full-time secretarial or office
staff, was run on less than £18,000 a year. People did different jobs;
Valerie was secretary, registrar as well as ethnographer, and the artists
were also conservators and technicians.

In 1961 MAMA convened a larger conference in Livingstone in
Northern Rhodesia. Delegates came from West Africa, from both the
London and South African Museums Association and there was a
representative from the museums and monuments division of UNESCO
in Paris. Just holding it in Livingstone was an achievement, for we
encountered racist and homophobic opposition to several of the
participants, including the American Hiroshi Daifuku, of Hawaian
descent, from UNESCO whom several local hotels turned aside as being
Asian. At the time it seemed that the conference was a success because it
resulted in a larger Museums Association of Tropical Africa, with the
acronym AMAT/MATA (in French and English) and UNESCO initiated
a training programme for museum technologists at Jos in Nigeria.

Looking back I felt we took a wrong turn. Instead of depending on
their own resources the museums in Africa had allowed UNESCO to
internationalize the situation and somehow the cooperation lost its
momentum. Museum assistants were sent off for training, much of the

12. At MAMA conference in Livingstone, Northern Rhodesia with
J. H. Chaplin left, Eunice and an American diplomat.

instruction was provided by specialists with little knowledge of Africa
and more than two-thirds of the trainees took the opportunity of
overseas training to slip away from museum work. I firmly believe
that training can only be done at the museum level and should involve
hands-on work in the collections with instructors staying for years
rather than weeks, passing on their skills to ensure that good practices
developed. UNESCO also invited senior personnel to conferences,
mainly held in Paris, who regarded their attendance as a way of
obtaining *per diem* overseas allowances but felt no obligation to give
feedback to the museums from which they came. Senior personnel
came to regard certain jobs as beneath them and grumbled about the
lack of resources to replicate the practices they had seen in the
overseas museums. For nearly 30 years museums receded in influence
and activity.

The principal weakness of African museum personnel in the late
twentieth century was their lack of interest in basic conservation.
Preserving and recording what museums already possess does not
involve heavy expenditure, but it does call for constant attention from
concerned eyes. Consequently, labels fell off, cockroaches ate the

numbers from objects, and exhibits were lost, stolen or sold to greedy outside visitors. Governments were giving very little attention to museum management and visitors were often targeted by new antiquities ordinances that demanded export licences for even modern crafts. In short, too many posts had become sinecures.

Apart from recording rock art,[6] my main research focus at the museum was on what archaeology could tell historians about state formation in the interlacustrine area. I excavated Bweyorere in Ankole in 1959 and Bigo in Buganda in 1960. At Bweyorere I demonstrated how oral traditions could be used to locate sites and archaeology could throw light on the physical nature of those sites. We found a huge royal house, probably of conical form and perhaps more than 50 feet across, within a set of earthwork enclosures made largely out of piles of animal dung. We discovered the early significance of pipes and found blue beads, then a precious trade commodity. We were also able to distinguish the use of a finer, thinner royal ceramic. The approach I adopted at Bweyorere called upon the researcher becoming familiar with the oral history before embarking on the archaeology. In this sense it was historical archaeology and claimed so by one of my early protégés Peter Schmidt[7] who worked in Karagwe in northern Tanzania in the late 1960s. The Bweyorere dig was my first with a sizeable number of African students; we lived in a glorious grass-roofed rest house at Gayaza and interacted with the local community.

Our objective in 1960 was to ascertain the age and nature of the huge earthworks at Bigo on the Kagera River. Bigo was reputed to have been built by the Bacwezi, the dynasty predating the later Buganda and Bunyoro dynasties, which Milton Obote's republican authoritarian rule was later to terminate. The earthworks, which stretch across two-and-a-half miles of land, comprise an inner and outer set of banks. Using a compass and chain and clearing our way through heavy vegetation, we completely remapped the earthworks. By cutting through the banks in several places we were able to expose their truly impressive form; the earthen banks originally rose more that 12 feet above the surrounding ditch and were cut to at least that depth into the parent rock. Working there was a logistical feat. We had to make a road, clear heavy vegetation, build a camp and feed a party that at its peak (when we brought in local prisoners as labour to supplement the Makerere students) numbered nearly 30. We ate very well, however, because hunters brought us game and fishermen sold us *ngege* (tilapia) from the river and a nearby dam. I lived in a trailer the geological survey provided, but we built several structures, including a large mess, and put up numerous tents. When Roland Oliver, the distinguished historian of East Africa, joined us for a time we held some exciting evening seminars. Careful mapping revealed the form of a royal capital; animal bones indicated a cattle economy; and radio-carbon dating showed that the site was probably 22–25 generations old, around AD 1350–1500. Though unable to confirm if the Bacwezi were a legitimate dynasty or mythical rulers, as some historians claimed, we had at least shown that there was a large state with a distinctive ceramic and earthwork enclosure predating the historic dynasties of Buganda and Bunyoro.

One abiding joy of my time in Uganda was the opportunity it gave me to link research with teaching. Graduate students became an extension in many ways of many of my own research interests. My first students joined me when I became assistant director of the British Institute of History and Archaeology in East Africa. Susannah Pearce, who worked on the interface between the Stone Age and Iron Age, dug an exciting site on Kansyore Island in the Kagera River where she found some of the earliest Iron Age pottery in East Africa, which we now know dates back 2000 years to the beginning of the Iron Age. The only access to the island, which formed part of the hotel grounds of a remarkable Italian woman, Toni Nuti, was by a cage pulled across on cables. Toni kept a civet cat called Martin Luther as a guard dog and had decidedly racist ideas about Africans whom she did not accept as guests. Nevertheless, her cuisine was superb and splendid faience ware, silver candlesticks and other ornaments from Italy graced her home. The Iron Age ceramics were found in the foundation trenches of a hotel extension she was building but destined never to complete. Alas, Susannah never completed her doctorate.

My first successful doctoral student was John Sutton who worked on the Sirikwa, who built the semi-subterranean houses I came across at Lanet. He dated them to the mid-second millennium AD and, from examining the traditions and ethnographic evidence, showed they were a population of southern Nilotic Kalenjin people and not Hamites or some mysterious folk from the northeast of Africa as had previously been thought. In 1965 John received the first Ph.D. the University of East Africa had ever awarded. I also had a hand, as co-supervisor, in the first master's degree awarded by the university to Gordon McGregor who wrote a history of the early days of King's College Budo.[20]

Another of my MA students, Jim Chaplin, wrote on the rock art of the Lake Victoria region. Jim did not have a university education, but gained experience as a meteorologist and participated in the British Antarctic Survey. Later he became inspector of ancient monuments in Northern Rhodesia and I first met him when he undertook research on East Africa's mountains as part of the 1957 geophysical year. In 1961 he helped Eunice and me when we went to Northern Rhodesia to run the Museums Association conference. We noted that he lived in the township and not the European area and that many of his colleagues shunned him. Only years later did we learn that his isolation was because he belonged to UNIP, which supported African nationalism, and had emerged from the closet, thus beyond the colonial pale on both counts. In Northern Rhodesia he became particularly interested in rock art. To get around not having a degree he decided to take a diploma in archaeology at the London Institute of Archaeology; with the diploma he was then able to register for a master's degree in the Makerere African studies programme. While studying with me he became part-time inspector of monuments for a year in our newly created commission. In 1964 he joined two of our research expeditions to Lolui Island[8] where there was both rock art and rock gongs.[9] He became a close family friend and our daughters loved him. Sadly, the week of his graduation he died in a car accident, a very promising career unfulfilled.

When I was assistant director of the British Institute we attempted to expand interest in archaeology by organizing first training schools and later field schools in archaeology. In 1962 we held a successful two-week course at Makerere and invited luminaries like Louis Leakey, Glynn Isaac, Bill Bishop, Bethwell Ogot, Aidan Southall and Neville Chittick to give lectures, which I later edited into a book.[10] We took the students, many of whom later became historians or archaeologists, on a field trip to sites like Bigo, Kansyore and Ntusi.

In 1963, to introduce students to the practical side of coastal archaeology, we ran a four-week field school at Kilwa on the Tanganyikan coast where several helped excavate a Swahili stone house. The students enjoyed the new experiences, like eating *mboga ya pahani*, seaweed soaked for days to rid it of the salt. Two lecturers to join us there were Hamo Sassoon, the Tanganyika inspector of monuments who was later to take over the Uganda Monuments Commission, and James Kirkman, my old colleague from National Parks in Kenya who had devoted his career to working on such coastal sites as

Gedi. The same year John Sutton also held a field school at Moiben in Kenya. Archaeology was thus developing rapidly and when I took over the African Studies Programme at Makerere in 1964 it was only natural that archaeology was one of the first graduate disciplines introduced.

In 1964 the University of East Africa was was being developed as an umbrella for the three independent colleges at Makerere – Uganda, Nairobi and Dar es Salaam. I was asked to draw up a memorandum on teaching archaeology, which the university council adopted. In 1965 Dr John Sutton became the first lecturer in archaeology at the University of Dar es Salaam's history department. Nairobi followed with its first appointment a few years later and I was invited to draw up a proposal for teaching archaeology at the Haile Selassie University in Addis Ababa where Richard Wilding became the first archaeologist. Sadly, much of this momentum petered out during the periods of political instability in the 1970s and 1980s and no successors to the original posts were appointed, except at Nairobi, but by the end of the 1980s even that had lapsed.

In 1966 and 1967 two trips enhanced my knowledge and under-standing of Africa's past. The first, to an international colloquium on African archaeology in Fort Lamy in Chad,[11] was organized by Jean Paul Lebeuf whom I had met in Brazzaville in 1959. He was a man of great charm and though Chad was, and is, one of the poorest coun-tries in Africa, he had managed to develop the national museum and undertake numerous archaeological excavations. He had also managed to persuade the authorities to produce postage stamps depicting the country's art, particularly its rock art, funerary terracotta figures and prehistoric artefacts. Most of his own work was on a series of mounds where a long since departed people, the Sao, had lived. He discovered their wonderful art, their strange funerary figurines with flat faces and huge pot burials. The conference, which UNESCO supported, attracted many Nigerians, including Thurstan Shaw and Graham Connah whom I had met earlier in the year when I passed through Nigeria on my way to the USA. At the time Lebeuf was interested in setting up an organiz-ation to parallel the Pan African Prehistory Congress and the tensions among the French prehistorians, who had taken different stands on the war in Algeria, were being played out at the conference.

For me, one presentation stood out from the others – the des-cription by Théodore Monod, who had been director of the Institute francaise d'Afrique noire in Dakar, of his discovery of the Macden Ijafen lost caravan in the remotest part of the desert. Monod had seen some brass rods sticking out of the sand in 1962 and when he went back to excavate in 1964 he found more than 2000 brass rods in bundles wrapped in matting and cowrie shells. The site dated to the eleventh or twelfth century AD and firmly established the brass trade to West Africa. Monod was a remarkable man. His skin was wrinkled like a prune and he often crossed the Sahara by camel accompanied by only one or two local assistants. Although not a man of many words, he was a wonderful naturalist and definitely made an impact. He later visited me in Kampala.

Lebeuf had good government contacts and President Tombalbaye invited us all to an open-air dinner at the palace. Three whole sheep were roasting on spits and when the meal was served we were helped to couscous that had been cooking inside them. Fort Lamy, now named Ndjamena, was still a town with a sizeable French presence. It contained an army camp and French traders who had fled from Algeria ran many of the small shops. There was an open market selling attractive brass figures of antelopes and exciting jewellery made from semi-precious stones and amber brought down from the desert. The town was divided into distinct quarters, with the army, adminis-tration, market and African town clearly set apart.

On an excursion to the Tibesti Mountains in the far north of Chad close to the Libyan border we travelled in an old Chadian army DC-3 Dakota. Our first stop was Fayeau Largeau where the local adminis-trator invited us to an interminably long lunch. We still had time, however, to visit the market in an open courtyard with most of the traders seated on the ground rather than behind stalls to sell their bags of spices, dates and leather crafts. We spent several nights at Bardai in the Tibesti Mountains in an old French Foreign Legion fort. The three-foot thick walls ensured that the interior was cool in the day and warm at night. We travelled in an open truck to see the rock engravings and paintings and I do not think I had ever been so cold. Huge sand dunes, some over 50 feet high, were slowly spreading to overwhelm small oases. In all this dryness and cold we also inspected the remains of beaches from a time when, only a few thousand years back, Lake Chad had been ten times larger than it is at present. Engravings of huge giraffe, elephants and rhino testified to a wetter Sahara; we saw the polished stone artefacts, barbed bone points and ceramics of people who had thrived 5000 years before.

The remarkable cast of characters on the trip included Shaw, Connah and Ekpo Eyo from Nigeria, Henri Lhote, who discovered many of the paintings of the Tassili Massif, Helmut Ziegert from Germany,[12] who showed us some of the geomorphology and large numbers of Neolithic tools he had picked up on the desert surface, and Carleton Coon, an eminent American anthropologist whom I shall always remember wrapping himself in a thin, shiny, silver, solar blanket. Richard Nunoo of the Ghana National Museum was there too. The excursion brought home the importance of the Sahara, the untapped nature of its rock art and the reality of climatic variations in the late Pleistocene and early Holocene periods.

At the end of the conference Connah, Shaw and I visited many of the Sao mounds, which were similar in age to a huge mound Connah was excavating, more professionally, at Daima on the Nigerian side of Lake Chad. By staying on I learnt much more about the Sahel. The trouble with conferences is that one stays in a big hotel so has little contact with the local community or town. Unfortunately, we stayed on rather too long. First, my flight back to Uganda was delayed and then, when I did eventually leave on Christmas Eve, our Sudan Airways flight crash landed at El Fasher in Darfur. We spent more than two days at the airport, which was ill-equipped for visitors, though the regional district commissioner and Sultan of Darfur both sent us gifts of whisky. Being only 13 passengers and crew, we got to know each other quite well and, with the hills bathed in a purple light when the sun went down, we were in a hauntingly beautiful place. Then, because I had missed the connection to Entebbe, I had to be put up in Khartoum, where Sudan Airways spared no expense and where I was surprised to see Christmas decorations. Although a message had been sent to Eunice that I was delayed, it was worrying for her not to know what had happened.

By 1966 changes were occurring in Uganda. The Obote revolution had caused the Kabaka of Buganda to flee and, with the universities expanding, money for archaeology was growing tighter and it looked as if the Rockefeller Foundation would withdraw its support for the African Studies Programme. The trend in Makerere was moving against interdepartmental programmes and in favour of graduate research undertaken in the individual department. My job was on the line; I could either become a university administrator or look else-where. Fortunately, a vacancy came up for the chair in archaeology at Ghana and, with few qualified applicants around at the time, I was appointed. I thus had a chance to combine my two interests in teaching archaeology and conducting research. Ghana presented me

with a wonderful challenge. A. D. Lawrence, the classicist brother of
the famed Lawrence of Arabia, had started the department in 1951 at a
time when the Gold Coast museum and department were located
together in Achimota. Then, on independence in 1957, a decision was
made to turn the museum into an independent national institution
with a Ghanaian director, Richard Nunoo. Lawrence felt let down and
resigned; and Peter Shinnie, who had just left Uganda, replaced him.
He found Ghana more to his liking because at that time it had enough
resources to enable him to dig in the Nile Valley in Nubia every year.

In early 1967, before I left for Ghana, Mocha Abir, the dean of arts
at the Haile Selassie University in Addis Ababa, asked if I would be
willing to go to Addis at the beginning of our long vacation to take his
classes for three weeks while he visited East Africa. I had also been
invited to the Hebrew University in Jerusalem as a visiting professor
and decided to seize both opportunities. To travel to Israel before the
Six-Day War I had to fly through Cyprus and return via Tehran. I
could thus take a flight from Asmara in Ethiopia to Beirut, see a little
of Lebanon and visit Iran on my way back. David Stronach,[13] with
whom I had been at Cambridge and who had joined my dig at
Lockington in 1954, was director of the British Institute in Tehran. I
had seen a little of Egypt, but now I was able to link the northeast of
Africa and part of the Middle East in one visit.

I arrived in Addis on the day students challenged the government
for the right to demonstrate and were savagely put down. The police
and army invaded the campus and the university was closed, so I had
plenty of time to see the museum, visit the surrounding area in the car
Mocha had lent me and travel south of Addis to what was called the
Lake District. There, on the surface, were vast amounts of obsidian
flakes that gave me a good indication of the past importance of early
human societies in the area. The time I spent in the museum helped
me appreciate Ethiopia's connections through art with southern
Arabia; they had the same script, iconography of bulls and statues of
rulers from Axumite sites. Raymond Anfray took me to some of his
sites nearer to Addis. The university came back into session the day
before I left and I ended up giving only one lecture.

On my way to Israel I travelled to Gondar and saw seventeenth-
century castles built under Portuguese influence. The countryside was
beautiful and the climate good enough to roam around in a Harris
Tweed jacket. From Gondar I flew to Lalibela to see churches dating
back to the thirteenth century hewn out of solid rock and still in use.

At over 10,000 feet, the air in Lalibela is thin, but I was fit. Its churches are one of the greatest wonders of medieval Africa. From Lalibela I went to Axum where the impressive variety of standing monuments made me realize that the Axumite civilization was much mightier than I had ever believed. Wandering around, I was offered Axumite coins. Being poor and believing they should remain in Axum I turned them down, which I now regret because I could have obtained them for the museum before they were lost to less scrupulous tourists. I left Ethiopia via Asmara, which, as the old capital of Italian Eritrea and the present capital of the now independent state, was still a rather Italian colonial town with broad boulevards, palm trees, little pensions run by Italian widows dressed in black, and restaurants serving pasta and Chianti on tables with red-checked tablecloths. I particularly enjoyed visiting the Adulis museum. It housed material from excavations early in the century of Hellenistic and Roman remains of what had been an important port and town on the Red Sea and an important link in the spice trade.

I was fortunate to visit Beirut before it was riven by civil war. I saw Byblos and visited its national museum where, with so many Egyptian objects from Lebanese sites, I grasped the importance of Egypt in the eastern Mediterranean. Seeing the school children in their uniforms and the many small boutiques imprinted on my mind the Frenchness of Beirut, for many of its streets were reminiscent of ones I had seen on the Riviera. In Israel I lectured at the Institute of Archaeology, where the lack of interest in Africa disappointed me, and in the history department where there was a nucleus of scholars interested in Africa. I talked to guides at the museum and felt sorry that most of them detached Africa's art from its cultural context. With my sister I climbed up to see the citadel of Massada, built partly by Herod but eventually overwhelmed by the Romans. The preservation of artefacts, as in Egypt, was superb and made one realize why volunteers often prefer to join digs in dry areas with great civilizations where they are sure to find walls, pots and other relics from the past. The National Museum of Tehran was also an eye opener; in fact, it inspired me to read Mortimer Wheeler's *Flames over Persepolis: Turning Point in History* when it appeared in 1968. In Tehran I was surprised to see broad, well-surfaced highways and a very modern city. Being April, the views of the snow-clad mountains gave it a romantic air, though I now gather that population, smog, war and pollution have taken away its glamour. I was fortunate to see Iran because ours was the last El Al flight to stop off in Tehran; the Six-Day War broke out in the same week.

After this exciting trip I only had one term left before leaving Makerere, but I felt at the time that archaeology had a future in Uganda. We had set up a historical monuments commission, my student Jim Chaplin was the inspector of monuments, the history department had a commitment to archaeology and we were attracting foreign scholars to work in Uganda. Jim Chaplin's death just before I left, however, was a great blow to archaeology in Uganda and the university offered no instruction in it after I left.

The department in Ghana was still basically a research unit when I arrived in 1967. In 1961, before the Volta basin was flooded to create the Akosombo Dam, money had been obtained for the Volta Basin Research Project (VBRP), one of the most ambitious multidisciplinary projects in Africa. After 40 years the biological work on the lake still continues. The archaeological component had as its task the survey of the basin before flooding and the rescue excavation of threatened sites. Two young researchers were recruited from Britain to help with the project. When I arrived in Ghana there were four full archaeologists working on sites assisted by an equal number of technicians. Some good work was accomplished but it was at the expense of other research in Ghana, of teaching and of space for storing or working on new materials and advancing in new directions. My immediate goal was to introduce teaching at all levels.

We already had one MA student registered, a Nigerian, Hudson Obayemi,[14] and we spent the year 1967–68 getting our BA and Ph.D. programmes approved. The members of staff were unenthusiastic about training Ghanaian undergraduates. The grounds for their objections were that there were no suitable texts, that the two designated lecturers were committed to research and had no time to teach, and that there were no jobs for archaeology graduates. Although the latter objection was valid and, sadly, applies to all graduates in African universities, textbooks can be provided and we began an ambitious programme both to expand our library resources and to translate articles about sites and archaeology in Francophone Africa from French to English. We had enthusiastic first-year students, the two leading lights being Leonard Crossland and Kofi Agorsah. Leonard eventually chaired the department in the 1990s and did sterling work on the historical archaeology of Accra, while Kofi later worked at the Ghana Museum, taught archaeology in the department, initiated archaeology teaching in Jamaica and had a distinguished career at Portland State University, where he made a reputation for himself as the proponent of new world Maroon archaeology. Contrary to predictions, students were willing to come into the field. From 1970 regular field schools were held, the first being on a settlement site by one of the Dutch forts at Sekondi and thereafter in the Begho area where I was to work.

As the department grew in student numbers it became important to expand the teaching staff and by the time I left in 1976 we had six lecturers and two teaching assistants, enough to allow us to offer a wide array of teaching options. Though our main focus was on West Africa, we included world archaeology among our first year options and, in the absence of an anthropology department, also attempted to cover cultural and physical anthropology. In 1969–70 we received a grant from UNESCO to upgrade our museum and I introduced some of the features that had made the Uganda Museum so attractive. Many people from outside the campus visited the museum. We held compulsory practical classes on how to make stool tools, on the different aspects of ceramics and on how to recognize different metals and appreciate the importance of such items as beads. Students were taught to draw pottery and for several weeks learnt surveying in the university grounds. Towards the end of my time we introduced classes in archaeological photography.

It was exciting developing a department. We cooperated with our colleagues at the University of Ibadan where Professor Shaw introduced archaeology as a teaching subject in 1971. It seemed as if a brave new world was dawning for archaeology when in 1968 Ibadan and Legon, along with the Ghana Museum, launched the *West African Journal of Archaeology*. Adequate funding was provided but during the 1970s, when the economy nose-dived, the journal was forced to struggle on largely with Ibadan funding and the enthusiasm of its Nigerian editor, Bassey Andah. In 1974 the British government began to phase out its expatriate supplementation schemes; and US and Dutch programmes were also severely cut or ceased altogether. As the value of the Ghanaian cedi crumbled Ghanaian salaries tumbled in real terms. The unavailability of foreign exchange meant that libraries in Ghana could no longer maintain their runs of journals and disciplines dependent on field research could not finance research, for their vehicles were old and spare parts difficult to obtain. Our children who went to school in England complained of being weighed down by having to carry spare parts for either our own or the department vehicle when travelling back for holidays in Ghana.

13. Merrick examining painted Begho pottery, 1980.

One of my proudest accomplishments at the University of Ghana was my role as chairman of the university bookshop committee, a role I took very seriously. We had two problems, students could not afford textbooks and the bookshop had no foreign exchange to obtain books from overseas. From constant meetings with overseas publishers like Longman we made our point that more texts had to be published locally. We also took advantage of lower priced books, many probably produced in violation of copyright agreements, from India and Eastern Europe. East Germany was particularly active in Ghana and provided gramophone records of classical music at very advantageous rates, which were a great attraction for customers from outside the campus. I also negotiated with the UNDP office for UNESCO book tokens to obviate the long, frustrating process of trying to get foreign exchange. Through a survey we ascertained from students actually how much they were willing to spend of their declining allowance on textbooks. Lecturers had been in the habit of ordering unrealistic numbers of books. The bookshop sold stationery, greeting cards, international and national weeklies, and the best array of children's books available in Ghana. Some of this trade helped us to defray textbook costs and keep the bookshop viable for longer than had one time seemed possible. The bookshop also had a remarkable asset in its manager Mr Kofi, who had a great deal of personal integrity and commanded the respect of his staff.

Though I went to Ghana hoping to initiate historical archaeology on the coast, the vice-chancellor and others convinced me that there were more pressing priorities. It was felt that my predecessors had paid too little attention to Ghanaian concerns. When I arrived in Ghana a lively debate was in progress on the nature of northern influence on the Akan world. Some scholars, like Eva Meyerowitz, even went so far as to claim that the Akan, of which the Asante were the most celebrated members, had come from the north. Others, like Ivor Wilks, emphasized the role of Mande-speaking Muslim traders in bringing change to the world with which they traded. Though a relatively late northern influence was clearly demonstrable in the area immediately to the east of the Akan from Arabic chronicles like the *Khitab Gunja*, and had been recognized archaeologically by Oliver Davies and members of the VBRP in the Volta basin, the relationships between the Akan world and the north still needed archaeological verification. From what I had read and from the brassware from the Islamic world I saw still existing in Brong Ahafo villages, it was obvious that trade had been a major stimulant in state formation. Long-distance trade thus became a key, but not the only, component in my theoretical approach to the origin of the first Akan states. The Nuffield Foundation in England funded the project, including money for excavations at Begho and for graduate research by students trained at Begho field schools.

The West African trade project was launched at Begho in 1970, with seven further seasons of excavation between then and 1979. In addition to the more than 50 Ghanaians, students from Nigeria, Germany, Britain, the USA, Zambia and the Ivory Coast participated in our work at different times. In 1971 we built a permanent field centre where we kept excavation and camping gear. We also undertook some ethnographic work upon which I have touched in another chapter.

In all, we excavated on five different quarters, or sections, of Begho and were able to show distinct differences between them – the Brong quarter contained items relating to Brong chieftaincy, including a shrine room, ivory side-blown trumpets and numerous clay spindle whorls used by women cotton spinners; the *Dwinfuor* or artisans' quarter contained clay crucibles for brass casting; the *Kramo* or Muslim traders' quarter contained extended burials, dye pits and a different food regime; and the market quarter contained a mixture of materials. Begho clearly dates to a period from AD 1350 to the early nineteenth century. In its heyday in the seventeenth century it may have had a population of between 5000 and 10,000, making it the largest town in the Ghanaian hinterland and famed for both its market and products. Its brassware, textiles, painted ceramics, and occasional cylindrical drainpipes suggestive of some flat-roofed houses, were all indicative of the transference of technologies from the middle Niger in the Jenne area to the edge of the forest where traders from the south brought their gold, skins, kola nuts, forest ivory and other products to trade with the Mande. Many stayed on and intermarried with local women.

Students from the Begho training school went on to develop their own interests. Roderick McIntosh from Yale studied decay patterns in swish houses at Hani and later excavated sites in the Jenne area, which was from where the Mande traders came down to the Begho area; Emmanuel Effah Gyamfi examined the contemporary city state of Bono Manso and J. Boachie Ansah the old town of Wenchi. Dr Joanne Dombrowski and Emmanuel (later Kofi) Agorsah investigated the Neolithic sites we found when researching the origins of the Begho population. Hani oral traditions pointed to the significance of holes in the ground from which it was believed ancestors emerged.

The holes turned out to be *bilegas*, bell-shaped cisterns dug into the hard laterite, on which their ancestors had to rely for good water in the rather high open country they called home. Bedrock mortars in the immediate area were presumably used for grinding grains like millet and the artefacts of the Kintampo industry date back to more

14. Excavating at Begho, 1979.

than 1000 BC. Also uncovered were the remains of circular swish houses as well as hollow-based arrowheads, stone bracelets and other stone artefacts reminiscent of a northern and Sahelian origin, as well as distinctive tools named 'cigars' (from their shape) and rasps (from their possible function).

Though I worked on sites on the frontier between Islam and the

south, between a northern Gur and Akan south, between forest and
savannah woodland, I had never abandoned my original interest in
historical archaeology that at that time comprised the narrower
definition of sites representative of the contact between the European
and African worlds.[15] Dr Albert van Dantzig from the history
department at Legon, a Dutchman and soul mate – like me he had a
wife from Africa and devoted his life to its study – presented me with
a major opportunity. He knew all the main western European
languages and had written books in Dutch and French on the
companies that had built the trading forts that graced the Ghanaian
coast. He and a graduate student had written a very readable guide to
the forts and castles of the Ghanaian coast[16] that went beyond
Lawrence's dull architectural descriptions to evaluate the lives of those
who lived both within and outside their confines. He lobbied the
Ghana Museum and Monuments Board to do more to develop the
forts as a sustainable historical and tourist asset.

I was interested in the forts and in 1970 had encouraged our chief
technician, Bernard Golden, to conduct a survey of them. In 1973, I
helped Doig Simmonds, then curator of a planned Cape Coast
historical museum, excavate one of the underground dungeons in the
castle,[17] the only such slave holding area so far excavated on the coast.
In 1975 Albert invited me to see many of the forts through his eyes.
The most memorable of our visits was to Fort Ruychaver, built in
1654 and the only fort erected far inland from the coast. It survived
four years and was destroyed in mysterious circumstances that
involved self-immolation by the limping factor who controlled the
trade but could not satisfy local demands for imported goods. We
trekked 28 miles in a single day down into valleys and up steep slopes
to get there, but found it covered in forest and its remains completely
overgrown.

Fort Ruychaver presented a challenge I could not resist. In
December 1975 and January 1976 I excavated it with the help of the
Brathay Exploration Group from England and included in our team
several sixth form students from Ghanaian high schools. Though the
fort is not far by boat from the company mining town of Prestea, the
river was so polluted by cyanide used in roasting the ores in the gold
extraction process that we had to carry everything to our camp over
land. Our camp was deep in the forest and dark until around 10.00
a.m. because high vegetation obstructed the light. Humidity was high
and when I washed out my singlet it took two days to dry on the tent

guy ropes. When I took the students to visit the gold mine, involving a descent of nearly a mile below the surface, we had to wear hard hats, metal-toed boots and overalls. Bent low to crawl along the three-foot high shafts we had to walk half a mile to the face where the temperature and humidity were over 100 degrees. Miners felt lucky to earn $2 a day, but deserved a lot more. We were exhausted after only two hours of visiting without doing any work.

The life of the people who traded with the Dutch was far easier as their adits were shallow and they extracted the gold by pounding the ore in rock-cut hollows that abounded in the area. To reveal our site involved nearly a week of clearance. Mahogany trees, three feet across, had grown up over mounds of stones brought up from the river once intended to build a substantial fort. But before that fort was built there had been a tile-roofed mud-walled building. We found its reddened collapsed walls and the roof tiles were scattered for at least 100 feet beyond the fort, thrown up in the explosion that had marked its end. The intensity of the heat was such that the tiles had vitrified becoming in some instances naturally glazed. The tiles were identical in form, and later we found in composition, to the Dutch tiles that had roofed the contemporaneous forts in New Amsterdam and Cape Town.

Chapter 6

Career: coming to America, new directions

B
Y THE END of 1973 UCLA had approached me with a view to applying for a professorship in history. Though I was enjoying Africa, the economic situation meant that the writing was on the wall. Also, I had health problems and hospital services in Ghana were in a calamitous state and patients had to supply their own sheets and cutlery. The opportunities for research in Africa seemed greater from the United States than in Africa.

I let my name go forward and, at the end of my 1974 sabbatical year in Cambridge, received the offer of an appointment, which I accepted with the proviso that I would be unable to take up my appointment before 1976. The year 1975 proved to be a very busy one archaeologically and the department was doing well, but 1976 came all too quickly.

My visa for entry to the United States, however, did not come as quickly. The US immigration authorities had to get clearance from the criminal investigation bureaux of every country in which I had lived for more than six months. This included Uganda, Kenya, Ghana and Great Britain. My friends were convinced that the delay was most likely in Uganda, where Idi Amin was president at the time, but it turned out to be Britain where my papers had been lost in the US embassy.

Fortunately, I had a resourceful sister in Dora, who approached Senator Cranston, and my niece Marie contacted Shirley Temple Black, the former US ambassador to Ghana. I was quickly learning that in America knowing people means a lot more to one's advancement than one's qualities as an individual. Since that time I have always felt sympathetic towards immigrants arriving in the United States without either a job or relatives with any influence. The six months I spent in Cambridge waiting for a visa proved invaluable. I had enough leisure time in which to read, give a few guest lectures, plan classes, help with the children's education, see museum material and think about the future.

Caribbean archaeology and the archaeology of the African diaspora

An archaeological opportunity arose as soon as I got to Los Angeles. Roderick Ebanks, a graduate student in Ghana but now at the Institute of Jamaica, had returned to Jamaica excited by the continuities he observed between Ghana and Jamaica. Working on folk pottery in the old capital of Spanish Town, he noted that vessel forms, potting tools and even linguistic terms were similar to those he had seen in the coastal plain in Ghana, particularly in the populations that had been evicted from the Shai hills. He invited me, along with Professor Kwabena Nketia who had also been in Ghana, to participate in an African Caribbean summer school. It is no exaggeration to say that this visit changed my career.

Each topic had one person dealing with the African background and another with the Caribbean side. I dealt with African history and archaeology and Eddie Brathwaite, who had spent time at the University of Cape Coast, dealt with the Caribbean. We examined continuities in language, art, folklore, music, religion and social behaviour. We attended an all-night Kumina possession rite where several of the people collapsed in a trance; we marvelled at the use of African words from the Congo and Akan words in the songs, many of them hardly understood by the participants. I later explored a little of the interior on my own and noted how the traps used for snaring birds were identical to those I had seen in Ghana. I realized that there was tremendous scope for African archaeology in Jamaica, looking at ceramic forms on slave sites, at ethnographic practice, house forms and the spatial patterning of material culture. I arranged to go back for a field survey in 1979 and to involve one of my graduate students trained in Ghana. A field survey by Douglas Armstrong led ultimately to his doctoral research at the slave village at Drax Hall. We held a field school when he was at work there in 1981. I wrote several well-received papers[1] and launched diasporan archaeology as a field pursued ultimately by five further doctoral students and several students for master's theses.

My feeling was that, although there was a growing interest in African-American archaeology in North America, far too few of its practitioners knew much about the Africa from which the Africans had been transplanted as slaves. In 1980 Montserrat, the Dominican Republic and Jamaica were the only places where serious archaeological work was being conducted on African communities in the Caribbean. Kofi Agorsah made a breakthrough in Jamaica when he stimulated a great deal of interest in the Maroons, the slaves who had gained their freedom by running away into the remote inaccessible parts of the island. He obtained Jamaican government help to fly his team by helicopter into the Blue Mountains where they investigated Nanny Town. He has subsequently gone on to work in Surinam. Another of my students, Candice Goucher, worked on African iron working traditions in Jamaica and Trinidad. Still others have gone on to work in the Bahamas and Guadeloupe. Unfortunately, many of the scholars who pontificate on black American archaeology still have little idea about Africa. In other disciplines like art history, linguistics and folklore there has been rather more cross-fertilization between the continents to good effect.

A positive effect of becoming involved in the Caribbean was that it opened my eyes to historical archaeology as a discipline. In the late 1970s it was still nascent and the annual conferences of the Society for Historical Archaeology, to which Douglas Armstrong had introduced me, attracted fewer than 500 participants.[2] In 1982 I held my first class in historical archaeology at UCLA with rather more history than anthropology students involved; by the time I taught my last class 20 years later anthropology students outnumbered history ones by nearly two to one and the enrolment was rarely lower than 65. I began to present papers on the archaeology of the black diaspora,[3] which had been previously ignored, though there was plantation archaeology dealing with the archaeology of African slaves on plantations in the southeastern states of the USA. The names of Charles Fairbanks and his student Theresa Singleton were closely associated with plantation archaeology and their work in Florida, Georgia and the Carolinas built up a critical following. In 1989 Theresa organized a seminal conference at Oxford, Mississippi on digging the African-American past. I also realized that the archaeology of African slavery had to be slotted into a wider African context, which I later defined in a survey paper on Africa at the Williamsburg meeting of the Society for Historical Archaeology. With my then graduate student Christopher DeCorse, I eventually augmented my views and published the paper in *Historical Archaeology*.

In 1984 the Williamsburg archaeologist Ivor Noel Hume came to

UCLA as a visiting professor. This gave historical archaeology a great fillip and encouraged our growing team of students. He was the first of several dynamic speakers and in 1986 the Institute of Archaeology published a special issue of the *Journal of New World Archaeology* devoted to several emerging themes in historical archaeology. In its introduction I was able to express ideas about the importance of a comparative approach. The journal had had a poor track record for sales but it was flattering when that particular number sold out quite rapidly to historical archaeologists who had access to few anthologies of recent research outside the colonial period New England–Virginia cradle of English contact. These areas had been made accessible particularly in the writings of Jim Deetz[4] and Noel Hume.

Historical archaeology

When I became more interested in historical archaeology I also realized that I was more of a cultural historian than a straight-forward archaeologist. Over the years I had become disillusioned with some of the theoretical aspects of archaeology. What interested me now was how our discipline interacted with others to expand our knowledge of people in the past and of their behaviour. I could see a difference in my interests just by looking at what I enjoyed reading. I began to prefer journals like *History Today* to *Archaeology*. For me humans were more than the creators of a transforming technology. I grew tired of pottery classifications and repetitive descriptions of material culture. Articles in journals like *Historical Archaeology* with their descriptions of some relatively unimportant farmhouse or urban quarter seemed pointless. What I wanted to know was the big picture, the bottom line.

I realized that the vignettes archaeologists produced added up to the bigger picture but I craved more adventurous uses of the data. I was attracted to the writings of archaeologists like Jim Deetz. He used the fullness of the human experience to reach his conclusions; he asked pertinent questions and, like my original mentor Sir Mortimer Wheeler, he wrote with clarity and a certain lyricism. At UCLA I perceived the importance of folklore and folk culture, which scholars like Don Cosentino handled so brilliantly. Folklore has been rather denigrated as a fringe subject; it was seen as verging on an imaginative whispiness that down-to-earth archaeologists found difficult to nail down. When I came to UCLA I suppose I fell into such a category because I was unsure of the writings of the well-established Maria

Gimbutas, but in time I realized that her breadth allowed her to seek answers to bigger questions of how societies transformed and created their value systems.

Archaeology, metal working, goldweights and students

One of my abiding interests has been in technology and at different times I have written about both iron working and brass casting. At Begho we found an early iron furnace that predated the later city state by 1000 years; in 1979 we discovered numerous slag heaps and furnace remains at Dapaa, two-and-a-half miles from Begho, presumably dating from the town's heyday.

Candice Goucher researched iron working at Hani in 1979 and tapped into the latent knowledge of the villagers to make charcoal in a traditional fashion. Two trees were felled, cut into logs and burnt for a week under a mound of earth, producing three sacks of usable charcoal. She also studied the smiths in the nearby village of Brawhani, possibly descendants of the smiths at Begho. For her doctorate she studied iron working in Togo, providing invaluable insights into its impact on the environment by looking at the end products and estimating the amount of charcoal, and thus trees, and iron ore required to produce a given number of hoes and other artefacts essential to an iron-using population. Her interest in experimental archaeology led also to her making a film (*Blooms of Banjeli*) on iron working by replicating past practices by aged iron workers in Bassar.

Another of my students, Philip de Barros, also worked on Bassar iron working in Togo but from a strictly archaeological viewpoint, locating the past iron furnaces and slag heaps and working out their chronology. He clearly showed that that area of Togo had been a powerhouse in iron technology between AD 1300 and 1800 and had overlapped in time with other great iron-working areas in the Cameroon, Mali and Senegal.

Another doctoral student, Tim Garrard, who had come to West Africa in 1967 to join the Ghana legal service, worked on brass casting in northern Ghana. He became interested in the brass weights the Akan people, largely the Asante, fashioned for weighing gold dust. When the weighting system derived from medieval Arab traders from North Africa, using simple shapes, hit the Akan world, weights began to be made in limitless designs, often termed geometrics, and later in natural designs. The latter represented the animals around, the paraphernalia of chieftaincy, basic household items like pots and even designs that depicted proverbs. Tim wrote papers about the weighting system and demonstrated its origins in first Islamic and later European weighting systems. He weighed thousands of weights and showed that his classification system worked. He also showed how seeds were used as small weights and found that on my Begho sites people had fashioned discs from potsherds that conformed to the weight grades and they had also made decorated cubes of baked clay that mimicked brass weights. Since that time many of my students have identified such weights on their sites, including Cameron Monroe in Dahomey.

Garrard eventually wrote a book[5] and registered in the department of archaeology to take an MA and write a thesis on the brass trade. We became friends and he infected me with his addiction to collecting gold weights, which have sometimes aptly been termed masterpieces in miniature. The design would first be fashioned in wax, and then turned into brass using the *cire perdue*, or vanishing wax, process. By this procedure the wax original is invested in several coatings of fine clay and made into a mould; the wax is then melted out and the brass poured into the cavity in which the wax had previously been. He came on several excavations and followed me to UCLA where he registered as a doctoral student, undertook fieldwork among the Frafra and completed his degree in a record three years.

UCLA, the archaeology programme and Institute of Archaeology

I am eclectic in my interests and when I came to America I was able to sample different archaeological orientations. I was drawn to the archaeology programme at UCLA because it combined archaeologists from ten different disciplines and attracted students with backgrounds in science, linguistics and art, as well as in anthropology and history. I chaired the programme from 1979 to 1981 and enjoyed the inter-disciplinary contact.

By 1984 I and others were distressed by the weakness of the Institute of Archaeology, which had been designed to bring campus archaeologists together. It was grossly under-funded and, in the face of a robust group of archaeologists in the anthropology department, it had difficulty demonstrating its claim to represent archaeology at the university. It was in effect an organized research unit made up of faculty members from any departments in which archaeology was taught, however peripherally. It provided archaeologists with basic services they could not necessarily find in their home departments.

These were a publications division, special laboratories for dating and for analysing bones and seeds, an archive for the rock art of the western states, a public programmes division to promote lectures to the southern California community, and an archaeological survey to deal with the immediate practical needs of research archaeology in the area of California served by the university.

The survey and an obsidian hydration-dating laboratory brought small sums into the institute, but we were a classic nickel and dime operation. There were two support groups, the Friends of Archaeology, which mainly supported research by graduate students and the Fellows of the Institute, a group of rather better heeled patrons whose support largely went to the publications division. We were housed in dispersed offices in Kinsey Hall where space had been allocated to our different activities. I was appointed with a clear mandate to increase the institute's visibility on the campus and turn it into an organization that attracted support from both scholars and the community. It was a tough call as many of the archaeologists were hardly pulling together.

Our ultimate salvation came with the news that there was to be a new building for the Museum of Culture History and that there was a possibility of obtaining space within it if we could get the ground floor partly funded through state and university money outside the donations that had made the museum into a reality. In numerous meetings we wrangled over how we would use our space and sell the idea of the institute both to the university planners and ultimately to the various state officials. I saw it as a fantastic window of opportunity – a new institute where all the archaeologists would be together instead of in seven separate buildings, where all seminars and public lectures would be in one place, where archaeologists could get services and where we could build up resources for everyone to use. It was coming at just the right time as the institute gained its first IBM computer in 1984 and we could see how the coming IT revolution was going to change our old ways of working.

From 1984 until I handed over to my successor Tim Earle in late November 1987, preparatory to my taking up a Fulbright fellowship in Ghana in 1988, we had to change the institute. We hived off the survey and made it into a California information centre, improved our publications by obtaining new university funds to professionalize the leadership, and acquired a grant to buy Macintosh technology to improve, speed up and expand our in-house publications. The biggest shift was in our public programmes. Previously, everything had been on an *ad hoc* basis. If we knew a suitable speaker was coming to UCLA we would arrange a meeting, canvass funds from interested departments, find a room and put on a talk. From 1984 we began to schedule talks in advance, publish a programme of what we were going to do and let as many people as possible know about our activities. In three years we promoted more than a hundred lectures and special talks.

We held quite a few joint programmes with university extension, thus ensuring adequate financing and, best of all, we made decisions on what to promote. Though talks on ancient Egypt, the Maya, astro-archaeology, early human origins, and Stonehenge or places about which people had heard were the most popular, we also introduced our public to new methodologies, and to the archaeology of the Pacific, Australia and Africa. We increased our average attendance from fewer than 20 to nearly 40. We also sought to involve our support groups in the institute's work and produced merchandise such as T-shirts, tote bags and caps with institute logos. The fellows' and friends' organizations were merged and we began to produce a regular newsletter *Backdirt* to keep our friends and supporters well informed. *Backdirt* is still going strong. In 1987 we passed an administrative review of the institute with flying colours, thus ensuring that the institute had a future. This allowed the institute to move into its new premises with confidence and to thrive under my successor.

The archaeology of the East African coast

Being in a well-respected and established American institution enabled me to see much more of Africa than was possible when I was working there. I was fortunate in my UCLA career in being able to visit Africa virtually annually for research, conferences or on US government contracts, mainly for the United States Information Agency. I visited Kenya in 1977 to attend the Pan African Prehistory Congress in Nairobi, but was able to spend a week on the Kenya coast beforehand with James de Vere Allen.

Jim Allen, as he was better known, whom I first met when he was lecturing at Makerere, was one of the best historians in Africa. He was born in Mombasa where his father had been warden of the Fort Jesus prison. After studying for a degree at Oxford, he undertook research in Southeast Asia and maintained an abiding fascination with Indian

Ocean culture. He later bought and furnished, in an authentic manner, a stone house in Lamu and was for a time curator of the Lamu Museum. He did much to revive, sustain and encourage traditional crafts and became an expert on the great ivory side-blown trumpets (*siwas*) that were so important in Lamu ritual. Jim helped change perceptions about coastal history by pointing out the connections between families in stone and thatch-roofed houses.[6]

Visiting Lamu helped me understand the logistics of Indian Ocean trade, for along the shore were red mangrove poles neatly stacked and ready for shipment in beached dhows awaiting the arrival of the winds that would blow them towards the Persian Gulf. Lamu was a living, thriving Swahili town with wood carvers and other craftsmen, a town proud of its ancestry yet welcoming to visitors who mostly came by air in small planes or by a laborious road route from Malindi, having got there by 'Happy Taxi' from Mombasa. On the same trip I visited Hamo Sassoon, the curator of the Fort Jesus Museum, and saw the finds from the *Santa Antonio*, the Portuguese ship sunk outside Mombasa harbour in 1696, a complex operation he was helping to coordinate. This was the first major underwater archaeology excavation in East Africa. I also visited his excavations in old Mombasa, a site that provided textbook examples for dating coastal archaeology. The wealth of imported ceramics and the even greater quantities of local pottery brought home how much activity in trade and settlement there had been in late medieval times on the Kenya coast and clearly demonstrated Mombasa's importance, which had somehow been overlooked in the excavation of more celebrated abandoned cities like Kilwa. Both Allen and Sassoon, both sadly deceased, were scholars whose work on the Swahili coast has not received the recognition they deserve.

Somalia, archaeology, museums and Mogadishu
In 1978 UNESCO invited me to undertake a reconnaissance of the archaeological resources of Somalia and, specifically, to report on the condition of, and suggest improvements for, the national museum in Mogadishu. I spent just over a month in Somalia. I had known about the museum from Italian experts in the 1950s when it had a reputation as a good general museum covering everything from natural history to archaeology, ethnography and history. By 1978 it had fallen on lean times. There were no trained personnel, the well-kept registration cards had been lost or mixed up, and many of the more

valuable artefacts, including medieval gold and silver coins from hoards, had been stolen. In an attempt to improve matters after the departure of the Soviet advisers, the museum had been painted but without removing any of the objects, so there were paint splashes on stuffed animals and dusty artefacts. The library was infected with bookworms and many of the archives, documents and books were badly damaged with pages stuck together. In the 1940s the Italians had published a catalogue and only a few were in any way usable. The museum was housed in a nineteenth-century building dating from the period of Zanzibari control and still had a fine carved door. While I was there I set about teaching a small class of Somali students about simple museum techniques, including how to accession materials, but we first had to buy pens, Indian ink and varnish to protect the numbers, in fact everything needed doing, even the most routine jobs. In Mogadishu at that time simple shopping took hours because most shops had only limited inventories.

In Mogadishu I stayed in the old colonial Italian-run Croce del Sud courtyard hotel and was surprised at how much of the Italian influence still remained. In 1978 Mogadishu was a wonderful and very peaceful place. Most evenings I would wander through the old town of Himarweyn near the shoreline, admiring its nineteenth-century architecture and chatting with residents sitting in doorways lit by small flickering oil lamps.

In Mogadishu there was still a residue of Swahili speakers. Many houses had distinctive carved windows and doors and, as in so many Islamic towns, they were built round courtyards and hidden from outside gaze. I visited several mosques, including Fakhr ad-Din, the oldest, where one had to walk down steps to get in because the town had risen more than seven feet since the mosque was first built. However, it still retained its thirteenth-century inscription on a coloured marble panel. I found the shops fascinating. There was a whole row of goldsmiths making filigree jewellery and the stalls selling incense, as well as incense burners carved from soft white rock, were reminiscent of the frankincense and myrrh of biblical times. I had several shirts made from the colourful striped Benadir cloth woven on horizontal looms set into the ground. For lunch I ate fresh fish fried on the beach with roasted plantains, bananas and oranges. The students took me to see banana plantations on the Webi Shebelle River near Afgoi. Somalia was a beautiful place to be at that time.

This was a time when Somalia was in the ascendant, with an

infectious sense of nationalism and energy everywhere. People were translating literature into the newly-adopted Somali script and making glorious, colourful and patriotic posters. I particularly enjoyed an opera cum ballet at the Chinese-built national theatre where tickets were priced to admit even the poorest Somalians. The *brise soleil* walls of the theatre let in the evening breeze, thus obviating the need for air conditioning. There was a great vitality in the performance depicting the struggle against imperialism and glorifying the ongoing revolution. The audience was clearly enjoying the patriotic singing.

Though people were proud of Islam, it was less restrictive than in Khartoum and less formal than on the Swahili coast. There were bars in Mogadishu and many young women wore jeans. There was a stress on education and on creating new symbols to remind the population of the splendours of their forgotten history, particularly of Mohamed ibn Abdullah Hassan's struggle against the British who bombed his desert fortress of Taleh in 1920. Stamps depicting Taleh appeared in 1980; the site still has its boulder ramparts and is well worth archaeological investigation. Everyone felt proud of the role of women in the revolution and pointed with pride to the prominent statue of Hawa Osman, the stone-throwing Somali nationalist who led a riot in 1948 to protest against the Allies sending a commission to decide on Somalia's future political status.

At the university, where I gave a lecture, the students were enthusiastic, but had few facilities and the library was pitiful. With the help of the American cultural affairs officer, I arranged for two students to obtain grants to come to UCLA. From this beginning sprang a successful link that UCLA maintained with the faculty of arts for the next five years. In 1980 I attended the first international congress of Somali studies and was impressed by the progress that had taken place in two years.

The British Institute in East Africa had begun excavating in the middle of the old town and had gone down through nearly 15 feet of cultural deposits, indicating an occupation at least as far back as the eighth century, several hundred years earlier than previously been thought. There were more tourists and the shops had more to sell, but tourism had the usual deleterious affect on life in the city by bringing in more bars, open prostitution and an increase in people wanting to change money on the black market, sell antiquities and ingratiate themselves to the casual visitors.

While in Somalia I also had occasion to visit Hargeisa. The town was situated on a high plateau and, with tin-roofed stores and a catering rest house serving English dishes, retained its English colonial atmosphere. There was a new Chinese-built museum in a round structure containing quite a lot of objects, but all of them new. There had been little attempt to look for old well-worn artefacts that could speak of traditional practice and the walls were painted in garish pinks and greens. I went from Hargeisa to Berbera by road, but broke down near Sheikh. I took the opportunity to explore the countryside and was astounded by the richness of the late Pleistocene stone tools lying on the surface made out of some of the most attractive coloured chalcedony I have ever seen. I showed a little of the material I collected to Steven Brandt, Desmond Clark's student at Berkeley, who was sufficiently attracted to work for several years in Somalia following up the pioneering research of Desmond Clark who had written a remarkable book while exploring Somaliland during his time off from the military during the Second World War.[7] It was also apparent at that time that many more people were drifting towards the smaller urban areas. I also took the opportunity to visit several of the other towns to the south of Mogadishu like Merca and Gondershe. They reminded me of the Swahili towns further down the coast in Kenya and Tanzania. Even their inhabitants looked more like Swahili townsmen than like the very distinctive Somalis of Mogadishu or Hargeisa.

Somalia's collapse brought sadness to those of us who had had such high expectations in the early 1980s. Television coverage in the early 1990s of the destruction of many of Mogadishu's old buildings, the irreparable damage to the museum and the collapse of the physical infrastructure made depressing viewing. Somalia collapsed because old clan and family rivalries resurfaced following the Russian pull-out and President Siad Barre lost sight of the delicate balance he needed to maintain between the old British and Italian parts of the country. Each of these areas had different clan affiliations, different educational backgrounds and looked to different outside patrons. Each had had different official languages, English in Somaliland and Italian in Somalia. The president tried to unite the country in an impractical struggle with Ethiopia for the desert province of the Ogaden, but this was a war his new American friends were unwilling to endorse. A terrible drought in the early 1980s and a downturn in world trade followed the Somali retreat. Eventually, southern Somalia became a failed state fought over by ruthless warlords; the north, with Hargeisa its capital, claimed back its independence, but no other state accepted it. Many of the brightest and best-trained Somalis fled to the emirates, worked in unskilled jobs in Saudi Arabia and Djibouti, or became refugees all over the world with significant numbers ending up in Scandinavia and the USA.

Beginning archaeology in Togo and linkages with Togo

In 1979 a new area quite unexpectedly opened up for me. I was working at Begho in Ghana when I received an invitation from the director of the United States Information Service (USIS) in Lomé to visit Togo before I went back to the United States. A Togolese scholar, Dovi Kuevi, had asked the USIS to send an American archaeologist to look into the potential for archaeology in Togo. As my French is not very good I invited my graduate student Phil de Barros to join me on a brief trip to Togo to investigate the possibilities before we returned to the United States. Phil had a Togolese wife and had spent six years in the Peace Corps there before joining UCLA, so had a wonderful network of contacts. In two days we went to several sites. When a storm broke out on our way back from Tado, felling a tree on our route, I thought we were doomed to miss our plane but, being in a government vehicle and relying on the cheerful cooperation of Togolese villagers, we got to the airport muddy, travel stained and with only minutes to spare.

We arranged to go back for a month and had a highly memorable trip in August when Dovi Kuevi and I covered the whole country. We looked for sites, followed up leads, met local officials and had a great time discovering sites from the middle Pleistocene to the modern period.[8] We wrote a 100-page description of our survey, which we presented to the minister of education when he visited UCLA the following year. The link led to two notable developments, plans to conduct a training excavation at Notse and the beginnings of an Education Abroad Programme from the University of California, both to commence in 1981.

The Notse excavation was particularly significant because it attracted participation from Benin, so could be said to have started archaeology in both Togo and Benin. All the future archaeologists and leading historians participated – Theo Gayibor, Adimado Aduayom, Dovi Kuevi and Angele Aguigah from Togo, and Père François de Medeiros, Alexis Adande and Goudjinou Metinhoue from Benin, a stellar group of influential future scholars and administrators.[9] It was a large excavation and included six American students and four UREP (University Research Expeditions Programme) participants. Seth Dankwa, the chief technician from the University of Ghana's archaeology department joined the team, as did Professor Ben Swartz from Ball State University in Muncie, Indiana. The Notse excavation involved mapping the 2.5 mile long earthen walls of the town of Notse. A peculiar aspect of the town wall was that the ditch lay on the inside of the wall. The wall had never been completed and there were several entrances to the town. The original town site was quite small and marked by potsherd pavements that indicated where old courtyard town houses had existed.

Angele Aguigah continued with the work and found what appeared to be a shrine with several superposed floors and a more elaborate series of decorative floors. Using tobacco pipes and radio-carbon dates she clearly indicated a seventeenth-century date for the town that was the ancestral site of the Ewe people. Local legend had it that a rather vicious king, Agokoli I, forced his people to build the wall. It was tough work because they had little water to mix with the earth and on occasion used their own blood. In time, they rebelled when the women conspired together and threw calabashes of water against one section of the wall to weaken it. The people of Notse escaped from the town to settle in southern Togo more than 50 miles away in what is now eastern Ghana.

We demonstrated in our sectioning of the wall its immensity and the fact that it had a puddle core rather than being formed of layers of soft earth. We also found many areas where people had created oval shaped bedrock mortars and long narrow grooves in the rock, perhaps for shaping, polishing or sharpening Neolithic stone tools. It was apparent that Notse had been an important settlement area long before the Ewe people came there from Tado to the east. Aguigah went on to find many more bedrock mortars and grooves on stones, similar potsherd pavements in Tado and, both at Tado and to the east of it, a huge agglomeration of iron furnaces. Tado and Notse marked two spots on the expansion of the Adja–Ewe peoples, whose ancestry lay in eastern Benin where the walled town of Ketou still exists with a 40-foot high rubbish heap going back hundreds of years. To the east of Ketou lay the medieval state of Oyo in eastern Nigeria whose first collapse, perhaps in the fourteenth century, had set the original migration in motion.

Phil de Barros stayed on in Togo after the end of the excavation to

initiate a University of California Education Abroad Programme (EAP)
link with Togo. It lasted 11 years and involved me in more than ten
further visits to Togo to help direct our teaching programme in 1983,
direct EAP summer programmes at Notse in 1986 and 1992, conduct
research in 1985 and 1986 and organize two international conferences
in 1984 and 1987. From 1982 until 1987 we ran a linkage programme
with the university from the African Studies Center, published a
newsletter called *Togo Togo*[10] and hosted five different Togolese faculty
members. We built up our Togolese library collections and earned a
reputation for being the main centre for Togolese studies in the
United States. I was often called upon to comment upon current
affairs in Togo for the Voice of America and in 1986 spearheaded a
campaign by Amnesty International to have one of our Togolese
cooperating faculty, Adimado Aduayom, freed from prison and the
threat of death.

Notse market and Notse cloth

I returned to Notse several times and grew to like the town. Years ago
it had been renowned for its bad water, but a series of wells and
pumps brought up a ready supply of some of the sweetest artesian
water I have ever tasted. We stayed at the Evangelical training centre,
which had simple rooms, a classroom and a kitchen where group
feeding was possible though on several occasions we hired our own
cooks. Notse was famous for its market where artisans sold ceramics,
baskets, metalwork, and leather goods. The vendors came from a
range of ethnicities. For example, the butchers and dealers in second-
hand clothing, colloquially known as dead Europeans' clothes, tended
to come from the Zongo (foreigners') quarter where northerners, often
Hausas from Nigeria, lived. Local remedies, sometimes called fetishes
and used to cure all manner of physical, mental and possibly imagined
illnesses, were sold by men whose stalls included shrivelled up
chameleons, monkey heads, bored stones, pots, lumps of clays and
soft rocks for dysentery, as well as roots, dried plants and
miscellaneous powders. Women mainly traded in foodstuffs and
Western medicines. Bars and outlets for palm wine and local foods
were on the fringes of the market with the charcoal sellers and bicycle
repairers on the most outer edge. There were tables for games of
chance, a watch repairer, women who dyed hair and others who
plaited it. The richest of the women sellers were those who sold cloth,
many travelling from market to market.

The big market was on Saturdays, but a smaller one was held daily. Most villages had a regular market day. Unlike Notse, which had a partly covered permanent market place with fixed numbered stalls and access to running water and toilets, local markets were held on rickety thatch-roofed wooden stalls. The bus park was close to the market, as were the larger wholesale stores and the Fan milk depot where the students and I would go for yoghurt and ice cream. The railway line was also nearby and traders would arrive by train with huge pottery storage vessels, mats and large quantities of foodstuffs to sell. Transport by rail was less expensive and easier on their products than travelling over rough roads in overloaded vehicles. Lorries, however, were faster and provided access from remote villages. We compiled statistics, took inventories, interviewed as many traders as possible, recorded different sellers' details and noted how many people entered the market. This helped American and Togolese students become acquainted with the locality's produce and the traders' attitudes; it gave them a sense of the town and the way it interacted with its catchment area. A trader in second-hand clothes saved coins for me that he found in old clothes. Mostly they were recent and I changed them into francs, but on one occasion he brought to me a 1906 Edward VII silver florin from Britain.

In 1986 I became interested in Notse's weavers, all old men in their sixties and seventies. One occasionally saw their blue striped narrow strip textiles at funerals and important festivals. While one saw modern Ewe cloth woven from machine-spun thread dyed with modern colours, it was rare to see the older cloth woven from locally spun cotton, though the Chief of Notse wore it on special occasions. On a few occasions I noticed balls of pounded indigo leaves for sale. In 1986 and 1987, with the help of Agbenyega Adedze, I set about finding out as much as I could about Notse's textiles. In some ways it was like saving an endangered species. I knew that the industry was dying out, that its practitioners were old and commanded little respect and that their product was uncompetitive in the market. At less than half the price, one could buy striped indigo cloth that was lighter, could be washed without running and came from China. With difficulty we tracked down 12 weavers, all of whom wove only on an occasional basis. They farmed or whiled away their time, as old men do. At independence there were more than a hundred weavers in a population a quarter its present size. We also located the women who spun and dyed the threads. They also ran the commercial aspects of the business, found buyers, brokered commissions and kept cloth to sell at their homes in special emergencies such as unexpected deaths. The women were also elderly, some even in their eighties. Spinning was something they could do at home when they were too old to farm; dyeing involved knowledge of plants and fermenting processes to achieve the best results. Threads were hung out to dry after being dyed in several pots containing bark, urine and even animal dung.

From the limited collection of cloth in the Lomé Museum, it was obvious that cloth had been woven at Atakpame, 60 miles north, and in many of the villages surrounding Notse, but that the practice had died out during the last half century. Though on first sight all the cloth appeared the same with blue stripes ranging from pale blue to nearly black it was evident that there were consistent patterns. Many of the weavers and dyers had sample books from which customers chose the cloth they wanted. I recorded 50 different patterns. Many bore the names of proverbs, many had interesting stories and certain people wore particular cloths on specific occasions.[11] It was apparent from the association of the names they bore with local history that some of the patterns dated back to the eighteenth century or earlier. Ewe textiles have since become influenced by the more colourful *kente* cloths of the Asante with muted colours and heather greens predominating and with the old indigo cloths out of favour.

The study of the Notse textiles taught me a great deal about textile technology. The Ewe weavers of Notse used wooden weights for their spindle whorls; they dyed their home-grown, home-spun threads in pots very like ordinary large domestic vessels. This means archaeologists in the future will be unable to find clues to their activity. This is in contrast to the clay spindle whorls and dye pits found in the Akan world to the west or in the great Hausa towns to the northeast. The weaving sheds were particularly ephemeral and often the only substantial material item was the pottery disc with two holes that gripped the heddles lines to the weaver's toes. Like the weavers in the Akan world, particularly the Baule, weavers had beautifully carved wooden heddle pulleys. Many of them became close friends and one of them, Koffi Baeta, made the smock, pants and cap worn by the first president of Togo, Sylvanus Olympio, in 1960. He made me a similar smock, which remains one of my most treasured mementoes of Togo. Each time I visited Notse he greeted me warmly. I think the attention I paid to Koffi and some of the other weavers spurred interest in the weaving tradition locally and I was pleased that by the end of the 1980s two younger men had taken an interest in weaving and were working with their elder relatives.

Denou terraces

In 1985 with the help of a president's youth exchange grant I took a party of six American students to conduct excavations at Denou on the Dahyi plateau on the western side of Togo. We joined up with an equal number of Togolese students under the direction of my then doctoral student Dovi Kuevi. We stayed in the house of a Togolese UN official who was out of Togo at the time. The Dahyi plateau rises to nearly 1000 metres; the early mornings are deliciously cool and often the hillsides are shrouded in swirling mists until nearly 10 a.m. The area is relatively prosperous, growing coffee and cocoa as well as oil palms and mangoes. Most of the towns are situated on narrow ridges and the people speak what are known as the Togo Remnant languages, which are quite different from the Ewe spoken on the plains below. Many languages are spoken only by one village of several hundred adults, so it is possible they will be extinct in another two generations. As we travelled up to Denou we passed village markets where potatoes, carrots and other European vegetables were sold alongside the plantains, yams, taro and groundnuts. With its hills and valleys, the area reminded me of the Celtic regions of Britain and, like the Welsh, the villagers were blessed with beautiful singing voices. Often groups would walk to our house singing as they came and we attended several concerts in their little church where the singing of hymns was positively angelic. On another occasion we visited the palace of a chief whom several communities acknowledged. They were holding a celebration, partly to mark our visit, and we were entertained by a brass band playing with a liveliness and vigour to match any New Orleans group.

The archaeology consisted of surveying and making plans of a stone circle of 35 upright stones on a high flat piece of ground. A flat stone abutted each standing stone and the whole enclosure may have been a ceremonial meeting place where chiefs sat in a circle. The hillsides were heavily terraced; the flat surfaces of the terraces were often little more than five to eight feet wide and the stone walls sustaining them rose three to four feet above the terrace below. Locals and visitors assumed they must have taken hundreds of years to build, so we tried a little experimental archaeology and found that two untrained students, selecting stones from the hillside, were able to build 200 feet of three-foot high terracing in three days. In past times, with soil being exhausted rapidly, new terraces would have been constantly created. Most of the work could be undertaken in the dry season when the vegetation was low, when fire could have been used for clearance and when the farmers had few other obligations. Probably in the past, sorghums, millets, highland rice and perhaps yams were grown. With the introduction of the more profitable tree crops grown in the valleys or on the lower slopes, the steep hillside terraces were abandoned. There are terraces all over Africa from Ethiopia to the Elgeyo escarpment in Kenya to the Inyanga area of Zimbabwe. Once it was believed they were the work of a people with an aptitude for (or cultural tradition of) using stone, what one authority referred to as Megalithic Cushites. It is obvious that terraces are the result of a fairly normal adaptation to hillside problems. Slopes are often well watered and contain loose soil that would have provided obvious agricultural possibilities.

What had brought Dovi Kuevi to the area was the discovery of a man-made cave, or *caveau*, found beneath one of the terraces. It was covered with slabs of stone up to ten feet long and the walls had been carefully lined with dry stone walling. Several slabs and soil above hid the cave from both the front and top and we presumed it was a kind of 'bolt-hole' to which frightened people and their small livestock fled from attack at the height of the slave trade in the eighteenth and early nineteenth century. The slave trade at that time had a big impact on adjacent areas of the plain. Unfortunately, except for a few potsherds nothing was found in the *caveau*.

Female circumcision

In 1996 my expertise on Togo was put to good use when I was asked to help in an asylum case. The case involved a young woman, Fauziya Kassindja from Tchamba whose Muslim father had moved to Kpalime in western Togo to run a transport business. Her father died in 1993 while Fauziya was in secondary school in neighbouring Ghana and her aunt, her father's sister, as his heir, became Fauziya's guardian instead of her mother. The aunt decided that Fauziya should leave school to marry a much older merchant, but before the Muslim marriage ceremonies could proceed, Fauziya would have to undergo female circumcision, which is commonplace among Togo's Muslim population. Fauziya did not learn of this until the last minute. Her sisters had not undergone the operation because their father, who was alive when they married, was less of a traditionalist. On the eve of the marriage Fauziya's mother and sisters spirited her away to Lomé and put her on a plane to Germany.

She had no approved papers and in 1994 the German authorities sent her to New York to be looked after by relatives. On arrival, before she could see her relatives, she was placed in a detention centre where she spent nearly two years. She claimed asylum on the grounds that if she went back to Togo she would undergo female genital mutilation and be forced into an unjust marriage. This was considered insufficient reason to delay repatriation, but a Georgetown University legal clinic took on her case and contacted me as someone who could possibly verify her story. This I did and provided a lot of supportive anthropological and historical evidence. Finally, her case went to the Philadelphia Appeals court in 1996 and she was granted asylum. The case provided a precedent that allowed other women similarly threatened to claim asylum. Her story[12] was frightening and indicated how someone, in her case a juvenile, could suffer incarceration without trial for two years. I later helped several other young women win asylum cases.

Benin

In 1990 I was asked to participate in a proposed national history of Benin. Benin had been one of West Africa's most closed areas since its military government took over in the 1970s, but when the cold war ended in 1990–91 and the West adopted a more realistic policy towards Africa by offering aid through the IMF in return for good governance, it was one of the first countries to be resurrected. A national conference was convened and a constitutional assembly worked out the parameters for new national elections, which took place without rancour. General Kérékou, its dictator for the last 15 years, retired gracefully to the north of the country and a former World Bank official took over with a cabinet that included many technocrats. The atmosphere changed immediately. Benin became an open society and its people were proud that a transfer of power had been accomplished peacefully. I liked Benin and returned several times, the most recent being in 2004 for the meeting of the West African Archaeology Association in Porto Novo.

I felt that Benin was an unpretentious country. It had many attractions, which we enjoyed seeing when we first visited in 1968. At that time we had stayed at Ouidah on the coast. Ouidah had been a bit of overseas Portugal. From it were sent the largest number of slaves to the New World. The town was separated from the beach by a lagoon and a sandspit. On the spit the slaves had been traded and kept in enclosures or stockades known as barracoons. One of the last of these still existed in 1968, a crumbling set of mud brick walls.[13] All along the sands one can still pick up pieces of glass, beads, tobacco pipe stems and other debris of a couple of centuries of intercourse with the Europeans based on trade largely in slaves. In 1968 we stayed near the old fort in a rest house that had ceased to exist when I returned in 1990.

Ouidah had two other claims to fame. First, it was a centre for voodoo religious practice. There were over 150 small temples and shrines often decorated with pictures of the spirits to which they were dedicated. The largest, opposite the Roman Catholic cathedral, was the python fetish house where, for a small fee, tourists could pose for photographs with pythons around their necks. The market was full of fetish pots, strange pots and figures that brought luck to the possessor and occasionally ill luck to their enemies. The second of Ouidah's claims to fame was that it was dominated by the descendants of Francisco de Souza (1760–1849), the *chacha* or custom collector and later, in the eighteenth century, the King of Dahomey's viceroy.[14] Born in Brazil of mixed parentage he was heavily involved in the slave trade, had many wives and concubines and sired more than 300 children. Many of his descendants held high offices in independent Dahomey and were men of substance and influence. They live in a special walled area of Ouidah, which contains as many as 2000 of his descendants. His tomb in his old bedroom is still one of Ouidah's principal attractions.

In Benin I enjoyed the food, the relatively inexpensive but excellent hotels, the feeling of never being overwhelmed by too big a city, and the mixture of people I met in Cotonou from all over West Africa. I particularly enjoyed the Hotel Croix de Sud's thatched-roofed rondavels, where I often stayed. Perhaps they reminded me of my own simpler rondavel in Olorgesailie, but it was nice to be in a room that is its own separate building.

At Ouidah I initiated my student Kenneth Kelly into his research. I have often gained vicarious pleasure from helping a doctoral student start off his or her research in Africa. One enjoys the anticipation of planning, the enthusiasm of helpers, the welcome from the local population and the joy of seeing an important site emerge from the initial clearance. It is a bit like being a grandparent because one can leave before the hard work begins of sorting through bags and bags of material, registering finds, classifying dubious objects and writing reports. At Ouidah we dug in a living town where house had succeeded house and yet there was little stratigraphy as the houses were of mud and the ruins of one house were used as the raw materials for the next. I found it fascinating that the mud walls of the houses contained the history of previous occupants in the form of pottery, pipe bowls and stems, glass beads, bones and all sorts of cultural detritus that had lain around. At Ouidah we introduced Beninois students to the mysteries of archaeology and I was excited in 2004 to find that several of those students were now the new archaeologists of Benin, giving papers and introducing another generation of students to what at times must seem a forsaken career, for no jobs are being created for archaeologists. One leading professional runs the arboretum in Porto Novo, but he has written about the history of the area and is transmitting his enthusiasm for local traditions and past highlights of a rich regional past.

Coleman African Studies Center

In 1988 I became director of the James S. Coleman African Studies Center. I was excited because I had loved directing the African Studies Programme at Makerere University College from 1964 to 1967. I imagined being able to recreate the magic of that time, but UCLA in 1988 was a different place from Makerere in the 1960s. In 1964 there was a hunger for Africanizing the university syllabus; the 1960s were when a brave new world awaited in which Africa was at last to be a major player. By 1988, the idealism had gone. Africa was suffering its 'lost decade' with an over-production of graduates, a brain drain of the brightest minds, decaying universities, bankrupt treasuries and everywhere a shortage of goods and a breakdown of services. The cold war was being played out in Africa, leaving a toll of death and destruction in such states as Angola, Mozambique, South West Africa, soon to be Namibia, and in the Horn of Africa. In US universities, money was tight and African studies were trying to run too many operations. The jewel in the crown, *African Arts*, had lost nearly $100,000; the Marcus Garvey papers scheduled for completion in eight years was both over budget and five volumes behind completion; and the student journal *Ufahamu* was eating up too many resources in staff salaries. I hoped to revamp the syllabus of the MA in African studies and build up a cohort of 'happy campers' to match those of Makerere a quarter a century before.

Unfortunately, I spent my first year away in Ghana and in my absence the MA in African Studies at UCLA was hived off as a separate programme. The chairperson was to all intents and purposes independent of the centre and the person appointed to look after the centre's administrative affairs had little allegiance to it. Black studies was gaining ground in US universities and many people felt that Africa and its past belonged to Afro-American Studies. With the end of *apartheid* in sight there was a fusion of African and African-American problems, and the struggle was overwhelmingly for African rights. This of course was simplistic and lost sight of the richness of the fusion of African and American traditions within American history and culture. There was still a struggle to be won in America and in some ways Africa could be a diversion. There were constant tussles at UCLA. The centre needed to reduce its expenditure, but what should be cut? Instead of working together, members of the centre, students, faculty and staff, began to manoeuvre for influence. My own African credentials were questioned and the African-American community became needlessly involved, with questions asked about whether the African Studies Center needed autonomy or could be co-joined with black studies. Many students actively encouraged the involvement of members of the black studies community. In the end I was happy to step down as centre director in 1992, by which time the MA programme had again been returned to the centre.

It was not all bad. We entertained many prominent African visitors at the centre, including the future Liberian president Ellen Sirleaf Johnson, convened several conferences that brought together Japanese and US Africanists, and the Society for African Archaeology held its biennial meeting at UCLA in 1992. We honoured our distinguished Africanist alumni, Hilda and Leo Kuper from anthropology and sociology, Wolf Leslau from Ethiopian and Semitic studies and Walter Goldschmidt from anthropology, all of whom had brought distinction to UCLA. We also managed to stay high in the triennial rankings of foreign area studies programmes, being ranked second among African studies programmes at a time when we had lost several distinguished colleagues, including three by death, John Povey the longstanding editor of *African Arts,* Hilda Kuper in anthropology and Derrick Jelliffe in public health. We had also strengthened ties with African universities with a federally funded link with the University of Ghana in 1992 and very active discussions with universities in Swaziland, Uganda and Benin.

After African studies I hoped to engage again in African archaeology, so was attracted by a chance to conduct research at Ketou in eastern Benin, 120 miles northeast of Cotonou, where an important Yoruba chieftaincy still exists. The town walls and huge gateways to the town with massive doors, still partly extant, give an indication of past importance. Nowadays it has lost its importance and visitors come to the town to buy the colourful Elegba masks that are still worn during festivals honouring their traditions. Unfortunately, events at home led me to abandon the prospects of active fieldwork and in 1994 I took the last of the University of California's voluntary retirement inducement programmes to retire with the promise of being called back to teach, but with the flexibility to look after Eunice. It was this abandonment of fieldwork that led me to return to a passion of my early career – postage stamps.

Postage stamp imagery

As a boy I collected stamps and when my brother Leonard went off to war in 1943 I took over his collection, but eventually sold it, which I have regretted ever since. When I went to Uganda I started to collect African stamps, alongside my collection of East African stamps and coins as part of the nascent historical collection of the Uganda Museum. At that time I was more interested in English coins, which I bought from places like Seaby and Spinks in London, but when we urgently needed money in 1961 to build our house on Makindye, I decided to sell my two most precious material assets – my Hasselblad camera and my coin collection. It was then that I began seriously collecting stamps again; some I bought from Asian dealers in Nairobi but most I obtained from correspondence at the museum. My collection was small, unspecialized, poorly curated and without much purpose but I slowly filled envelopes and tins with stamps. For some years other than collecting the stamps that came my way in the mail, increased in number during my time as director of the African Studies Center, stamp collecting was a dormant interest. But I suppose I was born with, or acquired at an early stage, the collecting bug. In Ghana after 1972 I had collected brass gold weights but ten years later I realized that I was too poor to buy such items from auction houses in the United States and stamps took their place. Stamps have the advantage of taking up very little space.

With Eunice requiring care, I needed a focus on which to work without a laboratory or research assistants and I began to realize the research potential of stamps. Most philatelists are interested in stamp rarities, in postal history, where stamps are posted and how many were issued and why? My focus is on the image. What does it tell the user, the buyer and the collectors about the people who issued the stamps? Why were certain designs chosen? Who designed the stamps? Why were some stamps chosen to commemorate events and other stamps issued to provide everyday coverage internally within the issuing state? I realized that stamps hold up a mirror to a country's propaganda, aspirations and achievements. I have always enjoyed a comparative approach to history and I became fascinated by the differences not only between African countries but between developed Western states.

France depicts its philosophers, chateaux, intellectuals and history. It has proudly displayed the Ice Age rock art of Lascaux, the ivory carving from Brassempuy, Abbé Breuil who is famous for his excavations and writings on archaeology, and the reconstruction of its *Homo erectus* find from Tautavel, whereas the USA ignores its Indian rock art, its huge pyramid-like mounds at Cahokia in Illinois, its early historical sites and its true archaeological pioneers. Donald Duck, deceased jazz musicians, film stars or golfers are more likely to appear on US stamps than intellectuals, yet intellectuals and scientists are the people who have made the USA great. Africans are proud of their past, so their diverse cultures and monuments, museums, hominid finds, rock art, stone artefacts, hunting techniques, crafts from weaving to basketwork and ceramics regularly feature on their stamps.

The different emphases different states places on different categories particularly interests me and I have given several conference papers on the topic.[15] Libya, for example, has used its stamps to promote propaganda, to proclaim its support for Palestinian liberation, while Tanzania has used its stamps in public health campaigns to create awareness of how to combat HIV and AIDS. After the mid-1960s many countries began to produce more and more new issues, and by the end of the century it was not unusual for countries like Tanzania, Sierra Leone, Liberia or the Comoro Islands to be bringing out hundreds of issues each year. Most of these stamps were commemorative and fairly large, often as big as two inches by one inch. The images were designed to appeal to juvenile collectors chasing stamps for their topical interest, so tended to depict celebrities, different types of animals, dinosaurs, mushrooms, boats, trains, cars, cartoon characters, flowers, art and popular sports. Very often these commemoratives were not sold in the issuing country, except in their philatelic bureaux, but to agencies in Europe or dealers in the United States. International agencies like the Inter-Governmental Philatelic Corporation controlled the issuance of stamps and profits from their sales went to unscrupulous leaders. This helped to explain why failing states like Sierra Leone, Liberia or the Comoros were issuing such large numbers of stamps. A collector can only collect a limited number of stamps and the profits from the sales to collectors might be the same from Tuvalu as from the USA, making it an exciting source of revenue in a small country.

I was surprised that people took an interest in what we were doing. At the 2001 Triennial African Art Symposium we convened a panel on stamps and, with the help of Dr Agbenyega Adedze, Jessica Levin and Lisa Aronson, attracted a good audience. When our paper in *African Arts* appeared in 2004, our approach attracted interest from political scientists as well as art historians. I began to scour the periodic stamp conventions with a view to buying any stamps on Africa that depicted African arts, material culture and archaeology. It was a wonderful way of increasing my knowledge of Africa. I have left the collection in my will to the Fowler Museum at UCLA and it will be the first museum-housed stamp collection in the western states.

Chapter 7

Hani

THE VILLAGE OF HANI, 270 miles northwest of Accra in Brong Ahafo, was completely unknown to me, even as a name, in 1970, but it has played an integral part in my life. Having arrived in Ghana in 1967 and established a degree programme in archaeology in 1968, I needed to find a suitable long-term research project. I wanted a site where I could train students, and where they could acquire skills not only in field archaeology but also in oral history and material culture. It needed to be far enough away from the university at Legon so that it would mean more to them than a weekend jaunt. I wanted to encourage them to undertake individual research projects and come to grips with the culture, traditions and whole ethos of the community in which we would be staying. It also had to be a place where the community was welcoming and where we felt we belonged.

Prior to my coming to Ghana virtually all archaeology in West Africa was undertaken in the dry season from November to April; in the summer months expatriates went on annual leave to Europe. Just before I arrived in 1967 the university instituted two-year terms of duty, which meant that I would be in Ghana every other summer. My new colleagues told me it was impossible to dig in the summer. It was too wet, the vegetation was so overgrown that it was impossible to see the ground surface, the roads were muddy and often inaccessible and the insects were at their most aggressive. However, I knew from East Africa that during the wet season, if one avoided the height of the rains, normally only about ten to twelve weeks, the air was fresh and everything was cooler. The earth was less compacted and easier to dig, the stratigraphy exposed in the trenches more discernable and the farmers were often in a good mood because their crops were growing.

Our work from 1970 began a trend that has continued and the old taboos about wet season archaeology have evaporated. New archaeologists to the region take it for granted that there is a period between the peaks of the summer or monsoon rains from around mid-July to early September in the areas of the southern savannah and nearer to the coast when it is drier. From the late 1970s foreign teams began to come to Ghana in the summer, a period that was very convenient because it coincided with the long vacation. For a West Africanist the big advantage is that students are also on their long vacations and can freely participate. Before 1968 local students had not been encouraged to take part in excavations except as privileged individuals. Students from 1970 became the key labour component in excavations conducted by universities.

After reading the research of historians and anthropologists like Ivor Wilks and Jack Goody, both of whom I knew and greatly respected, I decided that one of the big unresolved problems of Ghanaian archaeology was to discover the first state, find the first town on the edge of the forest where the Muslim traders came down from the north to buy gold, kola nuts, ivory and hides from the Brong peoples.[1] Hani had been suggested as a possibility as the site of the first town of Begho mentioned in chronicles in Arabic and in the reports from the early European companies on the coast and in June 1970 I arrived there to search for the site of Begho. Three of us, Mr J. Quansah from the department of archaeology, Cleophas the Institute of African Studies driver, and I travelled through Asante at an intriguing time, the day before the funeral of the late Asantehene, Sir Agyeman Prempeh II. We stayed in the Asante capital of Kumasi for a night and were warned not to go into the streets because it was still customary to capture people and cut off their heads so that they could accompany the dead chief in the afterlife. This had happened in 1943 when the last great chief in Ghana had died, the Omanhene in Kibi. My companions were cautious but I tested the waters. I noticed that few people were brave enough to venture out that night, but I certainly saw nothing amiss except that the streets were deserted and there was little to excite my interest. The taxis still ran and I went back to the rest house near midnight. I may have gone to bed before the excitement began, but I doubt it.

The road to Hani was and is still difficult. Getting from Kumasi to Wenchi, which is Brong Ahafo's main town, is fine because the road is paved, but west to Nsawkaw is over a very corrugated road. The first few miles are surfaced because they lead to the village where the then prime minister Kofi Busia's father lived, but the last 12 miles after Nsawkaw can take an hour, with huge stones sticking up, deep ruts and an unevenness that even a Land Rover finds difficult to handle.

Hani is at the end of a feeder road. From the north there is a road from Namasa and to the south the road eventually peters out after a small daughter hamlet. It is this detachment that makes Hani ideal for research. It is just accessible yet out of the way.

In our search for Begho Hani had not been our first choice. Some years before, Bravman and Mathewson[2] had described some mounds north of Namasa that they ascribed to the Dumpo Quarter of Hani. To get to those mounds we visited the chief and elders of the Muslim town of Namasa, but the chief seemed more interested in what we could give him than in assisting us. Eventually, we explored the area where Mathewson had dug. Though it was evident from the mounds that there had been a settlement, there were too few of them to suggest a major medieval town. In contrast to Namasa, when we visited Hani we instantly felt at home.

The *hanihene*, Nana Kofi Ampofo II, was more interested in helping us than asking for gifts. He arranged for 17 of the townsfolk to accompany us to what they remembered to be the quarters of the old town. Being the rainy season the elephant grass was high, in places more than ten feet tall. Clearing a way, looking at the surface was a slow business but the chief and his followers were enthusiastic and soon we had visited three of the known quarters of the town of Begho. At each quarter there were mounds, many as high as five or six feet, associated with depressions, which we interpreted as the collapsed walls of houses and their courtyards. Underfoot there were numerous potsherds, some with red slip painted designs that signified the ceramic forms introduced from the Middle Niger that previous archaeologists working in the southern parts of the savanna had described as 'painted pottery'.[3] There were also many animal bones being turned up by burrowing cane rats known as grasscutters in West Africa, as well as fragments of locally made ceramic smoking pipes recognizable from other sites as dating to the seventeenth century. It was evident from the number of mounds, the density of surface finds and the rich traditions related by the chief and his elders that in all probability we had located Begho. I arranged to return in July to dig at Begho and explore the area. Our first major field school, the first of eight, began in mid-July. The area we chose to work was the Brong quarter where the elders claimed the Brong chief had lived.

I arrived a week earlier than the students to set up camp and decide on a course of action. I am always happier and less flustered if I can plan the fieldwork, recruit local labour, arrange a camp and feel in control before the main group arrives. Hani was then a relatively small village in Ghanaian terms with between 600 and 700 inhabitants and about 70 houses. It was laid out in an open fashion with two broad intersecting main streets with the chief's palace (*ahemfie*) at the conjunction. To some extent the streets defined the geographical distributions of the three main clans. Beside the chief's house there was an old tree under which people rested and near it the only functioning well, which more often than not was empty. The houses were made either of coursed mud (also called swish in Ghana and known elsewhere as tauf), or of upright posts woven with flexible horizontal withies plastered with mud, known in Europe as wattle and daub. During my time in Hani the number of wattle and daub houses declined substantially from over 20 per cent in 1970 to less than 10 per cent in the late 1980s. Most houses, including the palace, had thatched roofs, though corrugated iron was beginning to be used. Thirty years later most of the houses had metal roofs. The largest houses were built around courtyards, though in many instances the courtyards were open because either a final room had never been completed or the walls of at least one or more rooms had collapsed and had not been rebuilt.

There was a small general store, poorly stocked with just a few bars of soap, tins of mackerel and sardine, locks, building materials such as nails, hinges and occasionally cement, cutlasses (machetes), rope, paraffin lamps, sewing items and some minor medications. In the good years they sold a little cloth. It also served as the main bar, with warm beer and soft drinks available on an intermittent basis, depending on whether the *tro-tro* (passenger-carrying truck) had been to a neighbouring town to pick up supplies. There was a covered veranda and courtyard where people could dance and the shopkeeper sold cloth; we bought baft (undyed cotton cloth) and had it sewn into sample bags for our archaeological finds. Two other small rooms in private homes sold locally made beer or spirits when their owners were not on their farms and there were two houses that sold a few assorted items on an occasional basis.

There were two churches, the more popular Methodists on the west side, with an adjacent football field, and a very small open and somewhat decrepit Catholic church at the southeast corner of the village, with open windows and a thatch roof. Nearby was a small shrine, with a ritual smithy, consecrated to the iron smiths (of the *kronti* clan) and their role in breaking out of the hole in the ground from which the original ancestors of the clans had emerged. Offerings of dried food often hung from its roof with occasionally a chicken left between the furnace and anvil stone. In 1970 there was a primary school going up to the sixth grade on the northern side of the village and a further football field. On the west side of the rough road to Namasa, behind thick vegetation, were the graves of villagers, but with no conspicuous markers. On the edges of the village were rubbish dumps. Every day young girls swept the debris from within the courtyards and around the houses. The swish swish of brooms made from stout grass in the early morning is one of my abiding memories of life in a Ghanaian village. Also on the fringes of the village were the communal toilets. These were grass-roofed walled structures erected over deep narrow pits across which strong poles were laid on which one crouched. They were smelly, buzzing with flies and among my least pleasant memories.

From going round greeting friends and stopping by their open hearths at night to help families shell their groundnuts, over the years I got to know the village very well. I monitored changes in the village, recording new houses, collapsed walls and new communal buildings. When I came back to Hani I would often bring small gifts of soap, bread, biscuits and, in the early days, tobacco and cigarettes, which would take me several hours to distribute. The following morning, often as early as 6.00 a.m. the same people would call to thank me for visiting them the previous evening. Whenever I went away I was given gifts that ranged from chickens, even a sheep from the chief on a few occasions, to roasted groundnuts, yams, eggs, pineapples, limes and plantains. At the time of my last visit in 1998 many changes had occurred.[4] In all I made 24 different visits to Hani, where cumulatively I spent over a year. Eunice, our children, friends and many scholars from the university visited it in those years. From being an unknown village it acquired a certain local and national notoriety. We persuaded two regional commissioners to visit, the first in 1972 to open the Archaeological Research Centre and the second in December 1974 to open a small library for the middle school funded by the Lions Club of Gary in Indiana.

In our first year at Hani I lodged in the village with Peter Tekyi, the elder in the Methodist community. As a successful farmer, the roof of his courtyard house was made from sheets of corrugated aluminium. They looked nice, reflected the sun and protected the structure from rain, but metal does not breathe and by nightfall the house was always airless and hot. As the metal cooled it crackled and when it rained it was very noisy; also, every sound, sniffle, cough, bed turn and creak was amplified. Curiously, though everyone knew each other's business, there was a respect for basic privacy. In lieu of a shower one stood on stones in a walled off area about three feet across and, with a calabash, threw water from a bucket over oneself, which then drained into the street. In some houses the washing areas had only flimsy thatch walls, but enough to preserve one's modesty. Towels were draped over the low walls for easy access and sometimes left there to dry.

People ate on a veranda around the inside of the courtyard, but except for a possible cup of tea there was no breakfast. Real sustenance came in the mid-morning on the farm with boiled yams and a tasty onion and red pepper relish. Those who did not go to the farm were served a similar meal in the courtyard, often around the hearth. Staff members and students stayed in other houses. We put up some tents for expatriate helpers, though in our first year Sian Hughes, a lively young Welsh woman who came for six weeks between school and college, stayed with a family and so charmed the young villagers that, after 30 years, they still remember her. We employed two young women to help us prepare and serve food for the group. Each year the women changed and sometimes strange things happened. On one occasion, at the end of a dig in 1970, the chief had given us a sheep and the students were looking forward to roasting it on a spit. However, when we got back to camp they found that the women had chopped up the sheep with machetes, skin and all, and stewed everything, resulting in a lot of disappointment.

In 1971 we all agreed that Hani was an ideal place for annual field schools so decided to build a field centre. The archaeology department's technical assistant Mr Seth Dankwa had building experience, so he served as the contractor and spent several months in Hani in 1971 and 1972 supervising the work. The centre was 'L' shaped and made of layers of swish. Two workers came from Togo to help us with that, for Atakpame men had a good reputation in Ghana at that time for swish construction. The building consisted of a director's room with attached store, which also served as a private bathroom, a large lecture hall cum dining room with windows on both sides and a store attached for camping gear, a kitchen and, in the perpendicular wing, three student bedrooms. Behind the building there was a store for field equipment such as wheelbarrows and shovels, and at one side a small toilet with a box seat above a deep pit, a concession to my own sensibilities I suppose. To the back of the wing a further toilet was set up with a large pit covered with planks with just enough space for very rudimentary squatting and seating. The walls at the centre were plastered and the floor cemented. The roof was covered with aluminium sheets and around two sides there was guttering leading off to a 3200-gallon underground tank to contain rain water. At the time this was quite revolutionary and, seeing the efficacy of the system, quite a few villagers followed suit to save their women the tedium of fetching water daily.

Throughout the building there were abundant windows with fixed wooden slats and mesh screens to keep out insects. We built an outside hearth for cooking with firewood collected from the wooded areas around the village. There is a wide veranda on the north side of the building where classes could be held and a further veranda in front of the student rooms. When at full capacity, around 15–18 individuals, several students slept in tents covered with grass to keep them cool, though some of the department personnel preferred the greater privacy of staying in the village with a family. The building, which was set 30 feet back from the road, was approached via a driveway edged with flowering plants.

The village community

When we first arrived in the village we went to see the chief to whom we had to speak through the intermediary of the linguist, *okyeame*. Everyone who visits the chief in an official capacity, even if they speak the same language, has to greet him through the *okyeame*. In larger villages the *okyeame* carries a six-foot long black staff of office with a carved wooden figure on top. On official occasions the chief sits in the middle on a studded chair or intricate stool with his elders on either side. On his left sits the *ohemaa* or queen mother. She is not the chief's mother, but the spokesperson for the women of the community, normally chosen for her social status, political sagacity or educational achievement. A second queen mother when we were there was a young woman in her late teens chosen because she was one of the few women who had completed middle school. Also seated by the chief were the *akwamuhene* and *krontihene*, the latter being the head of the clan from which blacksmiths are drawn. He has custody of the iron hammers credited with breaking open the hole in the ground from which all ancestors emerge. In his compound he also looks after other iron implements, including a set of bellows and more hammers.

15. Haniheni with his wing chiefs, 1972.

In 1975 I felt honored to be elected *ahohohene,* chief of strangers or foreigners. My deputy was the *tro-tro* driver Kwesi Brew who, though born in a village only ten miles away, was still considered an *ahoho.* Other *ahoho* in Hani were the Dagarti labourers who came from northern Ghana, some as early as the 1950s, to help with yam cultivation or cocoa farming in the forest areas to the south where they had been granted land to build houses and farm. Their children had been born in the village but nevertheless formed an independent community. Also in my community were the Ewe schoolteachers from the Volta region or Accra area, many of whom stayed on for years. Though their pay was low, they were given land to farm, houses were inexpensive to build, food was available and there were many willing hands to help them on their farms, carry produce to the village or assist them with all sorts of duties. Officially, they had to address their concerns to the chief through me, as did all outsiders who came to the village while I was in residence.

On several occasions, notably on visits to the village in 1979, 1983 and 1986, I convened an *ahoho* day when I entertained my people, gave out food, palm wine, beer, sweet biscuits, soft drink, cigarettes and sweets for the children. In a relaxed mood they played music on drums, pipes, whistles, xylophones or a sort of fiddle. They sang and danced and I made a speech with Mr Dankwa or Mr Firempong, also from the Legon department of archaeology, translating my remarks into Twi. In 1975 there were perhaps only 65–70 *ahoho*, but by the time of my last visit that number had grown to at least 200–300 with most of them living in a distinct zone on the north side.

My enstoolment was one of the most moving moments of my life. Dressed in my cloth and wearing my traditional sandals I walked slowly, with Mr Dankwa as my *okyeame* beside me, to the centre of the village where I sat surrounded by my students and staff; Eunice and our daughters had come from Accra for the occasion. Libations were poured to honour the ancestors and to tell them what the chief was proposing to do. Greetings were exchanged and speeches made. I was installed under a decorative, colourful, traditional umbrella with gold tassels; a small boy sat at my feet holding my sword of state, with its handle covered in gold foil, across his knees. A band of drummers, gong and horn players provided constant music and the chief and elders danced, as did I and several of my entourage. Finally, as the light faded, a number of villagers hoisted me into the air, dusted me with white powder and ceremoniously carried me on their shoulders to the research centre, nearly a quarter of a mile away, accompanied by the musicians and women waving cloths and dancing in front. A little later I was presented with a ceremonial stool and some impressively decorated traditional sandals. I never sat on the stool and in the passage from Ghana to the United States it was damaged by water and developed spots of mould. Until I cleaned it I felt unwell. In many ways it represents the soul of my office and I hope that when I die it will not be used as a stool but kept as a memento of my relationship to Hani. After several years in the United States I told the chief that I should perhaps renounce my position; the elders were horrified and told me that my position as a wing chief could only be revoked if I did something bad or died.

An Akan village in many ways is a very democratic institution. Everyone is a member of a clan and each clan is represented on the council of elders. Everyone has access to the elders whether they are men or women. Different religious persuasions are also represented. While I was in Hani there was only one Muslim family in the village, but its head was a member of the elders. Each clan is responsible for at least one local festival a year when they receive a certain prominence. The strangers have representation through the *ahohohene* or his deputy. In meetings of the chief's council there are no limits to the length of the deliberations, no votes are taken and discussion is continued until there is consensus. The queen mother is the 'king-maker' in that it is through her that a new chief is chosen. Though there is a royal clan, the *ahemfie* in Hani, there is no primogeniture so that there can be no succession from father to son or even matrilineal succession from royal aunt to nephew. Since chiefs are often chosen from the ruling clan from outside the village, they have little knowledge of past history and precedents, so the system has weaknesses as well as strengths. Chief Ampofo II's successor, Nana Adika II, for example, was educated, knew English, had useful contacts outside the village but did not control or listen to the pulse of the community. He was often away as he had a family and developed interests elsewhere. His reign was relatively short.

The *hanihene*

Nana Kofi Ampofo II had come to the stool, as chieftancy is termed, in 1946 and sat for 40 years until his death in 1986. He was a young man aged 26 when he assumed the chieftaincy and became the model of what a chief should be. He was an ordinary farmer who worked his land daily and, though he had more to farm than some, he never tried to pretend he was any different. His difference came from his wisdom, care for his people and understanding. He knew and had time for everyone. His palace had two courtyards, a formal one for his position as chief and an inner one for his family. He had five wives, three of whom lived with him, and 36 children. In his inner courtyard he would see guests like me without ceremony and there we often sat of an evening talking in the dark in an informal, friendly and spontaneous manner. In the formal courtyard, where he kept his palanquin on which he was carried on very formal occasions such as the accession of a new wing chief or for special ceremonies, he sat on a chair not a stool and spoke through the *okyeame*.

By his sheer presence the chief commanded discipline in the community. On many Fridays the villagers had to perform communal work, such as repairing the road or clearing vegetation from around or within the village. Every villager paid a small sum in taxes to the chief to pay for this work, but a special levy would be made for larger projects, such as digging wells or making dams. The chief and elders also allocated land to farm and for houses and when I first arrived each clan inhabited a particular quadrant of the village. Though the chief attended the Methodist church ceremonies, he did not formally belong to any particular church, for he represented all the denominations. Earth priests would hold festivals for key events like launching the yam harvest in which the whole community would participate. He not only kept his ear to the ground, but also listened to the radio, so knew what was happening in the wider world. He was open to new ideas such as my thoughts on the advantages of growing beans, creating a water hole, or encouraging villagers to catch rainwater.

Religion and tradition

Religion was and is important in village life. I never knew how many of the people were Christian, but suspect that some of the older ones were only nominally so because their children attended schools with a religious affiliation, but it is probably safe to assume that more than 80 per cent of the villagers are Christian. The daughter of the single Muslim in the village attended the Methodist school, taught in the Catholic school and now regularly attends Catholic services. I am not, however, trying to imply that Hani people no longer have beliefs based on traditional practice, or even that they are insincere attendants at the church. In 1984 I was surprised, even mortified, to discover that after the 1982–83 drought some of the beautiful old trees in the village had been cut down on the prompting of a traditional priest brought in from Techiman, 50 miles away, who said that the evil spirits that had caused the drought dwelt in such trees.[5] Many of the participants at the new yam festival are Christians, even though earth priests preside over it.

One rapidly learns in an African community that villagers have allegiances to family, clan, the village community, tradition, the chief, religion and occasionally when a national election is in the offing, to a political party. In other words, their loyalties span many informal barriers. Many of these barriers are weakening. In 1970 most villagers were exogamous, marrying outside their clan and the clans were geographically distinct, but by 1998 the boundaries were blurred. Some of the *ahemfie*, the royal clan, including at least one of the chief's sons, lived near the research centre, or *brunikrom* (town of the Europeans) as it was sometimes termed. Many Dagarti had shifted south from their restricted area. In the same way, as long as the family relationships were not too close, some young people were even marrying members of the same clan.

In 1970 there was one main church, the Methodists, to which the primary school was affiliated. It was on the western side of the village, had cement block walls and a metal roof, and attracted the largest congregations. It could be regarded as the established church and its elders, of whom Peter Tekyi was the most prominent, conducted the services. The swish-built Roman Catholic church on the east side of the village was much smaller than the Methodist one and close to the traditional *kronti* shrine. In the 1970s some outside Catholics provided funds for a larger building between the village and *brunikrom*. It has a higher roof, an imposing doorway at the top of a flight of stairs and a new private nursery and primary school alongside it. The expanding village population, the improved facilities and its position on the main road into the village attracted new converts. In recent years a small Pentecostal church has emerged, but by the late 1990s it had fewer than 30 regular members and there was some suspicion that its founders' motives were not purely altruistic. Many such churches have been used to attract largely poorer, particularly female, participants who are hoodwinked into tithing the little money they have as well as providing services for the organizing pastor who, like themselves, may be a poor, but ambitious, member of the community.[6]

Ancestors are extremely important in Akan society where time is perceived as circular rather than linear. They are not the forgotten dead but part of the community to be included in decision making. The elderly are respected for their wisdom and experience of life and ancestors are mentioned in routine conversation. Whenever someone calls on another person the ancestors have to be recognized by pouring a libation, an offering of recognition. Libations at the chief's court are in the form of palm wine, the sap of palm trees, but when a stranger comes from the town, particularly a European, it is usually in the form of spirits. Since the eighteenth century the preferred offering has been Schnapps or Dutch gin and it is usual to present this wrapped up and with an unbroken seal. The visitor declares why he or she has come, the seal is broken and a libation poured. The drink is then passed anti-clockwise around the gathered elders who individually pour a little drop to the ancestors before taking a drink. A single bottle can satisfy in such fashion up to 50 individuals and still leave a little for the chief to take home.

Since the ancestors ensure the success of an endeavour, a chicken would be sacrificed and a libation poured whenever we started a dig.

The ancestors would be asked to reveal their secrets of the past to the villagers and researchers. When I first came to Ghana I was told that one was expected to bring gifts to chiefs and that the gesture was never reciprocated. In fact, if the gift is consumable it is always shared with both elders and visitors. Being a chief can be difficult, for it carries obligations to entertain the community, give gifts to visitors, and take time off from farming or other private or family activities. As the soul or representative of the community it is virtually impossible for a chief, who is obliged to sacrifice animals on ritual occasions, to be a fully practising Christian. When my friend and colleague Seth Dankwa was invited to return to his home community to be chief, though highly honoured, he had no hesitation in saying no. He felt that he could not be a loyal Methodist, remain a good father and husband and also be the chief. He would have had to renounce too much, including quality time with his family and church.

Rites of passage are when traditional religion plays its most significant role. The people of Hani pay most attention to funerals and births; they are not big on marriage. Many otherwise observant Christians have several wives, each with individual quarters, often in a separate building. Children born out of wedlock are recognized rather than stigmatized. Births are recognized by name giving and outdooring ceremonies eight days after birth. Outdooring in towns has become a major social occasion with entertainment, gift giving and feasting, but in villages where people cannot afford such excesses, the occasion is still marked. Children are named after the day of the week on which they are born such as Kofi for Friday or Kwesi for Sunday for a boy, or Afua and Akosuwa respectively for a girl.[7] Naming is when the ancestors give permission for the child to join the ranks of the living.

At funerals, however, the whole village takes part. Initially, the body is laid out on a brass bedstead (if possible) and cloths displayed on and around it as marks of respect and to show what the family can afford. Within the day everyone pays their respects, conveys condolences to the bereaved and burial takes place, by inhumation, normally in the forest fringe area on the western edge of the village, though in the old days prominent people were buried under their houses. Then, to allow relatives and friends from outside the village time to make their plans to return, 40 days will elapse between the time of death and the main funeral ceremony. Immediately after the death relatives and members of the deceased's clan or lineage begin to wear mourning cloths, which are normally a deep orange ochre colour, maroon, black or occasionally a dark magenta. People keep special cloths for mourning often decorated with adinkra patterns that are scarcely visible against the dark backgrounds. Funerals are expensive, possibly the most expensive item in their lifetime for people who want to demonstrate their respect for their parents.

Costs include food and drink for the visitors, notices in the press, payment for the musicians, sometimes hire of special equipment like chairs, though in Hani people build grass shelters and use benches from the schools or churches. Sometimes special funeral cloths are ordered bearing the image of the deceased. Posters are made, receipt books printed and letters written. Funerals usually last up to three days. Visitors arrive in taxis, trucks and tro-tros. Sometimes audio equipment is brought in. Friends are sent out to procure palm wine. Life is hectic for the bereaved. In fact they get so tired that by the end of the ceremonies they usually feel a sense of anti-climax. They are left to ponder over how much they have spent and whom they have seen, which no doubt diverts their thoughts from the enormity of their loss. Visitors and family give cash gifts with the larger sums announced to everybody. There is much drinking and some sedate dancing; in a way the funeral serves as a family and community reunion and it is at such functions that small children learn the traditional dance steps and become incorporated into the community. Until one lives in a Ghanaian community it is hard to realize how pervasive music can be, for drumming and the beating of iron gongs occurs on every occasion, whether sad or glad.

One problem with funerals in a small place like Hani is that everybody is either related to or knows each other so work stops for several days and disrupts the farming cycle. Upwards of 30 days a year are given over to funerals in Hani. The government in Accra has tried to persuade people to spend less on funerals and they all agree that they cost too much, but they find it difficult to break the mould.

Funerals can bring out the best or worst in a society. In 1986 my friend Hanihene Kofi Ampofo II died and I was not informed, which seemed strange. I later learnt that news had been withheld about his death because his funeral arrangements had not been clarified. His death was unanticipated. His predecessor Nana Appau I, who died in 1938,[8] had not had a funeral and neither had four queen mothers and it was felt that all should be honoured at the same time. A state funeral is a costly affair and the community rather than the family pays for a chief's funeral. The village did not have enough money for an appropriate funeral in 1986, for it was still recovering from the worst drought in its history in 1983–84 and the general economic slowdown that the drought had caused.

In 1995 I had occasion to make a brief visit to Hani and was surprised that the funeral had still not been held for the late chief who had been so loved and respected and who had ruled for longer than any other *hanihene*. He had inherited an impoverished village with no facilities and fewer than 300 people, and left it well endowed with boreholes, wide streets, three schools and a population close to 1500. It had acquired a good reputation in the area for its appearance, education and general development and was now recognized as the historical centre of the old city-state of Begho. His family was upset at being forced to leave the palace in which they had all been brought up as soon as he died and felt angry that their mothers had not been provided with a secure future. All the photographs I had taken of the chief and his family had been taken away from them.[9] The small state treasury, including a brass bowl wrapped in cloths and containing a few gold weights, was also missing. The new chief was holding court in a different house. The palace was being torn down so that a more splendid residence could be built for the new chief.

After meeting many villagers from different clans, with different lineages or families related to the slighted chiefs, we agreed that a single ceremony should be held for everyone. The villagers wanted to ensure that this did not happen until everyone who had lived or worked in Hani would be able to attend. It was decided that once the road from Wenchi to Nsawkaw had been improved and the road from Nsawkaw graded with the addition of culverts to divert the storm water, a fine funeral could be arranged and maximum attendance ensured. I agreed to attend, to provide some money for the event and make T-shirts bearing the chief's image for his family. Nearly two years elapsed; I heard nothing; I wrote several times and was assured that plans were being made. Finally, in 1998 I was told that the funeral would be held in March. I booked my tickets, made the T-shirts and printed hundreds of cards bearing the picture of the former *hanihene* to give as gifts. On arriving in Accra I learnt at the airport that the funeral had again been postponed. I nevertheless went to Hani. The road had been improved but there was still work to be done. The funeral had been postponed because the family organizers were unsure of the finances. The villagers had been approached just too many times for money for all sorts of developments, including the new chief's palace, so were disinclined to give more. The organizers probably had far too grandiose plans for the ceremonies that involved hired bands, furniture and inviting many chiefs from surrounding communities. Such a large affair would cost a lot in food and drink alone. In a village where more than 70 per cent of the population is younger than 25 many villagers either did not know or had ceased to remember Kofi Ampofo II.

With Ghana's expanding prosperity in the 1990s fewer village people were interested in traditions and two new committees now paralleled the council of elders. I was, as always, well received but the new chief commanded little loyalty and there was a feeling that the battle to hold the funeral was a lost cause. There were divisions in the Opoku family, the children of the senior wife, and several key children lived away from the village. Everyone agreed that the funeral should take place but at a reduced level. I said I would ask my daughter Tessa to make a film of it and she went to Hani in January 2000 with her video camera, but there was still no decision about the funeral nor has there been one since.

The farming cycle
Everyone farms – men, women, children, rich people and poor people. It is part of the fabric of their life. Land is communally owned and liberally allocated by chiefs and elders. No one has fixed boundaries, for they practise shifting agriculture over a catchment area of three to four miles from the village centre. One year the men will clear the land by cutting trees and shrubs and burning the cut vegetation, but carefully leaving some small trees for the yam vines to climb. The next year they will grow on that land either more yams or a less exhaustive crop like cassava or corn. By the end of the third year the land is tired and so they move to an adjacent plot, often not returning to the original plot for another 12 to 17 years. On their land they build a farm shelter where they and their family can rest during the heat of the day and it becomes a kind of home from home in which the farmer can meet his neighbours, tell stories, instruct the young helpers, and process foods like cassava by cutting them into strips for drying in the sun. The shelter is where they keep a hearth and cooking pots for preparing meals, as well as a modicum of tools and some people even keep chickens there. The tools are often kept in the thatch of the roofs to keep them dry. By the farm shelter they store their yams in carefully built piles covered with grass.

Nearly 90 per cent of the farmers are also hunters and trappers. They go out to farm carrying their dane guns,[10] often with a bark cloth bag on their shoulder, a cutlass in their hand and a calabash to carry water. They hope to hunt the small antelope, duikers and occasional guinea fowl that still live in the area but their preferred prey are the grasscutters or pouch rats, known as *agouti* in Francophone Africa. Grasscutters eat their yams and other crops, so are a constant problem. They set wire traps to ensnare them, occasionally up to 30 around the shelter and yam heaps. They have ingenious spring traps that consist of a frame covered with heavy rocks placed above a fenced in area. A few sticks, holding up the weighted flat bed, can be dislodged when a grasscutter drops by to see what is underneath. Often the attraction is only the smell of human urine. Grasscutters can grow up to 18 inches long and weigh 15 lbs. They are normally slowly smoked and dried and kept for sale in the towns or slivers of their dried flesh are added to stews. Birds are caught in the snares but normally eaten fairly quickly. The farmers rarely use their guns, but like the image of themselves as stealthy hunters. In the dry season they burn the grass to flush out the game.

A ceremony known as *nyifie* marks the beginning of the hunting season. This is when the chief and his elders go to a shrine in the bush, consisting of a few pots, sacrifice some chickens and light fires to refresh the vegetation. I was told that one reason why shrines are in obscure places is that if they were more in the open goats would disturb them. A young boy lights the fires three times; on the first two occasions the fire is extinguished but is allowed to burn freely on the third. It is an exciting day since early in the morning the elders scour the village looking for unattended chickens to seize. Most people secure their poultry in small wicker pens so the pickings are often slim. Whatever is caught is sacrificed and eaten and libations are poured. The government now frowns on these ceremonies and the attendant bush burning, for it believes that the devastating fires at the height of the drought in 1984 worsened conditions, destroyed vegetation and homes and added pollutants to the air, which exacerbated the harmattan[11] conditions.

Yam cultivation probably goes back a very long time. Basically, there are three main types of yam – a small, slender, very tender early variety; *puna*, a yam with a straight, smooth body weighing up to a dozen pounds; and the water yam, which has an ungainly shape, is often bifurcated, has a darker skin and is, to my taste, less palatable than *puna*. Water yams are boiled and pounded into a starchy staple called fufu that is eaten with stews. Men also grow cassava, maize, coco-yams (taro), plantains and an occasional cash crop the government might recommend. In the 1960s it was pineapples, but the buyers never came through; from 1974 to the early 1980s they tried tobacco, but it was labour intensive, greedy for firewood for smoking the leaves, and exhausted the soil; since 1995 the new crop has been cashew nuts. One minor crop is an upland variety of rice that does not need a flooded field and grows along the river four miles north of Hani. The chief grew rice, but most other farmers could not be bothered with it because its best locations were far away from their farms. Women grow groundnuts, peppers, tomatoes, onions, okra, garden eggs, aubergines, beans, pumpkins and spinach nearer to the village and do not have field shelters. Most women take their babies to the farm, light a fire, do some cooking and dry their peppers on exposed rocks nearby. They store their harvest at home and sell it for the benefit of the family.

Food production is cyclical. From January to March the farmers clear the land and build yam mounds and, at the end of the dry season, they collect the borassus palm nuts. These are boiled for a long time, sometimes up to 24 hours, to separate the palatable part from the nut; corn mush and sugar are added towards the end of the process to make a nutritious porridge called *kube*. The shea butter nut is a woodland plant that is managed rather than planted and used for making soap, though the butter can be used in cooking. The oil palm is planted but left alone until chopped down and tapped for its palm wine by lighting a small fire near the base to cause the sap to rise. Palm nuts are collected throughout the year. Towards the end of the dry season the river to the north of the village begins to dry out leaving a series of ponds where, in a good year, lung fish can be found, which provide a welcome supplement to their diet. The only other fish available is brought from the coast and sold in the Wenchi or Techiman markets, but it is normally dried or salted, extremely bony and in poor condition.

One exciting feature of living by the edge of the forest is to see the myriad of trees that blossom before the rains come. The rainy season brings fresh greenery and is not necessarily when shrubs and trees are at their most colourful. The rains start somewhere between late March and early May, though there are showers earlier that encourage farmers to plant and hope for the best. The rains come in heavy bursts

– sudden showers at the end of the dry season presaged by thunder and lightning and dumping several inches of rain are not unusual.

While people are delighted that the rains have come it is nevertheless a sorry sight to see villagers pulling out their mattresses,[12] bedding and clothes to dry in the sun. Thatched roofs dried and shrivelled by the heat of the dry season let through some of the first heavy showers and it is only when the roof has fully absorbed the water that it expands to its most waterproof stage. With the first rains dirt and creatures sheltering in the eaves also fall into the house and an indescribable good scent fills the air. Wet ground and drying vegetation have a particular aroma that is often mixed with the smell of the wood hearths that are so difficult to restart after a sudden downpour. May to July is a period of weeding. It is also when the villagers are most at risk, for they have exhausted their food stores and have to live off their sales of nuts or dried grasscutters. This is the time to appreciate collected foods such as the nutritious fatty white grubs found in oil palms and forest snails. People go in groups into the forest to collect the forest snails, which can grow up to a half pound in dried weight, though they are normally much smaller. On the roads leading to Brong Ahafo one passes innumerable people, mainly children, selling snails that are either alive in bowls or dried on sticks.

A few villagers, who were especially well known for their knowledge of the forest, were honey collectors. They occasionally hung hives, but usually collected the honey from hives in the hollows of trees using smoke to drive away the bees. They would collect whole cones and melt the honey in special colander-like pots with holes in their bases and another pot underneath. This was to allow them to skim the wax off from the top of the honey and again this was done at night to avoid interference from bees. As a result, Hani honey was dark and smoky in flavour. One had to handle these bottles of honey carefully, for normally their only seal was a plug of brown paper. As villagers put palm oil and honey in bottles, there was always a demand for empty bottles.

The hunters would stay out for several days and occasionally kill a large antelope, but that was rare. Though they knew a great deal about wild animals and plants I was always astounded by the average villager's knowledge of plants and animals. They would collect nuts from oleaginous trees in one season and other nuts in other seasons. They would tap the sap from various trees for medicines and knew of the efficacious qualities of well over a hundred plants, in some cases using the roots and in others the bark, leaves or shoots at certain stages of development. The honey collectors still knew how to make bark cloth. They would peel a long piece of bark, usually about seven feet in length, from the trunk of a kind of fig tree. They would then separate the rough outer bark from the inner bark and yield a strip up to three feet wide. Using special wooden mallets, they would then beat the bark on a large log for several hours, eventually stretching the original strip out to at least twice its width and an eighth of an inch thin. The bark is then washed, squeezed and left to dry out thoroughly. Unlike the well-known Buganda bark cloth in Uganda, it never becomes reddish and is nowhere near as fine. The finished product is used for shrouds, bags, mats and sleeping pads. With the advent of cheap imported mats, canvas and plastic bags the practice of bark cloth making is rapidly being abandoned and I doubt if it will still be made in another generation.

With the terrible drought of 1982–84 crops failed, tubers shrivelled in the ground, yams kept for planting were eaten, fires ravaged the landscape, water holes dried up and people suffered. At that time villagers collected the leaves of plants they knew were nutritious – if sheep could eat them so could they – and during this crisis their knowledge of wild plants came in handy. They survived in the same way as their hunter-gatherer ancestors of old had done and used their latent knowledge to good effect. The drought taught them hard lessons. After it they built more storage units, so they would always have some stocks to bide them over. One way to ride out the hungry days was to lessen the number of mouths to feed. Young men drifted into the towns; young women also went to nearby towns and even further afield to Abidjan in neighbouring Ivory Coast to find work as domestics, and in a few cases bar girls or even prostitutes. When I visited Hani in 1983 my friends insisted on giving me a few nuts, a yam or two and the odd small egg to take back with me to Accra, where food was also short and where they were greatly appreciated.

Some villagers had sheep and a few chickens, but that was the full extent of their livestock. Many houses had a small shed where they kept their sheep at night and an even smaller chicken pen. A few farmers kept chickens at their farm shelters. Neither the chicken nor the goats were regularly killed. They were kept for special occasions, for sacrifice or as gifts. The eggs produced were small but tasty and the chickens when eaten were extremely tough. People in Hani kept sheep but in other villages they kept goats, I never quite understood why they decided to keep one rather than the other. The sheep were never milked or sheared. Tsetse fly and various infectious animal diseases made it impossible to keep other animals. The lack of locally produced meat meant that the animals they hunted and smoked, like grasscutters, were extremely important because the smoke-cured meat could be kept for long periods and used to flavour their stews.

Crafts

Though several village men make baskets and all know how to build houses, few actual crafts persist. When I first arrived there was still a smith, an old man in his early eighties, who occasionally made a few items (omega shaped pieces of metal used with stones as fire lighters or tiny spoons for clearing wax from ears), but mainly I believe to show us that he still could. He said that when he was young there were several smiths but the availability of cheap iron goods in local markets had basically put them out of business except for occasional repairs. He was using a small bowl bellows, a stone anvil and had only a limited number of iron and stone hammers. By the time of my last visit to the village in 1998 there were two smiths making hoes, animal traps and repairing bicycle parts. Neither smith was a local man but had come to the village sensing an opportunity. Villagers still, however, buy iron goods from the village of Brawhani ten miles to the north or at local market towns like Wenchi and Techiman. At one time villagers also bought guns made from the steel frames of bicycles, particularly from markets at Seikwa and Berekum.

When I arrived I often saw women potters from Bondakiri, 12 miles to the northwest, carrying stacks of pots on their heads on the way to markets to the south or east of Hani, or to the tiny market at Hani. The most popular pots were large globular bowls for cooking and small ones for sauces, and they found a ready market for their wares. Over time, however, the trade declined. Now, the potters rarely visit and the villagers either travel to Bondakiri or buy their pottery at Nsawkaw or in other neighbouring villages. Women prefer to use cast aluminium pots for stewing and often find that the enamel ware bought in the town markets serves them better and lasts longer than the cheaper earthenware they used to buy. In 1970 it was usual for a woman to own more than 20 pots of different sizes, but by 1998 that number had dwindled to somewhere between five and ten, for enamel pots and basins, aluminium plates, plastics and glass have taken their place.

A kente weaver intermittently practised his art in Hani but only for a short while and only part time. At other times he worked as a farmer and school teacher. His shed was moveable. Like other craft people, he rapidly discovered that although there was a demand for kente cloth, the demand fluctuated and villagers preferred to travel to the market towns where they had more choice and they felt that the price was more negotiable than it was in Hani. It was strange that Hani could never maintain a corps of crafts people. Debibi, which is not that many miles northwest of Hani, had a thriving indigo-blue narrow-strip-weave cloth industry with women spinning and dyeing threads and up to six weavers active in producing good cloths, which were probably not at all that dissimilar from the cloths Begho had produced in its heyday. There had been some dyeing in the village as recently as the 1950s, which we established when we found two 'cement' lined dye pits not far from the palace. It was claimed that the crafts people of yore had belonged to other ethnic groups. As such people moved to Bonduku in the Ivory Coast or even to Debibi, whose people claimed a common ancestry from the sacred hole, the village became largely a Brong centre denuded of the skills of their neighbours.

Health and medicine
Hani is 32 miles west of the nearest government hospital at Wenchi and 30 miles northwest of Berekum, where there is a Catholic mission and hospital. In the 1970s Wenchi hospital had an approved quota of two medical practitioners, but very often there was only one. The hospital served a population of at least 180,000. In the 1970s and 1980s the University of Ghana medical school was producing up to 30 doctors a year. However, with inflation escalating, the economic situation spiralling out of control, imports of medicines and medical equipment restricted, and salaries at an all time low (often less than the equivalent of $200 a year for a fully-fledged doctor), more doctors were leaving Ghana than arriving from overseas or being trained internally. By the early 1980s there were more Ghanaian doctors in Germany than in Ghana. There were a few scattered health centres in Brong Ahafo, a few had beds and all had dispensaries, but again they were understaffed and under-equipped. There was neither the money nor transport for health assistants to travel around. When asked on our questionnaires what services the village needed most our Hani respondents always placed health care above education and far above agricultural extension services. On the rickety and uncomfortable

truck (the *tro-tro*) that Kwesi Brew drove twice a week from Hani to Wenchi and Techiman there was always someone seeking medical care or looking for medicines to treat a sick relative. Drugs were difficult to find; they were often outdated when available or sold as single pills in hot and sunny markets that had adverse effects on their potency. Health deteriorated during years of economic and environmental stress.

Water was always a problem. Even in the late 1980s it was being carried from a pond in a seasonal river more than a mile north of the village. Adolescent girls and women would collect it early each morning before school. When we first arrived earthen pots were still being used for carrying it, but by the mid-1970s lighter vessels like enamel and aluminium basins, plastic buckets and recycled kerosene drums had replaced them. Sprigs of leaves floating on the basins prevented the water from sloshing over. Come evening the whole process was repeated. Boys did not help. Unfortunately, when the well and river holes dried up during the horrendous drought, the water became infected, turned grayish and villagers came down with Guinea worm and other diseases. By 1984, I calculated that possibly up to a third of the population had been affected. With paratyphoid endemic – to which the loose stools scattered round the village were a clear testimony – there was a constant demand for help to obtain a more secure water supply.

In the 1970s we pestered the district administration and Ministry of Works in Accra to provide some boreholes. Being Ghana, the borehole diggers demanded money, so the chief taxed the villagers to pay for them and two boreholes were sunk, but neither produced much water. The water table had dropped both from over use because the population had increased and because, with erosion and tree felling, the surface water was running away too fast. A lot of trees were lost during the mid-1970s' push to increase tobacco cultivation. In 1980 the *hanihene* decided to build a dam and raised money from the village to hire a bulldozer for the purpose, but the dam was too shallow and failed to collect water from a wide enough catchment area, so this project too was unsuccessful. The water problem was only solved in the late 1980s when World Bank money paid for three deep boreholes fitted with efficient concrete casings and hand pumps. Though clean drinking water is appreciated, the idea of boiling and filtering water is a difficult message to impart. Natural drinks, like palm wine, were normally kept in a calabash, which is absorbent so retains microorganisms on its rough internal surface. Often quite dirty water was drunk and unless made into tea would retain its own quotient of bacteria.

On the whole, by Ghanaian rural standards most villagers were relatively healthy, though childhood diseases were common because of waterborne parasites and, during any period of economic or environmental stress, simple infections like measles could prove disastrous. With malaria and other fevers endemic, as they are in much of Africa, the mortality rate for children under five was quite high. Children catch fevers many times before their fifth birthdays. Those who survive build up a resistance that protects them from mortality, though they still experience recurrent low-grade fevers that sometimes last for days. From our observations, it was obvious that relatively few villagers were over 60. Some, like the chief's mother, who died in her early eighties, were exceptional, though not knowing exactly when one was born often led people to assume they were older than they were. Many presumed that centenarian mothers left behind children in their fifties and sixties, even though most women had their first children in their teens and births after the age of 30–35 were uncommon.

In 1981, by which time we had stopped visiting the village as a large team, the University of Ghana decided to donate the research building to the village for use as a health centre and adjunct to the middle school (now JSS) next door. The chief persuaded the district medical authority to pay for a part-time health assistant and some rudimentary drugs. Peter Tekyi went away for some short-term training and thereafter functioned as a medical orderly. Periodically, he would travel to Wenchi to pick up medicines or buy supplies and a district medical assistant would occasionally visit the clinic. Peter rapidly became known as 'doctor' and gained a great deal of local respect, though very often he had only headache tablets, malaria pills, cough mixture and some liquid stomach disorder medicine to dispense. Infrequently, he had anti-fungal and antibiotic creams and occasionally a general-purpose antibiotic tablet such as Ampicillin. With these he performed miracles and provided a sense of physical security that had previously been lacking.

After 1985, when political stability returned and, with the help of World Bank loans, the economy of Ghana rebounded, the general health of the village improved. Commodities like drugs, antiseptics, plasters, which were mostly obtained from abroad, became more freely available. With slight improvements in the roads, particularly after 2000, and more vehicles available, the markets and medical centres became more accessible.

Though falling short of starvation, except in the hunger year of 1983, malnutrition was, and probably still is, certainly present. Many children under seven had stunted growth, pot bellies, herniated and pronounced belly buttons and sometimes mangy hair, several of which are signs of protein deficiency. Children are fed on a mush of fufu, pounded yam, plantain or coco yam. They have no access to milk after breast-feeding, and the protein intake of most villagers is severely limited. I tried my best to promote bean growing. Groundnuts contain some protein, but the average villager obtained most of his or her protein intake from stews in which bony bits of goat or chicken provided the flavour. Grown ups, particularly the men, eat the meaty bits and, with any luck, the children are left to suck the bones. Vegetables and fruit that could easily grow in the area are not encouraged. Pineapples and papaya seem to grow accidentally or, if planted, are regarded as a worktime snack rather than a necessary part of the diet. There are many mango trees growing wild, but their fruit is small and stringy. Oranges would be brought in from outside, but they were small and full of pips; the limes and lemons that grew around the edge of the village, often near the trash heaps and toilet facilities, were used as much for washing, because of their good smell on the body, as for food.

Childbirth took place at a relatively young age and most young women started to have their babies between the ages of 14 and 16. Out of the first batch of six middle-school female students in the early 1970s, four had to drop out because they were pregnant, some, alas, because of the forced attentions of their instructors. By the 1990s the number of junior secondary schoolgirls had increased and, either because there were more of them or because the social climate had changed or government propaganda had taken effect, there were fewer pregnancies, thus allowing the more successful girls to proceed to secondary schools outside the village.

Villages and the Ghanaian economy

For me Hani represented a microcosm of rural Ghana. Being there and communing with its people taught me a great deal about Ghana's political economy. Though my data were on material culture, attitudes to a changing situation, crafts in nearby villages and social interactions, much of what I learnt had relevance for a far wider area. For many years politics focused on towns, with many outside initiatives to increase Ghanaian living standards and economic development being urban based. Foreign experts came for short periods, stayed in the few functioning Accra hotels, travelled between the major urban centres on roads badly in need of repair, visited foreign embassies and aid organizations for advice, gathered statistics and imbibed opinions, but rarely left the main centres of population. Occasionally, they spoke to academics at the universities, but many had already joined the brain drain and those who stayed were too busy supplementing their miniscule salaries to give them much time. Few experts, particularly from the World Bank, stayed for more than a month, so the wheel kept being reinvented.

Earlier reports from similar missions remained in ministries to gather dust on shelves like abandoned party favours from long for-gotten dances. It was too easy for government departments to get aid for feasibility studies, for proposals for action rather than for action itself. Sadly, most of these missions came out of much heralded aid budgets and represented extremely expensive advice. If organization A was approached for a million dollars, the costs of the evaluation by overseas experts and all their direct and indirect expenses, as well as those of their hosts, were deducted from the final grant. In addition, Ghana was normally not allowed to spend the money as it wished, for it was often tied to purchasing agreements stipulated by the funding authorities. Too much money went into collecting data and far too little into programmes bringing together foreign experts and local personnel to work for extended periods on critical problems.

Few foreign experts went to rural areas. They visited selected farms, research institutes, regional headquarters and extension services, but spent no time in villages. They were led to where local consultants had pet projects and the situation persists. For many years, it has been policy to placate the urban masses, who are easily mobilized politically, by providing social services in the towns and ensuring cheap food. Foods such as flour, hops, barley, evaporated milk, sugar cubes, tinned fish and meat can be provided more cheaply from overseas than from rural areas, which need good roads to make them accessible to urban consumption.

In the 1970s, prices of essential commodities were kept artificially low, which meant that food from rural areas had also to be under-priced to find a market. In the 1980s the situation improved, but then there was less money for social services at the village level. A more radical government demanded more services but could not provide the funds for them. Parents in Hani found that if they wanted their children to go to school they had to pay for a chair and desk, and dispensaries no longer stocked subsidized medicines. Much of the foreign aid was used to fund burgeoning urban bureaucracies and to develop and rejuvenate export-oriented industries. The little aid for farmers was siphoned off through corrupt practices[13] and the small amount available at the village level often had to be bought through inducements to operatives who, although sympathetic to rural needs, felt that their pay was inadequate and they seldom had either the funds for travel or the vehicles to get to remote areas.

Ghanaian farmers are the backbone of Ghana's economy. At independence, Ghana, Malaya (now Malaysia) and South Korea were economic equals, yet the latter two are now ten times wealthier than Ghana. Ghana has gold, timber, bauxite and various other mineral resources, and a fertile tropical belt suitable for cocoa, palm oil, nuts, coffee and other crops. The race to industrialize and develop a cash economy in the late 1950s and 1960s has been deleterious to farmers at the village level. Ghana's strength should be based on its human resources, particularly the knowledge and adaptability of its farmers who coped remarkably well with the economic stress in the 1970s, environmental disaster in the 1980s, and political changes and fickle state mandates. They know how to farm without exhausting their resources, experiment with new plants, substitute honey for imported sugar, and trap and hunt animals and birds. They use local building materials, are economical with their water, retain their local pharmacopoeia and run their lives in a sound common-sense way.

They are socially functional, retain their communal solidarity and have superb coping mechanisms, which the government should value. Ghana's villages are capable of increasing their output, but the authorities need to recognize that helping the villages is an essential key to national development. Ghana's village sector has been let down. Rather than subsidizing urban social services or removing price controls on imports, the moral of any village study leads to the inescapable conclusion that priorities have in the past been misplaced. President Rawlings (1992–2000) had the right slogan 'Grow what you eat and eat what you grow'. Much of what Ghana grows still has to make its way onto the Ghana market. Ghana has the ability to provide many nutritious foods and to reduce imports.

People in Hani were generous and open. They were prepared to talk about their families, beliefs, hopes and aspirations. Alfred Forkuo, who helped on all seven of my excavations, used to teach me Twi in the evenings and did not seem to mind that I was a poor student; I felt honoured when he called his eldest son Posnansky. I have such pleasant memories of chatting with friends on the research centre veranda with a smoky hurricane lamp to one side. I would often walk around the town in the dark and call on people seated around the embers of a hearth or shelling groundnuts. On a weekend there was often drumming coming from the town and I was welcomed as they say in Ghana 'to be among'. It was expected that I play my part in village life and this on occasion included going to services in the church and showing up and bidding at the harvest festivals. These were good fun with villagers tempting me to bid on such items as huge yams and bottles of honey. Sometimes the bids went up to the equivalent of $20–30 for one item. The proceeds of these sales went to the church and its promotion of the welfare of the students in their village school. Villagers in Africa are as loyal and generous to their own communities as any people in the world and I have often been amused by Americans' conceit in thinking that they are the most generous people in the world. They may well be in total contributions, but in terms of the percentage of their wealth or the significance of their giving I have never met more generous people than the villagers in most parts of Africa.

A little bit of my soul will always be in Hani, even though I cannot be buried there, as many of my friends wish.

Chapter 8

Africa: Kenya and Uganda

A FRICA PLAYED no part in my education or aspirations when I was growing up. I envisaged my future in England near my family and everything familiar. I dreamt of a book-lined study and a future of quiet scholarship, so how did Africa creep into my life and take hold of it so completely? Britain in the mid-1950s was an austere place; there had been rationing until 1953, universities were not expanding, and archaeological jobs were few and far between. I had lived in a protected environment and had not travelled much. In effect, my life was restricted and I began to feel that I wanted to see something of the world before settling down.

Some people I knew at Cambridge, like Jack Golson, had gone to New Zealand and later Australia. In 1953 I applied unsuccessfully for an English-Speaking Union travel scholarship to the United States and in 1954 turned down an opportunity to join the Israel department of antiquities, which had invited me to apply for a post. My tutor Graham Clark had alerted me to the importance of world prehistory as opposed to just European prehistory, so I decided that if a suitable job came up anywhere in the world I would apply. Some of my colleagues in the geology research laboratory at the University of Nottingham had gone abroad. Bob Newton had gone to Northern Rhodesia and Penny Touche to British Somaliland and they both wrote glowingly about their lives in Africa. I knew I wanted to go, but had no real preference for any particular country.

In early 1956, when I was starting to look for a job following my anticipated doctorate later in the year, I received a letter from Graham Clark informing me that he had heard from Dr Louis Leakey, the curator of the Coryndon Museum in Nairobi, who was looking for a research archaeologist to be warden of the prehistoric sites of the Royal National Parks of Kenya[1] and Graham wondered if I would be interested. I immediately wrote to Leakey asking for more information. I was excited by a possibility I had never really thought about. Everyone, particularly my mother, said 'Why Kenya?'

At that time the Mau Mau insurgency was in the news and everyone had heard about the panga-wielding Kenyan Africans who took oaths to a secret society and savagely killed white farmers. The news focused on terror, on the use of blood in oath taking and on the bravery of British troops hunting down terrorists in the forests. However, the more I read the more I realized that the peak of the emergency was over, that there was law and order in Nairobi, that the trouble was highly localized in the Kikuyu area around Mount Kenya and that Kenya was an exciting place to live. I also began to realize that the popular news I heard was slanted, that the uprising was a struggle against white colonialism and that not all Kenyan Africans were uncivilized. It was also obvious that except for a few farmers on remote farms and a small number of African soldiers, it was largely Kikuyu who were being killed.

Miles Burkitt at Cambridge had introduced me to rock art and the prospect of boundless opportunities and wonderful scenery stimulated my imagination. I immediately accepted the terms I was offered, which I later realized were far from generous, for my salary of £720 a year was about half what geological students who went out to work for colonial geological services in Africa were getting. I was to be given a contract of 42–48 months with no home leave, whereas graduates without higher degrees in the colonial service were getting larger salaries and home leaves every 21 months. Anyhow, I was still excited. I anticipated going out for only one tour and perhaps even returning after two years. I stayed in Africa for 20 years!

Kenya
In 1956 it took 26 hours to travel to Nairobi by turboprop Britannia planes, stopping *en route* in Rome, Cairo, Khartoum and Entebbe. My discount ticket cost £216 for a one-way flight, about half what it might cost today, though an equivalent starting British academic salary is probably 20 times the one I received. Cairo was a bit scary because it was in the period immediately prior to the Suez crisis and troops were everywhere. The airlines rigorously enforced the 20-kilo luggage allowance, so my limited household items, including a set of crockery I had just bought, had to go by sea. Alas, the crate never arrived because the ship to which it was consigned was sunk in the Suez Canal. Two items I distinctly remember bringing with me were a tea cozy and egg cup. Now if I were travelling I would still take my tea cozy, for I drink a lot of tea, but my second item would be a down

pillow because I have come across some rather stiff and occasionally smelly pillows in my travels.

Louis Leakey met me at the old, but convenient, Eastleigh airport and whisked me to Ahmed's on Government Avenue to order essentials such as a bush jacket, which I still have, khaki shorts and a sort of bib overall, which I never liked or wore but which Louis insisted was essential because it obviated the need for braces or belt and was more comfortable for fieldwork. I also ordered mosquito boots, soft leather-lined boots up to the knee, which one changed into after one's evening bath and wore without socks. They were comfortable and effective, but a houseboy stole them in 1963 and I regretted never having replaced them. Leakey then took me to the Norfolk Hotel for lunch, which, with a wide veranda, lots of woodwork and very green garden, was very colonial. At that time there were still five-course set lunches including an appetizer (avocado or corn), soup, fish, main course, dessert, savoury (like cheese on toast) and coffee. On many of the tables patrons had placed their revolvers, which people coming down from upcountry still carried.

At the Coryndon Museum I was introduced to my first Land Rover, a rather ancient model with no trafficators,[2] noisy windscreen wipers and a hand crank that I had to use a great deal over the next two years. Later, I went to Leakey's house in Langata where I was to stay on and off for the next six weeks. The house, built of grey lava blocks, formed three sides of a compound with a shallow pond in the centre in which there was a 14-foot python. There were stables behind the house for their horses and in a special room under the eaves of the house Leakey raised tropical fish, which he shipped by air to European buyers. At that time money was tight. Museum salaries were particularly low and the Leakey household, with its ponies, horses, assorted other animals and servants, was expensive to maintain. Louis was for ever on the lookout for alternative sources of income, which came when his discoveries in Olduvai Gorge and the *National Geographic*'s coverage of them made him a highly sought after and well-paid international public speaker. Seven frisky Dalmatian dogs were Mary's pride and joy and occupied all the comfortable chairs in the living room. Everything was covered in a fine film of red dust, which blows in from the red lateritic soils that dominate tropical Africa. Sundowners with whisky and water took a couple of hours and we did not as a rule eat until after 9.00 p.m. As someone used to my dessert, I had a surprise in that Louis did not believe in eating fruit at night. He considered it, particularly pineapple, too acidic for good sleep. I got used to hard cheese.

On my second day I signed in at the entrance kiosk to the governor's lodge, a requirement for all new Britons. I was told that it might result in my eventually being invited to a garden party; it never did. Because of the emergency I also had to sign in at the district office in the town. I acquired a driver's licence, given on the basis of my British one, and picked up my clothes, which had been made within the day. Nairobi was then a highly efficient commercial centre. Indians, a term that included anyone hailing, even after three generations, from what are now India, Pakistan, Sri Lanka and Bangladesh, provided a highly competitive marketing world in which everything was available and artisans were quickly able to sew clothes, make boots, create tents, repair cameras, manufacture custom-designed tools, build furniture and do everything with a minimum fuss. The city was at its most beautiful as the glorious purple jacaranda were in bloom. Princess Margaret was expected on a visit to open the Royal Technical College, the nascent university.

On my third day I had to pick up permits from the district office for the three Kikuyu who were to help me rehabilitate the museum at the Royal National Parks of Kenya prehistoric site of Olorgesailie, 46 miles to the southwest in the Rift Valley. Olorgesailie, which was to be my base for the next 19 months, consisted of a series of remarkable Stone Age sites. Discovered initially by the geologist Gregory in 1919, the Leakeys, particularly Mary, had been excavating it since 1942. The excavation areas had been turned into a 42-acre national park with several sites exposed under grass awnings (bandas) and with a walkway connecting them in a circuit of nearly a mile. There were four round single-roomed thatched rondavels for overnight use by visitors and I was to live in one of them. Louis took me on a very quick tour in his Land Rover and explained his theories about the evolution of the site, which involved Stone Age foragers camping at the edge of lakes that existed during the middle Pleistocene period. The Stone Age settlers lived on a superimposed series of at least 17 distinct land surfaces with each separated by lake deposits. Several cataclysmic events had disturbed the sequence and were marked by the spread of ash from a nearby extinct volcano and by flooding caused during periods of very heavy rainfall, which he called pluvials. He pointed to huge rocks spread by the floods.

My job was to rebuild all the buildings, make a field museum,

16. Merrick in front of his Olorgesailie *banda*, 1957.

provide painted signboards explaining all the sites and put back into
action a water supply from a borehole at a small *duka*, or trading post,
five miles away.

The following day I began my mission impossible. A truck carrying two 44-gallon drums of water, my newly recruited houseboy Mulei, son of Nthuka, four workers and a few tools, including pipe wrenches, accompanied me. Except for one of the Kikuyu, Kanyugi, none of the Kenyans spoke any English and I spoke no Swahili, though in Nairobi I had bought *Up-Country Swahili* by Elisabeth Le Breton, which introduced me within its first seven pages to useful phrases like 'make way for the master', 'very potent witchcraft charms' and 'snakes are very numerous nowadays'.

Olorgesailie, 3000 feet lower than Nairobi, is in semi-desert with days reaching into the high 90 degrees Fahrenheit and rainfall normally less that 12 inches a year. Water is essential, so I determined that my priority was to make the water line work. I had never seen a pipe wrench before, knew nothing about the practical side of plumbing and had no idea how a pump worked. In my first week away I learnt enough Swahili to get by, repaired the pump by cutting my own leather valves, cleared airlocks in the long pipe, which we had to open every few hundred yards, and got a feel for the environment.

We were delighted; the people at the *duka* were delighted to have water again and even the Masai who frequented the *duka* seemed pleased that after several years of little happening there was some momentum. Olorgesailie was back in business and I took visitors around the sites at weekends. Within half a year I had composed and lettered explanatory boards with UNO stencils and varnished them with clear acetate varnish as weather protection. It was gratifying to go to Olorgesailie 20 years later, for the Pan African Prehistory Congress in 1977, to see how well everything had survived. After a few weeks of going back and forth to the Leakey's, Louis found me a room with the Coryndons, who lived in a museum apartment. Shirley was an exceptionally gifted zoo archaeologist and palaeontologist. She looked after two delightful daughters and a sick and inebriated husband who was the son of the former governor after whom the museum was named on his death in 1923.

I have many reasons to be grateful for having stayed with the Leakeys. First, I got to know Mary Leakey from whom I learnt a great deal and who helped me piece together potsherds from my excavations, improved my artefact drawing and acted as an excellent foil to Louis who, though brilliant, was intolerant and politically very paternalist in a rather missionary sort of way. Louis knew a great deal about wild life, the environment and the Kikuyu, but he knew very little African history and was disdainful of a lot of African culture. He also had a heightened idea of the importance of his views on African archaeology and Kenya politics.

Second, staying with the Leakeys introduced me to their library. There was nothing to do at Olorgesailie at night and there is a limit to how much one can listen to on what I still called the wireless because of the static. I had no electricity, no access to a telephone and no gramophone, so I read voraciously. Although there were very few books on Africa or on African art at the time – Basil Davidson's *Old Africa Rediscovered* was three years away and Kenneth Ingham's *A History of East Africa* six – there were a few archaeological site reports and some short books on African archaeology, like Leakey's 1936 *Stone Age* and Sonia Cole's 1954 *Prehistory of East Africa*. I concentrated on travel books, anthropology and biographies. About this time I also began to take the *Manchester Guardian Weekly*.

The third great benefit of my stay with the Leakeys was it brought me into contact with Richard Leakey, then a precocious but charming 11-year-old who forced me to learn to ride and took me into the Ngong Reserve on the fringes of the Leakeys' property. He told me the names of plants and animals in both Swahili and English, and opened my eyes to creatures I would not ordinarily have seen because they blended in so well into the environment. I have often found that young people provide one with a better introduction to new areas than their elders. They avoid overloading their information and use simpler prose with a more concise vocabulary.

Olorgesailie taught me many practical skills about life in the bush. I was on my own in a round grass room with mosquito mesh for windows; at night the kerosene pressure lamp gave enough light to read by but too much heat, and if I read outdoors on the veranda, hordes of insects would trouble me. A grass room may provide good insulation against the heat of the sun, but bits of grass or dirt period-ically drop from the unlined thatch and at the beginning of the rains, before the grass has a chance to swell, water drips through onto the bedding. Visitors from outside Africa often bemoan the passing of the attractive grass roof, but if they had to endure the threat of fire, the nuisance of insects and vermin sheltering in the eaves and the need to rethatch every few years, I am sure they would welcome the steady encroach of corrugated aluminium sheets. I had a small kerosene refrigerator with a wick that needed constant nursing to ensure good results and that required defrosting every week. I had primitive plumbing with a shower tank cut from an oil drum that had to be

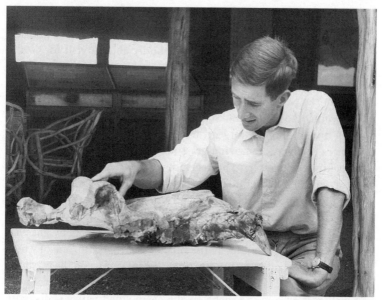

17. Preparing fossil hippo skull for Olorgesailie site museum, 1957.

refilled daily. Cooking was on an open fire with wood collected from the landscape. Mulei performed wonders on it, including baking bread in a four-gallon kerosene container known as a *debbi*. Abandoned *debbi*s were recycled in so many ways – they were opened up for roofing sheets, halved to make cooking pans and universally employed for storage and particularly for water carrying. I was overjoyed one day to come across an old cast-iron wood-burning stove on a dump in Nairobi. I bought new bolts, lovingly reconstructed it at Olorgesailie, fitted a chimney and painted it silver and, at last, I had a reliable oven and several top burners instead of an open fire. It revolutionized our cooking.

We spent the first six months at Olorgesailie rebuilding. We collected long grasses several miles away for thatching and went even further afield to collect suitable poles for uprights and roofing frames. Since most of the work was done without nails, we would bind the components together with rope made from bark. I quickly learnt important lessons in humility. The parks service paid my workers a minimum wage and all of them apart from Kanyugi were illiterate, yet they knew more languages than I did and had so many other skills, including making fires without matches. They worked tirelessly in the heat, could handle a range of different tools, had a knowledge of building, were excellent recyclers and from a wage of less than a dollar a day were able to save a greater percentage of their pay than I did for their families, whom they were only able to visit for two to four weeks once a year.

Being on my own I spent a lot of time in the cool of the evening exploring the neighbourhood looking for new sites. Practically every plant seemed to have spikes to scratch one's flesh or catch one's clothes and in both Olorgesailie and elsewhere in Africa I have memories of always removing grass seeds embedded and hooked in my stockings or trousers. The vegetation was often very dry and brittle and the wind had a distinctive soft whistle. Though our small park was in the Ngong National Reserve, I never felt nervous about game and was particularly fond of the long necked gerenuk that feasted on the leaves among the fresh spines of the acacia. I saw many gazelles, zebra, hyaenas, jackals and, a little further away, giraffe, one of which side-swiped my Land Rover in the early morning mist on the way back to Nairobi. We were both startled but neither of us hurt. There were klipspringers among the rocks on the steep-sided valley walls, with their dainty hooves adapted to moving up almost vertical slopes. Occasionally, on the flatter lands, I saw hunting dogs and cheetahs, both of which are now quite rare.

One night during the rains, when water formed pools along the bed of the normally dry Ol Keju Nero, the river that had exposed the sites by cutting through the old lake deposits, from a concealed bluff we watched animals come down to the water to drink and, in less than an hour, we saw 13 rhinos. Once when I had gone to bed I was awakened by a persistent crunching noise and less than ten feet from the perimeter fence, about 30 feet from my rondavel, I saw a pride of lions snacking on a Masai donkey they had caught nearby. I tried to shoo them off so that I could get some sleep, but they ignored me. By morning most of the donkey was dismembered and its bones dispersed; vultures and other prey were finishing off the last of the, by now far from juicy, morsels. Contrary to popular belief, insects and snakes were not a particular problem, though one morning while out walking a huge black mamba rushed across my path. It was both quick and quite alarming. One learnt to watch out for scorpions; they never troubled me but I always shook my shoes before putting them on. One weekend the two younger Leakey boys came to visit and spent a lot of time catching scorpions and trying to get them to race. Lizards were a constant source of interest.

I would often call on the warden of the Nairobi National Park on my way to or from Olorgesailie. Mr Ellis and his wife were very friendly and frequently looked after injured or young wild animals rescued in the park. One abandoned lion cub grew so strong that it knocked their German shepherd dog out with a playful slap of its paw. On another occasion they decided to wash it in Stogol, which they used to kill fleas, ticks and lice on their dogs, but it had an adverse effect on the lion by causing a minor skin allergy. Several years later I got lice from a dirty rest house and used my Irish terrier's Stogol in the bath; it worked splendidly and saved me the trouble or embarrassment of going to a doctor. The lion eventually was released into the park but not before it tried to sneak back several times. I learnt a lot about animals from these visits. Park wardens, unlike their popular image, do not go around with guns; they are supposed to know about animal behaviour and avoid trouble. Most animals are only a danger when frightened such as when one is between them and their young or blocking their passage to safety, food or drink.

Among my enduring memories of Olorgesailie are the sounds of the night – the high-tension tingle and buzz of insects, the honking of frogs, and the sound of human coughing or even whispers in the absence of a human presence. There are also the smells – the distinctive smell of the earth after the rains, the acrid smell of burnt grass, wood fires, decaying vegetation and sometimes even of unwashed humans. At Olorgesailie the air was dry and the light shimmered. It was possible on occasion to glimpse mirages in the distance. At first the evenness of the length of the days daunted me. There was so little variation. Darkness came so rapidly but when it did it was not as dark as I imagined it would be. The moon seemed brighter at Olorgesailie than anywhere else, perhaps because there was no other light or because the soils were whitish from the diatoms. I could read big writing in the moonlight. Masses of stars twinkled and were more vibrant than elsewhere. The Southern Cross was always visible, as were shooting stars on a few occasions. A storm in the distance would bring amazing displays of lightning, with the flashes of electricity lightening up the sky in ever-changing patterns. Living in a flimsy house of grass I should perhaps have feared the dark, but I felt quite assured. I would frequently sit outside my rondavel in a folding canvas chair, sipping tea and listening to the BBC. The reception was often surprisingly good at night and I loved the stories and plays. I began to appreciate landmark broadcasts like Alistair Cooke's *Letter from America.* I still enjoy the radio and listened to Alistair Cooke's broadcasts until he died in 2004.

There were many Masai in the neighbourhood, particularly after the rains in May and later in October/November when grazing was good. I would visit their *manyattas* (extended family settlements) in which low, oblong, dung-plastered houses bordered an open area in which the cattle were corralled at night. There was a smell of smoke and dung everywhere and the redness of their ochre-stained cloths and skins was pervasive. They gave me several items, including an ear-plug for stretching an ear lobe, necklaces and a gourd in which to store milk. They were friendly towards me and sometimes turned to me for help. I remember one young *moran*, a Masai of warrior age, turning up with a gaping gash in his leg that was already turning green. The wound, which was by then a week old, had been inflicted when he killed a lion with his spear. All I could do was send him to the medical centre 25 miles south at the salt-working factory at Magadi. I particularly remember the coming of age ceremonies for boys when they would dress like women in beadwork and feathers, or in one case with dried humming birds in their hair as decoration.

Life at Olorgesailie could be exciting. One Sunday I was awakened at 4.30 a.m. to be told that the chief secretary (whom I took to be some government clerk) had arrived to climb Mount Olorgesailie before it got too hot. I was not amused to be woken at that hour, so went back to sleep. It was only when I got up two hours later that I realized that the chief secretary was second in command in the Kenya government, later to be appointed Governor of Uganda as Sir Frederick Crawford. We had other visitors, including Charlie Chaplin, whom I missed by being away from camp, and some who came to see the sites, like Peter and Marilyn Kenyon, who ended up becoming lifelong friends. I wrote a guide to the sites and collected donations for an excavation fund that eventually helped me to conduct research away from Olorgesailie. Of particular popularity was my ice pit. We dug a pit, lined it with charcoal and straw and every Saturday when I came from Nairobi with the weekly rations I would bring soft drinks and large ice blocks to keep the drinks cold in the pit during the weekend when most visitors came.

One day we had some unexpected arrivals. I heard a loud spluttering noise and saw a biplane flying so low that it was evidently running out of fuel. I got into the Land Rover and as it crash-landed nearby I was able to get to it fairly quickly. Seven clearly shaken clergymen and one swearing pilot emerged from the DH Rapide, so I quickly ferried them to our camp for some tea, and a little medicinal brandy for the pilot. I then got one of my staff to wait on the nearby road to send a message to either Nairobi or Magadi. Often nothing would come along the road for hours on end, so we were lucky to get a message to Nairobi and have the 'victims' on their way to safety within about four hours. The pilot said it was just his luck to have crows, as he called men of the cloth, as passengers because he believed they always brought bad luck. The following day reporters arrived from Nairobi to photograph the crashed aircraft and I was credited in the *East African Standard* with having saved the passengers. A lorry came to haul away the wreck but as one of its wings was badly smashed they gave it to me and I used it as firewood for several days. The publicity brought more visitors to see the site.

In the twilight years of the colonial era, it was still possible to sample the good life in Kenya. British farmers still had large estates, loved Africa, and were hospitable and generous. When I dug several iron furnaces on the Kinangop on a high plateau near Mount Kenya, Mr Reynaud the farmer lent me horses to ride to the site and let me live in his beautiful home, which contained many antiques and fine porcelain from Europe. Like many of the farmers, he was a cultivated man, but there was no suggestion that my African assistants would get transport to the site; they were expected to walk.

Largely because most Europeans, as white people were called, had domestic staff or belonged to clubs, there were hardly any restaurants in the main towns apart from catering facilities in the handful of hotels, European clubs and rest houses. There was, however, a vigorous social and cultural life in Nairobi. There were two theatres, the Donovan Maule, a repertory with plays, and the National Theatre, which put on musicals and light opera. In the late 1950s the performers and audience all came from the relatively small white population, in which people had enough time on their hands to audition and rehearse. With little serious crime, it was still possible to drive at night in Nairobi without danger, but there was a fair bit of stealing. Thieves would push long poles with a hook on the end through the burglar bars of open windows to fish out a woman's handbag or man's trousers. There were razor blades at the end of the pole, so startled sleepers trying to stop the theft could cut their fingers badly. There were many sporting events, including polo, rugby, tennis and cricket, as well as a popular racetrack and frequent gymkhanas. These were paralleled in the pluralistic Asian communities, although there badminton, cricket, football, hockey and table tennis were often more popular. In many ways the white community looked on its counterparts in Rhodesia as their peers or competitors rather than the Asian groups in Kenya. In 1957 a combined Oxford and Cambridge rugby team toured Africa to reinforce links between the scattered white communities.

My time at Olorgesailie passed far too quickly. Each week I came to Nairobi for rations and after a time spent two nights a week in a one-roomed wooden house in Karen in the shadow of the Ngong Hills where Karen Blixen had had her rather unsuccessful coffee farm in the 1920s. It was then a very European suburb of Nairobi. Occasionally I would travel upcountry, as we called the area beyond Nairobi, either to attend to the other museum I looked after, Kariandusi, or occasionally to follow up leads on new sites. Travel was a problem because so many of the roads were unpaved, potholed and very rough. We often got stuck, even in a four-wheel drive vehicle, and had to get large numbers of people literally to lift up our wheels, or we cut branches and vegetation to serve as matting under the wheels to increase traction. With all the bouncing around in a Land Rover, the base of my spine became black and blue. Revel Mason, a great South African prehistorian with whom I visited sites in Tanganyika, Uganda and South Africa, talked about having a facetted butt, a play on the prepared platform stone cores he studied.

Among the highlights of my time in Kenya were the opportunities I took to see the varied human population. I was surprised at how uncurious many Europeans were about upcountry Africans. The Masai with their spears, flowing ochre stained wraps, beadwork and jumping dancers were possibly the only different group that many white Kenyans ever saw. But if one went east past the then largely European settlement of Eldoret, to which many Boers had trekked after the Boer War, one entered a very different world. In the Eldoret area one could in the 1950s still occasionally see the long trek carts hauled by up to 16 oxen. The road east stretched past Lake Hannington, originally named after a bishop of Uganda martyred in 1885 but renamed Baringo at independence, and across gorges of startling beauty. The descent down the Elgeyo escarpment, the steepest wall of the whole Rift Valley where the drop is over 6000 feet, is probably the most spectacular in East Africa and, in the drama of its vegetation change, somewhat similar to the descent into the American Grand Canyon. In the 1950s the slopes were still heavily wooded.

At the shore one enters a different, hot, humid world. The waters are pink, I am not sure why. The Njemps people, who are related to the better known Pokot and Samburu, still wore among the men elaborate painted mud-plastered hair pieces and carried their carved headrests, which served as cushions to prevent their headpieces being damaged in sleep. It was the beginning of the realm of Cushitic pastoralists stretching north through to Lake Turkana and southern Ethiopia. We slept in the open near the lake on two occasions and suffered the worst attacks of mosquitoes I encountered in Africa. There was still plenty of game in the area, mainly antelope but with the occasional giraffe and smaller felines.

Going down to the coast one saw the Giriama subtribe north of Mombasa with women wearing distinctive short flared skirts. Traditional art was limited in Kenya, but there was a thriving market in Kamba wood carvings, figures of antelope, solid but small wood masks that became characteristic of 1960s' airport art and that in ten years had even invaded large stores in Europe. I only remember one display of what was still called 'tribal' dancing in Nairobi; the lack of interest in dancing was to me quite staggering. Even in the otherwise exemplary Coryndon Museum the emphasis of the displays was on natural history, fish, insects, birds and animals and on the prehistory, particularly stone tools and rock art, of Tanganyika. Except for a few scattered shields and spears and some recently commissioned paintings of 'native types' by Joy Adamson, the former wife of the director of the East African herbarium, Peter Bally, soon to be famous for *Born Free*, her book about an adopted lion, there was nothing on the rich cultures and variety of peoples in Kenya or even in the vicinity of Nairobi. All this was fortunately to change after independence in 1963 but until the late 1960s the average tourist to Kenya got a skewed impression. A culture I regretted not sampling was that of the varied Asian communities. I knew no one from the Indian community and the only people I met were shopkeepers. Fortunately, my experience was enriched once I went to Uganda.

Uganda

In Kenya I was a naïve, inquisitive explorer sampling Africa for the first time. Even after 20 months I was far from an expert, though I was beginning to wonder why there was such a rich diversity of cultures, why colonialism was so blind to the African heritage and what was changing the so-called traditional structure that so many colonialists regarded as immutable. I was experiencing the dynamic nature of Africa. It takes time to savour a new environment, to grasp the significance of the diversity of environments, peoples, histories and human responses. It is only when one is employed in Africa, pays its taxes, reads its newspaper, tastes its foods, wears its costumes, faces its diseases and feels local concerns that one can be thought of as having served a real apprenticeship. Uganda gave me a chance to mature as an Africanist. I had already visited several other African countries, witnessed the last throes of the struggles against colonialism and experienced positive political and economic changes.

In Uganda, because I was brought into closer contact with people through my role as a museum curator, educator, scholar and eventually house owner with a Ugandan wife and extended family, I could at last feel that I was getting to know Africa from an African point of view. I had visited Uganda in 1957 and thoroughly enjoyed the liberating experience of being in a country that seemed more genuinely African. British Kenyans dominated the Kenya I had experienced. They talked about it being a small world and knowing everyone, which really meant that they knew the *Bazungu*, white people like themselves, who were a relatively small community of only about 50,000 in the whole of Kenya.

Many of them questioned why I was choosing to go to Uganda. They said it was a closed-in country, that it was impossible to see vast stretches of country because there were so many bananas, that the grass was too tall and that there were too many people and farms. I think that those Kenyans who counselled me against Uganda did not realize that the views in Uganda are just as awe-inspiring and exhilarating as they are in Kenya. When one drives north from Mount Elgon, one cannot help but be struck by the great northern plain stretching towards Karamoja with a few old volcanoes piercing the landscape, with its shimmering haze and purple hills in the distance offset by puffs of red dust thrown up by fleeting vehicles and wind eddies traversing the plains like miniature tornados. The same is true of many parts of Uganda; it is true of the southwest with its velvety rolling hills of grassland in Ankole grazed by graceful long-horned zebu cattle, or of the dramatic landscape of Kigezi further to the west with volcanoes and lakes lying deeply cleft between high ridges.

The greenness of Uganda or at least the part near Lake Victoria, the billowy cumulus clouds reaching their climax before a quick shower in the early afternoon and the blueness of the equatorial sky will always stick in my mind. The air seemed so clear; it always felt as if it had just rained, much like going into a flower shop after the blooms have been sprayed. I arrived in May 1958 during the rainy season, so I suppose the first impressions stayed with me. I was struck by the redness of the soils.

Kampala was still a small town of fewer than 100,000 people divided by its flat-topped hills, on which many of the main houses of religion were sited, into discrete neighbourhoods. As curator I had a modern two-storey, three-bedroomed furnished house on Kiira Road next to the museum. The house had a glorious view across the Kitante valley to the golf course and parts of Kampala, a view now lost through building development. There was a wide veranda on which I could sit and enjoy the view and entertain. For a bachelor coming from a grass rondavel, with all my possessions fitting into a newly purchased second-hand Peugeot 203 station wagon, it was exciting beyond belief. I still had the then princely sum of £70 left in England, some of it saved from the money given to me as barmitzvah gifts. With it I got my mother to buy pillows, bedspreads, towels and other household linen in Bolton, which she then shipped out. Today that sum would not even cover a quarter of the freight. I went down to Vallenders, the poshest drapery store in Kampala, and on hire purchase ordered curtains, couch and seat covers, and bought a few other items like cutlery, glassware and pans.

Having a big house with a garden and servants' quarters at the age of 27 was a heady experience. One of the first things I did was to install an electric bell under the dining table that rang in the kitchen. I had seen the English memsabs in Kenya summoning their servants with little hand-held tinkly bells and felt I could go one step better by summoning someone without anyone knowing. It worked; people thought I had the most prescient of houseboys. After a few months I brought my old houseboy, Mulei, from Kenya to help. He alas stayed less than a year because he missed Kenya and after a few days kept insisting that as I lived in a big house he needed a kitchen *toto* or small boy to assist him with the work. I resisted that idea because I already employed a part-time gardener.

Living by the museum I came home daily for lunch. Like many other expatriates my meals were absurdly British, a lot of potatoes, custard, sardines, baked beans, rice pudding, boiled and poached eggs, porridge and soup. Salad was still regarded as suspect, though washing in potassium permanganate was supposed to kill the bacteria.

18. Kampala, Museum House, 1958.

Anyhow, salad and most greens for me were a taste I only slowly acquired, so I stuck with carrots, peas, tomatoes, mushrooms and beans as my principal vegetables. I enjoyed branching out into the wide variety of fruits that were readily available. Few people in Kampala ate out; students ate in hall and most Baganda made use of local foods grown in their gardens or brought from home at the weekends. Outside the two main hotels, the Speke and Grand, there were few places to eat, though the missionary-run Uganda Bookshop had a tearoom for a time. Several bars cum snooker rooms served what would now be thought of as pub grub and there was a Greek tearoom and bakery on Kampala Road on the way to Makerere. Over the years a Chinese restaurant, the Canton, opened, which I still regard as the best Chinese restaurant I have ever visited, but that is perhaps because it was the first I had visited. With independence in 1962 several other restaurants slowly began to open as more international visitors arrived who did not cook at home.

Food shopping was frequent because most refrigerators were small, eight cubic feet being regarded as humungous. They had to be defrosted weekly, had very small freezer sections and, until the late 1960s, I never knew anyone with a chest freezer. One standard frozen item was Tufmac fish (filleted tilapia) from Lake George. As the years passed and I met more people from different ethnicities my diet changed to include sweet potatoes, groundnut sauce, various banana dishes like fried plantains, which I now prefer baked, and new seasonings stimulated from eating Indian and Persian food. I loved the tiny mushrooms (*obitiko obubaala*) that appeared after the rains, one could buy dried in the market and use for soup. I think I often surprised African women on the slopes of the Kitante valley when I turned up in the early morning to compete for the new growths. One seasonal delicacy for which I never acquired a taste was *nsenene*, a grasshopper that appeared a couple of times a year to swarm around the lamp standards along Kiira Road. People would stand underneath the lamps shaking blankets onto which the insects fell. They were collected in paper bags, sometimes eaten raw but often fried. Our children when small enjoyed them.

On arriving in Kampala my social life picked up immediately. The museum stood out in a community with few other cultural dis-tractions and I worked hard to enhance its visibility by organizing temporary exhibitions, giving public lectures and visiting schools. I was invited out and got to know people in official positions; I entertained, occasionally giving supper parties for more than 20 guests. I got to know people from different walks of life – government officials, diplomats, university personnel, missionaries and people in the commercial world. Being a member of both the Uganda Society and the Uganda Club brought me into contact with many Asians and Africans. At no other time in my life was I so involved. The innumerable drinks parties we attended at which guests stood around in suits for several hours drinking and eating savoury canapés, groundnuts and potato chips provided an easy way of meeting people. Most white people working in Uganda were relatively young; district commissioners were invariably in their thirties and there were very few men or women over 55, for by that age they had normally gone back to England to start new careers. Though one saw many very young white children being looked after by their *ayahs* (nursemaids) wearing starched pink and blue dresses and nurses' caps, there were very few older children, for they were at school in Europe. They came back for the holidays on the so-called lolly-pop express – flights on which government and employers had paid for many of the seats to retain their parents' services.

Though very different from Kenya, Uganda was still very colonial. Virtually all Europeans lived in houses and apartments that their employers provided; junior staff such as clerical personnel and

craftsmen, by contrast, normally had to find their own accommodation on remunerations a twentieth of that paid to their bosses, who
often came from Britain with paper qualifications but little experience.
Until independence in 1962 there were separate Asian and African pay
scales and hostesses could look up the pay scales of the people they
were inviting to their dinner parties. The standard of living was high;
there were car loans, mileage allowances, free medical services, a
separate white hospital and, to all intents and purposes, a white
Anglican church in Nakasero that few Africans attended. The cheap
availability of house servants facilitated a constant round of entertaining. The so-called boy's quarters often consisted of unfurnished
single rooms of 100 square feet or less with tiny windows, no
electricity and, if lucky, a single outside water tap.

Most government officials lived by the lake in Entebbe, whereas
commercial people lived in Kampala. There was remarkably little
racial mixing, for Entebbe had its own white church, social club with
amateur theatricals, golf course and tight social circles. Many
government officials were well informed about local culture and
would receive promotion and extra pay for learning the local
languages. Many were excellent scholars who contributed greatly to
the Uganda Society and wrote for the *Uganda Journal*, albeit with a
hint of benevolent paternalism. Intimate relationships with Africans
were rare, though many government officers took pains to help
Ugandans learn and acquire English ways. Needless to say, Africans
who conformed were more acceptable than those who aggressively
asserted their own culture.

There was a lot of criticism, much of it valid, of Asian exclusivity,
but many Europeans failed to realize that the African population
found British exclusivity just as condescending. Once the countdown
to independence had begun in the early 1960s, however, the British
presence could be discounted, but the Asians, who had been born,
bred, traded and built their homes in Uganda were a different matter.
Many Africans wanted to live like Europeans; they admired their style,
wealth and education, but the Ugandan educational system had not
exposed them to Asia's rich culture, multiple communities and varied
religious practices. This ignorance made them suspicious of Asians,
resentful of their material success and position between them and the
ephemeral white Ugandans. In many ways, the Asians became the
scapegoats for the abuses of the colonial system and paid a heavy price
in their 1972 expulsion. Incidentally, contrary to popular assump-

tions, their expulsion was neither inexplicable nor the sudden irrational whim of a mad dictator.

I became aware of the cultural importance of Buganda fairly early on in my time in Kampala, for the museum's core collection consisted of 'fetishes' taken from chiefs in the early part of the century; because they were used in warfare, their confiscation was seen as a conciliatory nation-building gesture. The fetishes had originally been housed in a small building with an imposing porticoed entrance in the centre of Lugard's fort in Old Kampala. Old Kampala was adjacent to Mengo, the seat of power of the Kabaka, the traditional ruler of the Baganda. Mengo and Kampala were centres of political activity and many Baganda wanted to assert their rights in advance of independence, which everyone knew was not far away. A brick wall enclosing an area of nearly three-quarters of a mile in diameter surrounded the royal compound (*lubiri*) in which the Kabaka lived and where his palace and the offices of many of his traditional advisers and musicians were located. Past a quarter-mile-long manmade lake on the western side of the *lubiri* was another hill, where the *lukiiko* (Buganda parliament) met at the *Bulange*. The *Bulange* also housed Buganda government ministries. Many of the Kabaka's traditional chiefs and retainers lived in large old houses along a broad road between the palace and parliament – *Kabaka njagala* (the Kabaka wants me). In the garden of one house there were giant tortoises, on which children could literally ride, brought back in the late 1920s from the Seychelles where Kabaka Mwanga and many of his advisers had been exiled after the Sudanese rebellion of 1897.[3]

Since the Buganda government gave the museum an annual subvention of £1000, I needed to maintain good relations, but I was also interested in the traditions of the kingdom and sometimes went to the *lubiri* to listen to the drum ensembles. All the attendants at the Uganda Museum were musicians and I wanted further recruitment to come from the ranks of the court musicians, for Buganda had the most evolved and intricate musical tradition in eastern Africa. Eunice and I once attended a ceremony at which dancers, with hips enhanced by many cloths and gyrating from the waist down, rapidly swept across the floor before prostrating themselves in front of the Kabaka. It was very exciting and I regret that, as the only foreigner there, I felt too inhibited to take photographs. Little did I know that the rich traditions I observed would be swept away in a few years.

As curator I also visited the traditional rulers of the two other principal hereditary kingdoms, Bunyoro and Ankole. I had an entrée to the Bunyoro court through one of my students at a University of Nottingham extra mural class in Derbyshire being a close friend of Ibrahim Mugenyi, the son of the Omukama. The Omukama was a good historian and, under the pseudonym KW, was the first African to contribute articles to the *Uganda Journal* in the 1930s. Like many older Ugandans, he served exceedingly good tea in his garden, which made for a relaxed experience. He invited us to visit his royal potters. Their black ware with a graphite 'slip' and highly polished with many of the forms based on wooden and calabash vessels was exquisite. The latter had thin, elongated necks. The best pots had delicate incised decoration. Sadly, in 1960 only two old men still made pottery for the court. One of their secrets was in the preparation of the graphite they brought from exposures near Kibiro on Lake Albert. We bought what we could for the museum, but the two pieces I bought for myself were unfortunately broken before I ever left Africa. I now content myself with marvelling at the wonderful pots the missionary John Roscoe donated to the Haddon Museum in Cambridge in the early twentieth century.

A saving grace for a Jew like me was that the Baganda ate neither pork nor shellfish; all their butchers were Muslims. The staple diet was *matoke,* steamed green bananas, and the average Muganda man could eat as much as 7 lbs of it a day. The bananas were skinned, steamed in their leaves and served in shallow basketry platters. The steaming could take as long as three hours, with the golden yellow mass kneaded from time to time during the process. One ate *matoke* with one's fingers after dipping it into different delicate stews, my favourites being made from mushrooms and sesame seeds. *Matoke* is an acquired taste and it took me ages before I could eat much of it; the same applied to *fufu* in West Africa, which is made from pounded yam, plantain or cocoyam. Other new foods included sweet potatoes, fried or roasted plantains, beans of various kinds and soups or stews made from groundnuts. If one asked people in either Uganda or Ghana what they had eaten, they invariably mentioned the carbohydrate rather than the protein component of the meal. The centrality of carbohydrates was brought home to me at my first reception at a Gombolola[3] chief's home. We were served pieces of roast beef, goat and chicken as well as roasted groundnuts and fried plantains, all of which I enjoyed, but many guests kept asking when the real food, meaning the *matoke,* would arrive. When I first went to Uganda many older women did not eat chicken, lamb or eggs, but the practice was rapidly changing as younger women began to realize that it was a ruse to keep the tastiest foods for men rather than a sanctified tradition with a justifiable rationale. Baganda were not great on desserts and, though they served fresh fruit, foreign guests were often the best customers for the rare sweet treats.

Though I had been interested in politics in Kenya, I did not know any politicians and was purely an observer from afar. In Uganda, however, I had direct contacts with many of the players. The period between 1958 and 1967 was one of intense change – colonial control giving way to self-rule in 1961, independence in 1962, the declaration of a republic in 1963, culminating in a clash of ideologies and violent coup in 1966. As a committee member at the Uganda Club, curator of the Uganda Museum, husband of one of Uganda's most important African women, and later director of the African Studies Programme at Makerere, I had opportunities to meet all the leading players. Eunice was a close friend of the Kabaka's companion Lady Sarah, who was the mother of his sons and sister of his official wife. The Kabaka became the first president of Uganda in 1963. Yusuf Lule, briefly the fourth president in 1979, had taught Eunice and she in turn had taught Miria, the wife of Milton Obote, prime minister at independence and second president from 1966. Yusuf Lule was the deputy minister in charge of the Uganda Museum before independence and later became the principal of Makerere College and again my boss. Some ministers had been at Budo or Makerere with Eunice. Several permanent secretaries or under secretaries played tennis at the Lugogo Sports Club and after a game we often gossiped over a drink. It was a surprisingly tightly-knit social world and we were part of the nexus. As embassies opened we were frequently invited to receptions where we met many of the same people.

A lively interest in politics, hidden agendas and visible apprehension characterized the last days of colonial rule, particularly among the Baganda who were afraid of losing their economic power, social standing and the integrity of their kingdom. Baganda missionaries, teachers and administrators had spread Christianity, education and hierarchical attitudes to other parts of Uganda in the early twentieth century. Buganda was the most Christian part of Uganda, which in turn was the most Christian country in tropical Africa. Baganda were enterprising professional people; they farmed cotton and coffee, which had brought them wealth and allowed some of them to travel. A few had gone to colleges in South Africa and India and by the 1950s there was a nucleus of Baganda professionals who had been trained in Britain. There were high-ranking Baganda clergymen, deans, canons and even bishops. The Baganda looked down on their more neglected northern neighbours whose food, dress sense and even cleanliness they sometimes disparaged. Baganda nationalists boycotted the Legislative Council before independence in the late 1950s to avoid a unitary as opposed to a federal solution.

The formation of the Kabaka Yekka (Kabaka only) party on the eve of independence split the Baganda vote between it and the Democratic Party led by Benedicto Kiwanuka. Many Baganda supported KY because they could not accept a Muganda politician having more authority than the Kabaka. Being federal, the Democratic Party had members from all the other regions, as well as experienced and well-educated politicians, but many voters were frightened because some of its most prominent leaders were Roman Catholics. Milton Obote, who formed an electoral pact with KY to defeat the Democratic Party, led the Uganda People's Congress (UPC), the other national party with support mainly in the north and east of Uganda. Like all politicians, he made believable promises and won over many Baganda voters, particularly those who wanted to see a progressive state emerge. In return for KY support, he intimated that he would propose and support the unopposed candidacy of the Kabaka to be the president of Uganda once a republic came into being after one year. The UPC became the dominant party and, within a short time, the power of patronage had led many KY MPs to cross over to the government benches and be rewarded with ministerial positions, committee chairmanships, as well as overseas trips for key supporters and scholarships for their children. It was thus obvious fairly early on that personal gain rather than principle would be the guiding element in the political game.

Independence was a time of great excitement. However, unlike many other African colonies, the manoeuvring between the Baganda and the British government probably delayed the day of independence. Tanganyika was weaker than Uganda in terms of education, economic development and trained personnel, but it had a strong political party, a charismatic leader with a strong political ideology in Julius Nyerere, and very little ethnic diversity. In Uganda there was a balance between Bantu speaking and non-Bantu speaking people, in fact Uganda's population was comprised of 26 different ethnic groups, or tribes as the colonists called them. There were divisions among the

Bantu-speaking people and between people with hereditary kingdoms like Buganda, Ankole, Bunyoro and Toro and areas without organized states like Busoga to the east of Buganda.

Nevertheless, most Ugandans prepared for independence with hope, optimism and unrealistic aspirations. Many believed that independence would mean not just running Uganda but also taking over all the rulers' appurtenances. Everyone wanted to see a massive expansion in social services, particularly schools and hospitals, improved roads and a cultural renaissance with a national theatre, national dance group and full representation at African and international organizations like the UN. Unfortunately, there were not enough resources for everyone to 'fall into things', to use a local expression, with new government officers obtaining the same standard of housing, health care and car loans that the departing colonial officers had enjoyed. Initially, services expanded and Africanization carried on apace, but over the years the export economy weakened; Uganda had to compete with other countries for investment capital; and tourism was slow to expand. Civil war in neighbouring Congo and instability in other African countries made the outside world wary of economic involvement. But this was still in the future. In 1962 everyone was excited. There was a new flag, an anthem to be sung, streets full of red, black and gold decorations, and reed arches appearing overnight over the roads leading to Kampala.

We attended the ceremony and saw the Union Jack lowered, the new flag raised, cannons fired, fireworks explode and the Duke of Kent, with Britain's blessing, usher in independence. Amid dancers from all over Uganda and the usual military tattoos, everyone felt a great deal of emotion – it was a ceremony one remembered for life. The following day we attended the garden party at State House and at the Uganda Museum the prime minister opened our new science museum. I sat next to Professor Mel Herskovits without realizing he was the doyen of American Africanists. No one was expressing doubts; all assumed that a new era of great prosperity was opening up. Ugandans were flattered by the new attention they received, with foreign embassies opening daily and scholarships being offered in a bid to buy favours. They felt proud of their talented athletes who were to gain Olympic medals, of playwrights like Okot p'Bitek and of their dedicated civil servants. It looked as if nothing could go wrong, but the blooms quickly faded. The honeymoon lasted about a year before the unravelling was noticeable.

Central to the unravelling was Prime Minister Milton Obote, a remarkably shrewd politician but an unattractive and personally unpopular individual. I met him several times and he never appeared relaxed. He clutched his cane tightly, rarely smiled and it was difficult to engage him in conversation even in relatively informal circumstances. He played his political cards in a similarly secretive fashion. He outfoxed the Kabaka who was hoping to reclaim the 'lost' county[4] of Mubende for Buganda before a referendum took place in 1965. Obote exaggerated the importance of the issue and used his control of the media to turn most Ugandans against the Baganda. He twisted the legal residency requirements to bar recent Baganda colonists in Mubende from taking part in the referendum and continued to use the government's patronage to ensure that support for the UPC led to rewards for those Baganda who supported his policies. Patronage was expensive. New boards were formed to control all manner of activities. Members of boards required fees and perquisites that Uganda could ill afford. Government was swallowing too much of Uganda's limited wealth.

After an abortive army coup in 1964 Obote rewarded the loyal army personnel by doubling their pay, ejecting all white officers and advisers and making the officer corps loyal to him personally rather than to the Kabaka, who had briefly served in the British army. Army officers like Idi Amin and Shaban Opolot[5] had too little moral fibre, education or leadership experience to play the parts expected of them, and the army became ill disciplined and unreliable. Obote nibbled away at Baganda influence and the prestige and duties of the president after the Kabaka lost the referendum over Mubende. In 1966 the army became embroiled in the Congo civil war, and many officers and government officials profited from seizing and smuggling Congolese coffee, gold and ivory. The situation developed into a scandal and, through the oratory of Daudi Ocheng, one of the few really independent minded and principled MPs and the KY's only member drawn from northern Uganda, a majority of the parliament, including all but one of the ministers, voted for government censure and an official inquiry. Obote, in a weak situation, struck first and decisively dissolved both the parliament and the constitution, arresting five ministers. Ocheng, a close personal friend of the Kabaka, died within weeks.[6]

Obote, perhaps sensing his vulnerability to an army coup, ordered the newly promoted commander of the army Colonel Idi Amin to storm the *lubiri* and, following a brief but unequal battle, the Kabaka fled to exile in London. Many Baganda, including several of Eunice's close friends, were killed in the palace; sacred regalia and countless musical instruments were destroyed; it was as if the cultural heart of Buganda had been ripped out. There followed two months of close control by an undisciplined army. Curfews were imposed from 7.00 p.m. and later from 10.00 p.m., which was nerve wracking, for one needed to avoid any contact with the soldiers and I was always frightened that I would blow a tyre or stall the car in trying to get back home in time. In early 1967 the Kabaka published his account,[7] which a British Sunday newspaper serialized. It became an offence to import the newspaper into Uganda and when Eunice's brother Lukonge unwittingly received a copy, he was arrested. We did not know where he was being held, but Eunice used her contacts to find out and, with great bravery, confronted different police officers and managed to have him freed from three gruelling weeks spent in terrible conditions without access to counsel and lying on bare concrete with virtually no food. It was the tension of the year 1966–67 that led Eunice to agree to our move to Ghana in 1967.

Eventually, in 1966, Obote used his power of patronage to convert the UPC government into a one-party state and together they oversaw the most corrupt era in Uganda life. Chairmen of government boards and directors of departments demanded and received kickbacks, with gifts from foreign contractors comprising holidays for officials and their families, expensive household appliances and money for the personnel providing the licences. With a downturn in the economy Obote became unpopular and his regime more repressive, particularly after an attempted assassination. In 1970 he tried to regain popularity with the *Common Man's Charter*, but since it confined benefits to those who had 'fallen into things' and denied them to new graduates who were about to enter the economy, it deceived no one. I was at Makerere in 1970 and the students' anger was very evident, so it came as no surprise when, in an exceedingly popular coup, Obote was overthrown by Amin in 1971.

In 1962 we built our own house on Makindye, a hill about two miles south of the town centre and just over three miles from Makerere College. It was thrilling to see a big signpost proclaiming 'house being built for Dr Merrick Posnansky'. It was on a sloping one-acre plot of land with a good view of Lake Victoria from our veranda, where we would sit watching afternoon storms build up, come over the city, and quickly drop their rain before the sky reverted to its wonderful blue. Among our neighbours, who were mostly Europeans at that time, were Colonel Bombo Trimmer, the director of the Uganda National Parks who, with his wife were keen bird watchers and opened our eyes to the rich avian fauna; the number two at the United States Information Service; Barbara Saben, an outspoken former mayor of Kampala and a feminist before the term was known in Uganda; the Indian owner of the Uganda Pharmacy; and one of Apollo Kagwa's sons[8] who had a European wife. Sadly, when he died the Kagwa family prevented her from inheriting the house and literally drove her from Uganda. Because it was normal in those days to go visiting in the early evening before it got dark, or on a Sunday morning, we got to know very well our neighbours and thus a cross section of Uganda's elite.

The Gombolola chief's home and office faced the end of our lane and at a church nearby women in the Mother's Union would sit on woven mats making endless coasters, gauze covers weighted with beads for jugs, or coiled baskets. The Gombolola compound included a small, though rather insecure, prison where people who failed to pay their poll taxes, had too much to drink, or fought with their neighbours served short sentences. We arranged with the clerk to loan us six prisoners to terrace our garden for 1/– a day. We made three terraces out of our slope, covered the flat surfaces with soil and planted grass root plug by root plug. The prisoners enjoyed being out, our small daughter Sheba loved them, and they her, and we were all sorry when the job was completed. Everything grew so quickly. I remember a colourful mass of canna lilies, sweet smelling frangipani, many hues of bougainvillea and hibiscus, as well as red leaved poinsettia, which in America are small pot plants grown for the Christmas season but were trees in East Africa. Our hedge was planted from cuttings that took root, some of impenetrable Christ's thorn and others of a form of cedar.

When we built our house we expected to live most of our lives in Uganda, so designed it bearing in mind that we may not always have servants. Our friend Kees Welter designed us an ingeneous burglar alarm, which involved a circuit around the house set into the plaster with a wire running through the insect screens of the windows so that if a window or door were opened the alarm would sound. When our Morris Minor was stolen from our driveway the dog barked, but I assumed it was because he sought attention so did not heed his warning, but the police caught some men a few hours later carrying

our radiator and sundry parts to Kampala to sell. We then bought an
unstealable car in the form of a 1954 Citroën and built a garage.

We had a glorious garden. We maintained an immaculate grassed
middle terrace on which we played croquet and organized some
wonderful children's parties. We grew different fruits, including
passion fruit and some vigorous pink ginger lilies that flourished at
the tail end of the kitchen sink down spout. Along one edge of the
garden we grew maize year round, four harvests, on a thin strip of
land fertilized with tobacco sweepings we collected monthly from the
tobacco factory from which we made our own compost. Only one
other faculty member at Makerere lived in his own home. We felt very
settled there. When the BBC interviewed us on our terrace at the time
of Uganda's independence, we spoke of our resolve to stay in the
country and to work for its future. We were so full of hope and I was
one of the few Britons who had been accorded permanent Ugandan
residence, the last step before citizenship. It was not to be. We kept
the house until 1988. Eunice hated parting with it, but it had caused
us a lot of worry during the difficult years in Uganda from 1972 to
1986 when tenants were unreliable and the water and power supplies
on Makindye were intermittent.

Chapter 9

Africa: Ghana

WE WENT OUT TO Ghana the old-fashioned way by Elder Dempster steamer, the *Aureol*, an experience we shall never forget. Leaving Uganda had been traumatic. First we gave up our home on Makindye in July to stay the last two months in a Makerere apartment. This meant packing up, selling many items, shipping some things to Ghana, trying to sell our car, which we failed to do so had to ship it at the last moment. We also went through the personal tragedy of losing our expected child at the last minute when its cord came out first and the baby literally cut off its own blood supply. We were devastated, especially since Eunice had wanted a caesarean but the doctor who had had a bad experience with his wife was set against it. Eunice was in shock, extremely depressed and yet leaving everything with which she had been familiar. We spent the night before our departure from England at the old Adelphi hotel in Liverpool.[1] It was great to experience the luxury of an old time railway hotel and the grandeur that was fast leaving Liverpool.

When we got on board we immediately began to experience the transition to West Africa. Other members of the University of Ghana were going back, as well as Nigerians and nattily dressed Sierra Leoneans. It was sheer luxury and a wonderful holiday. Slowly the temperature rose, so we avoided the abrupt shock that arrival by air entails. The food was good, there were playrooms and groups for the girls and we had a lot of time to get over our travails. We stopped *en route* in the Canary Islands, Freetown and Monrovia. President Tubman of Liberia was on board from Monrovia, a stately old man with whom we occasionally spoke. When we arrived in Accra, where he was paying a state visit, the army band welcomed him. It was a wonderful way to travel and enabled us to bring quite a lot of gear.

We were fortunate to work in Africa when we did because we had the opportunity to travel by ship. In the 1960s liners still served both the East African and West African coasts. I had travelled to Kenya by boat in 1960 and Eunice and the girls in 1966. In 1973 we travelled back to England in the *Aureol* and when it was taken out of service in 1974 an old era disappeared. It did not cost the university much more to have people come by boat, but for the traveller it meant a two-week paid holiday. The advantage of travelling when we did was that we had the modern convenience of air conditioning, which had been unavailable to pre-Second World War travellers. It also meant that one could ship a car to West Africa for less than $100. Most cabins had no private bathrooms so one had to book a bath; the baths were gloriously long and the water extremely hot, presumably because it came directly from the ship's boilers. One also received an early morning wake-up call with a cup of tea. The passage after the Bay of Biscay was warm and smooth and life on deck interrupted only by morning coffee and afternoon tea with scones and cake, a tradition I still uphold. There were competitions to keep one on one's toes and I was excited to win a general knowledge quiz, one of the few competitions I have ever won, and to receive a box of chocolates as a reward. A glorious ship tradition was that a single piper would play us out to sea as we left the various harbours *en route*.

The humidity in Ghana was a shock. Our beds smelled of mould, our kapok-filled pillows were lumpy and felt damp (we were glad we had brought our own) and cockroaches were everywhere. We were ready to turn around and go back, but our neighbours and members of the department of archaeology treated us with great friendliness. The exterminators came the next day, sprayed the whole house and swept up piles of cockroaches. Once the numerous windows were opened everything was aired and I bought an air conditioner for the study and later another one for our bedroom. Either we got used to the mustiness, or it dissipated when the dry season began in November. We lived at 25 Little Legon. The University of Ghana's campus at Legon was fairly new, mostly dating from after 1961. Before that the university had been at Achimota where many senior members still lived. It was a planned university, somewhat akin to an African Stanford. From a front gate a long double carriageway with bougain-villeas down the middle swept up to Commonwealth Hall and the administration buildings on the hill. Crowning it all was a tower above the Great Hall bearing a black star, the emblem of Ghana. The geology, geography, arts and social sciences departments and three of the five halls of residence were located on either side of the broad sweep. A roundabout beside a lake half way along the road led to the Balme Library, bookshop and banks on one side and the department of economics on the other. A slight curve at the edges of the tiled roofs gave the buildings a rather Japanese feel.

It was a beautiful campus with every amenity. There was a post office, telephone exchange, botanical garden, Ghana National Trading Corporation shop, guest house, primary school, chapels in each of the halls and wonderful flowering shrubs along the roads. Little Legon, a housing estate on the edge of campus, consisted of attractive bungalows with open gardens. Some houses were built around a courtyard; others were linear with the living/dining area in the centre and the bedrooms, kitchen and study on the outsides; a small courtyard behind the garage led to rooms for two house staff. All windows had outer wooden shutters, screens and glass sections. All the woodwork was made of *odum*, an insect resistant hardwood that was creosoted to resist the elements. Our floors were easy to clean terrazzo tiles. We felt very privileged. The grounds contained a cinnamon and an almond tree and the previous occupants had planted grapefruit, soursap (*guanabano*), tangerines and papaya, which we greatly appreciated. A stand of bamboo that creaked and groaned in the wind divided us from next door. Eunice, in her usual indefatigable way, created a lawn by searching for grass and planting it tuft by tuft. It provided a wonderful play area for the children. Leading from the living room was a semicircular paved area where we often sat in the evenings. With fairy lights strung above, it made a magnificent venue for Christmas parties and Seder nights.

The happiest years of our lives were spent in Ghana among the most open, welcoming and hospitable people I have ever met. We used to drive to town in the evenings and were amazed to see that even small bars had live music. Around 1970, however, when the economy began to decline, most of the musicians moved to other African countries and Europe. Large dance halls like the Lido, Tip Top and Star Hotel also closed and, in 1974, when beer became scarce, even the little bars began to decline as social centres. But in 1967 all that was in the future. We were impressed by the large department stores, especially Kingsway with its escalator, which was unknown in Uganda. At Christmas the top floor of Kingsway would be given over to Father Christmas, toys and a railway train to carry little children to see Santa. The only child of some friends of ours who spent a Christmas in England complained that he had not seen the real Santa because the one in England was white. At Christmas virtually every-thing shut down from around 22 December until about 2 or 3 January and the same is happening in many other parts of Africa. Christian religious festivals are better observed in Africa than in America where everything is over-commercialized. We always had a special dinner on Christmas Eve to which we invited strangers passing through the campus, foreign students and lonely bachelors. We employed one of the halls of residence cooks to help and those evenings held a special magic for us all.

Nkrumah embarked on projects that impressed us but bankrupted the state. Many were extremely useful like the concrete motorway from the port of Tema to Accra, the new airport that opened just after we arrived, Black Star Square where we watched the independence celebrations, the conference centre where the Organization of African Unity held its meeting in 1965, and the two large hotels that were bigger than any we had in Uganda. When we arrived there was an abundance of locally-produced foods – corned beef, pineapple jam, Golden Tree chocolate, tomato ketchup, baked beans, biscuits and various bottled gins and schnapps. East European contractors built many of the small factories and processing plants, but they were blamed for bringing in machinery for processing beets when Ghana depended on sugar cane or for building a single ketchup factory in the north of Ghana that could produce more ketchup and tomato paste than Ghana could ever use and had no reasonable transport outlets to distribute their products at a reasonable cost.

One problem was that when Nkrumah demonstrated his independence from the UK and United States and became an integral part of the Non-Aligned Movement, the Western powers began to shun Ghana's industrial hopes.[2] Also, by 1970 Ghanaians had lost their appetite for shoddily-packaged locally-produced foodstuffs and many of the factories became dilapidated and rundown. There was a lot of questioning about corruption during the Nkrumah years and commissions of inquiry were set up to look into past abuses. I served on one looking into the government's Volta Basin Research Project, which was far less efficient than our own at Legon. Serving on a commission was a pleasant chore; I was paid a daily allowance, was treated royally in the hotel at Akosombo and got to know many influential Ghanaians.

One survival of the colonial period was the rural rest house and in district capitals like Kumasi, Cape Coast, Sunyani and Bolgatanga, they provided food as well as accommodation. Bed and breakfast cost ¢3.30 a day, that is less than $3.[3] It was always a pleasure to come in from a dusty, sticky road trip to a proper afternoon tea. Smaller towns often had rest houses with furnished rooms for up to three or four travellers with a bathroom and kitchen costing as little as 50 pesewas (40 US cents) a night. Most rest house keepers were willing to make meals, run errands or do whatever they could to make one's stay pleasant. I often used to spend two or three nights at a rest house I could reach within an hour – at places like Aburi, Mampong, Kibi and Nsawam – where on a glorious wide veranda I could write without interference, prepare lectures and read. On the way home I would buy country produce such as yams, pineapples, oranges and plantains by the roadside at prices that more than offset the cost of the rest house. The rest houses were built at a time when district officers toured their smaller centres, and they also provided comfortable accommodation for circuit judges and inspectors of education. With independence many of these officers were moved to district headquarters and, as cars became available to more and more civil servants, the need for rest houses declined. By the end of the century they were virtually a forgotten amenity.

Travel in Ghana or anywhere in Africa was always memorable. The special names attached to even small journeys like going on 'safari' in East Africa or on 'trek' in West Africa were a reminder of different days. Roads deteriorated fast because few had the necessary number of culverts, a sufficient thickness of rock, gravel or other filling above the subsoil and the bituminized sealer was often thin. Good roads had a camber and, if well built, in the cities there was a concrete sill along the edges, but between the towns there was only a thin tarmac covering. As soon as it rained the soil beneath would soften, so potholes would develop, expand and break through all the topping. A good road seldom lasted in a perfect state for more than a year and the road from Accra to Kumasi was always in need of repair. Nkrumah's idea of a golden triangle with concrete motorways running from Kumasi to the ports of Takoradi and Tema and a coastal road through Accra joining them together made good sense, but it was expensive and alas was never completed. A lot of traffic on the roads carried heavy loads, which would break the edges of the bituminized cover. Some were timber trucks carrying two or three huge logs attached to the vehicles by chains; others were lorries overloaded with bags of charcoal topped with bunches of plantains. Gasoline-filled tankers were always travelling north from the ports.

When we arrived there were still *tro-tros*,[4] British Bedford trucks with wooden planked seats built in the back. There were no backs to the seats so passengers were crammed in five or six to a row on seven or eight rows. Everyone swayed with the motion of the truck. It was hot and fetid in the centre. One advantage of age is that older people are given the slightly better seats. On return trips to Africa I notice that my age counts in my favour; I am now assigned the front seat next to the driver in the mini buses that have replaced the *tro tros*. A mound of luggage would sit atop the trucks, including large yellow, blue and red plastic water containers; foodstuffs; an occasional hapless goat; chickens in bundles; mattresses and numerous sacks and holdalls. Occasionally one saw a whole 60–70-foot dugout being brought down from the forest.

Everyone drove too fast and cars did not last long. I replaced large numbers of engine mounts, exhaust pipes, brackets and items I never even think about in the United States. When we first arrived police still manned barriers outside towns on the pretext of controlling the transport of commodities on which duties were owed, but most Ghanaians believed they were to extract bribes from passing lorry drivers. Small markets along the side of the road sold local and seasonal products like plantains, pineapples and other fresh foods. North of Kumasi one could get mushrooms and giant forest snails in the rainy season and along the coastal road near Cape Coast there were always packets of *kenke* (steamed fermented corn mush) wrapped in corn leaves. Some places sold baskets, pestles and mortars and in one case the wooden stops (chocks) used to prevent trucks with faulty breaks from rolling away.

Road transport was, and still is, relatively inexpensive with fares normally lower than the equivalent of ten American cents a mile. In the 1980s enterprising Ghanaians began importing second-hand buses from Europe with air conditioning and aeroplane type seats. Though there were rules on how many passengers they could carry, one still found Japanese mini buses designed for 12 carrying 18 or more people and with gravity-defying luggage on the roof. Though the modes of transportation changed over the years the messages on them did not. Some slogans were simple like 'God's Gift' or 'Fear Woman', but humorous pithy proverbs in the vernacular often appeared on both the fronts and backs of vehicles. Because so many roads were earthen or laterite,[5] so dried rapidly, one always seemed to be travelling in clouds of reddish beige dust. A lot of accidents occurred because drivers attempted to overtake without seeing vehicles approaching that were shrouded in dust. If one kept the windows closed one became too hot so most travellers arrived with red dust on their faces and clothes. Being constantly hot meant that the dust stuck to one's perspiration.

City transport changed a lot. At one time there were *tro-tro*s and taxis with yellow-painted wings to demarcate them; then came buses and finally motorcycles. The municipal and government buses did not last long; there were too few of them and they were over-loaded and under-supervised. Taxis multiplied and became a standard mode of transport with distinctions made between those on set routes that picked up passengers and those chartered for specific journeys that were much more expensive. When I first arrived in Accra, taxis had limited access to the university, but by the late 1990s they were cruising all over its roads. There was an evident need for them since the buses the university once owned to bring its workers to and from the campus had fallen into decay. I always wondered how anyone made a profit from taxis, but they did by putting in very long hours. The taxi owner, often someone in a middle-class office job or even a university teacher, would lend the taxi to a driver with a proviso that he bring in a set amount of money each week. To make that amount the taxi had to be run virtually into the ground with mileages of up to 60,000 a year not unusual. The driver was responsible for all expenses. With oil prices rising it was not surprising that in Ghana, as in other African countries, the increase in the pump price of petrol usually led to demonstrations.

Perhaps the price of fuel played a part in the growth of motorcycle taxis in the 1990s. With engines often less than 100cc, without crash helmets for pillion passengers and little safety training, motorcycle taxis have become a feature of African urban life. Their evident advantage is that they are cheap and can be chartered to take you where you are going; they are also fast and can zigzag around traffic jams, but they have raised pollution levels in African cities and have killed or maimed countless people.

The postal service to Ghana was faster than in East Africa. I subscribed to the Sunday *Observer* and *Manchester Guardian Weekly* and both arrived by air from England within about two days; it was not uncommon to receive letters from England in three days (and they had been through the Accra and Legon post offices). There were problems with incoming packages, for there was a certain amount of theft. When Helen was born in January 1970 several friends sent us

presents from England and none of them arrived. We only found out
about the loss when we went on leave in 1971 and someone asked
how we had liked the dress she had sent. Telephone calls were good
internally until the mid-1970s. The university had its own exchange,
set up with equipment bought from a Lancashire town in the late-
1950s, but overseas calls were impossible. One had to go downtown to
book them and then return up to 24 hours later in the hope that one's
three-minute call would be on time, but there was no guarantee and
people often waited for hours to make or receive calls on a very open
line.[6]

The radio was our chief means of obtaining news and every evening
at 5.00 p.m. we listened to the BBC while we had our afternoon tea. At
lunch, and often in the morning, we listened to Radio Ghana, heralded
by the playing of *Atumpan* drums, sometimes referred to as talking
drums. We did not have TV until 1970 and only acquired it then to
stop our children roaming around and staying too long at the houses
of neighbours who had it. There was only black and white trans-
mission and the single programme began with vernacular news or a
public announcement at around 5.30 p.m. and ended at 9.30 p.m.
with a prayer. Last thing in the evening there was normally a drama or
situation comedy from abroad and we particularly enjoyed *Bonanza*,
Mission Impossible and several British mystery series. We took the
Ghana Graphic to keep up with local news and find out what was on at
the cinema. Until the foreign exchange ran out there were good films
in Ghana. We saw all the latest James Bond ones, but by the time we
left much of the fare was recycled Kung Fu and Godzilla. The cinemas
were all open to the sky, so one avoided them when it rained. There
was a good film club at the university for a time and we watched more
live stage performances than we did in the United States. Twice a year
Mrs Dawn Quist put on a ballet in which her pupils performed; since
our two older daughters were in them, we had a personal interest. On
the whole, life in Ghana was good even though the economy was
going downhill and we spent a lot of time towards the end hunting
and gathering, as some called it, picking up milk in one place, meat in
another and trawling the stores for occasional delicacies like baked
beans, steak and kidney pie, or poor eastern European wine.

In Ghana politics concerned us less than in Uganda. We knew few
politicians, though for a short time in 1969 and 1970 when there was
a Uganda embassy and we knew the ambassador, Brigadier Opolot, we
attended functions that brought us into contact with Ghanaian

functionaries and a few diplomats. In 1969 I had a chance to vote when the university was given representation in the constitutional assembly to draw up the new constitution and make way for a return to civilian rule. Everyone was excited. I voted for a neighbour with whom we shared a school car pool. He eventually won a seat in the new parliament and changed in character practically overnight – driving a Mercedes, dressing in fine suits, putting on weight and evidently sharing in the spoils of Busia's 1969 victory.

Everyone had high hopes for Busia's government. Busia, who had been the first Ghanaian professor at Legon, had been in exile and afflicted by Nkrumah's regime, but individuals in his government were quickly seen to be on the make and there seemed to be no controls on open corruption. On the occasion of a visit by the Council for Cultural Freedom in January 1970, which was sponsoring the East African magazine *Transition* in Ghana, I was invited to a state dinner at Christiansborg Castle. Eunice was terribly disappointed not to go, but was in hospital delivering our youngest daughter. I was appalled by the ostentation of the event, by the white-gloved servants, elaborate dinner with imported pears, exotic foods and numerous wines. I think it unlikely that the recipients were left thinking of Ghana as a country in need of aid for its culture.

In 1971, in a bid for popularity, Busia ordered all unregistered foreigners to leave Ghana under the Alien Compliance Order. This mainly affected small Lebanese traders, farm labour from Upper Volta and numerous Nigerian traders, pedlars and small artisans. It was sad to see their overladen lorries, pickups and cars trying to get out of Ghana before the deadline. Ghana needed those workers and its national reputation suffered a setback. Commodities became scarcer and the precedent was set to allow Nigeria to expel foreign workers, many of whom were Ghanaians, in 1983. Later in the year there was a showdown with state employees, particularly from the Ghana National Trading Corporation, trying unsuccessfully to sue the government for the loss of their jobs and for breaking legal contracts. The courts lost out to government power and the rule of law suffered a blow from which it has not yet fully recovered.

The nadir of government prestige, in my opinion, came on New Year's Eve 1971 when a state dinner was televised. Viewers saw army chiefs in ceremonial uniform and ministers in black tie listening to Busia call for belt tightening when, from the dinner table and array of bottles on it, it was clear that they were belt loosening. A devaluation of the cedi was later announced, which made foreign imports more expensive and caused a run on the stores. The coup of 13 January was, however, unexpected. There was little love left for Busia but the coup by a then unknown Colonel Acheampong was unnecessary. In a speech on TV announcing his takeover many people remember his shaking knees rather than the import of his words. A humorous article by historian Adu Boahen in the *Legon Observer* poked fun at the National Redemption Council, which to him sounded a bit like the National Cash Register, which at that time sold most of the cash registers in the country. The economic changes Busia implemented were largely the ones the IMF and World Bank had suggested as essential prerequisites for Ghana to receive a World Bank loan. A military dictatorship imposed the reforms a decade later. Had they been adopted in 1972 the troubled economic years, political crises and executions of the 1970s might have been avoided.

While the term military coup suggests violence, that was not the case. There was a small skirmish near the barracks but no breakdown of services or curfews. In fact, Eunice and I crossed town that night to have dinner with friends at Mulago Hospital. On another occasion, when there was a barrier on the large Tetteh-Quashie roundabout between Legon and the airport, a soldier stopped us and poked his gun into the car. Eunice was frightened and the soldier said smiling, 'Do not worry madam, my gun has no bullets.'

The military governments of the 1970s tried to impose a controlled economy that hardly matched the economic freewheeling style of Ghana and its market women. Strict import restrictions were introduced, foreign exchange regulations tightened and an attempt made to freeze prices and wages. Recognizing that price controls would push goods onto the black market, sanctions were brought to bear against hoarders, a measure that particularly hurt the market women. In the belief that some commodities were more essential to the majority of the population than others, shops received stocks of essential commodities to be sold at fixed prices, which the government set. Among these essential commodities were evaporated milk, sugar, flour, margarine, cooking oil, tinned fish, soap, soap powder and batteries. Unfortunately, shopkeepers gave more items to some customers than others, sold some things from the back door, sold and resold others at inflated prices and hoarded some to attract a higher price when the commodities became scarcer.

If this were not bad enough, the height of the essential commodities programme coincided with high oil prices after the Middle East war and rise of OPEC oil prices in 1973. With petrol rationed, queues of cars lined up at petrol stations, often for days for as little as three or four gallons and unscrupulous traders gouged customers with inflated prices. Many people found it difficult to disentangle the internal from the external factors. All they saw was that the good old days of the 1960s were gone, institutions like the university and schools were declining, expatriate teachers and traders were leaving, jobs for the young were getting more difficult to find, imports were frozen and motorcars were rapidly falling to bits for lack of spares. Even everyday commodities like paint, cement and building materials were in short supply. Ghana was becoming shabby. Though nobody wanted to admit it, everyone, expatriates and Ghanaians alike, were resorting to underhand practices.

There was little work ethic because working hard did not bring rewards, but efforts were made to increase food production with campaigns such as 'Operation Feed Yourself' to expand rice cultivation in the north and 'Food for the Millions' to encourage rabbit production. The second project failed because Ghanaians were not used to eating rabbits, knew little about using their skins and never went into it on a large scale. The rice cultivation depended on using huge imported combine harvesters that required large fields and enough technical know-how to maintain the machines. Many of the farms went to officers in the army, thus alienating peasants and chiefs from their land.

I got to know several military officers; in fact two regional commissioners came to Hani to open our research centre and later the library. They were well-intentioned but out of touch with rural communities. The new economy placed too much reliance on keeping the urban masses happy. Meanwhile, the prices of foodstuffs were declining in relation to other expenses; rural communities were finding it more difficult to obtain essential commodities and ended up paying higher prices. Because of import controls, items like hoes, cutlasses, cement, batteries and metal sheeting increased rapidly in price. The shortage of spare parts for lorries made transport more tenuous and expensive upcountry. Because prices in neighbouring Ivory Coast were not controlled, smuggling over the border increased throughout the late 1970s and 1980s.

While I visited from time to time, I was not in Ghana for the later army coups of 1978 or 1979, for the return to civilian rule in 1979, or for the imposition of military rule under the National Democratic Congress in 1981. Until foreign exchange bureaux were introduced in the mid-1980s, currency restrictions were vexing; visitors could bring in a set daily allowance of foreign currency and buy cedi vouchers, but all money had to be exchanged through banks and they charged commissions. Such complicated rules encouraged non-compliance; people were afraid to bring money in only to see it rapidly devalued as the cedi plunged from 2.5 to several hundred to the dollar within a short time. After a grim period from 1981 to 1984, which, as I mentioned earlier, coincided with the worst droughts on record, the economy began to stabilize with World Bank loans bringing trade liberalization, an end to harsh import controls, easier foreign exchange, and infrastructural improvements to roads, public buildings and social services.

Though Ghana went from the showpiece of West Africa at independence in 1957 to a virtually failed state by the late 1970s it was always a good place in which to live. The crime rate was lower than in other countries and one scarcely ever heard of murders or child abuse. It was possible to walk through Accra unaccosted and there were no gangs of street children. The only problem I sometimes faced was a mild protection racket in which a young man would offer to watch one's car at a busy city car park or at the airport, with the implication being that if you did not employ him something untoward might happen to your car. Though beer became increasingly difficult to obtain and restaurants catering to expatriates closed one by one, a reasonable social life still existed, particular for those with resources. However, many middle-class Ghanaians were being excluded from facilities they had previously enjoyed.

There were still private swimming clubs, like the one the Lebanese favoured at Labadi and the one Europeans frequented at Tesano, which also had eating facilities, and tennis and squash courts. As with the Ghana International School, which maintained high educational standards, the number of Ghanaian participants could only be retained by offering scholarships or fee reductions. The beaches still attracted visitors, with expatriates renting or leasing beach cottages east and west of Accra, but by the late 1970s the old signs of the former colonial era were rapidly disappearing. By the late 1980s there was a concerted move to encourage tourism to Ghana, with the old Labadi pleasure beach reactivated with live music and lifeguards. In the summer months Ghana attracted African-American visitors and several new hotels, including the four-star Labadi Beach Hotel, were built. Relaxed currency controls brought back many Ghanaians whose remittances aided the economy. With the extra tourism and improved telecommunications came new restaurants and fast food outlets. By the 1990s a sense of momentum and optimism was visible in new buildings, crowded roads, amenities like the forest sky walk, motorcar rentals and investments in enterprises to tap Ghana's timber, food and other natural resources.

Reflections

Being associated with Africa for over half a century brings many random thoughts about its changes, paradoxes and cultural characteristics. Extemporizing about such ideas was common among colonial administrators, missionaries and early visitors to Africa before independence. Although their thoughts often expressed their racial prejudices, they are important for the historian as they help us assess the more substantive writings of the same commentators. Historiography tells us as much about historians and their times as about their research findings. Since independence, foreign commentators, other than novelists and journalists, have felt constrained in their remarks, for they sense that their random thoughts might be taken out of context and prejudice readers against their more general work. Some would say that scholars are affected by the need to be politically correct and, while such approaches are conducive to a more objective stance, political correctness has at times been overdone. Only a few brave Africanists have been willing to call spades spades, among them John Povey, editor for over 20 years of *African Arts*, who was often very outspoken and misjudged for some of his criticisms of African artists, universities and a rather lazy attention to the detail he felt was so necessary to sound scholarship.

Phil Curtin of Wisconsin, later of Johns Hopkins, was another outspoken observer of Africa who was pilloried at the African Studies Association in 1995 for his comments about hiring African and African-American historians who failed to measure up to US academic standards to teach African history in American universities merely to achieve ethnically balanced faculties. Forgotten were his seminal studies in numerous well-received books on the Atlantic slave trade, plantations, and on trade and disease in Africa. Both scholars were judged not on the corpus of their work but on a generalized view of what opinions they should hold. Coming from a different background, different career and different residence experiences, my views were different, but I felt it important that they, as friends of Africa, should feel free to express their thoughts in public. America in this sense is less tolerant than either African or European academe. There is a lot of conformity of views and scholars in particular seem reluctant to rock the boat.

Its critics constantly bemoan Africa's slow progress, coups, diseases, wars and economic instability, but they fail to put their remarks in a spatial or temporal context. In terms of progress, whatever that means other than movement through time, the Africa I knew 50 years ago has disappeared; the changes are enormous. Populations in the countries in which I worked have more than tripled, or grown tenfold in capital cities like Kampala. Secondary schools, universities and hospitals have also increased more than tenfold, often not efficiently but medical centres and schools are nevertheless widely distributed. Instead of tiny universities with small numbers of students being taught a European syllabus, there are now multiple centres of higher education, some state run and others private, with literally tens of thousands of students. Professional schools of medicine, architecture, law and business administration have all been established and African businesses are rapidly growing in importance. Growth has been most active in the informal sector, with motorcar repairs, electrical stores, and furniture and clothing workshops of particular importance.

As rural Africans have moved into towns and peri-urban housing grown with few controls, it has been difficult to secure an urban tax base. The limited funds available are not enough to maintain the streets, public gardens and museums, let alone all the pressing demands from the expanding social services. The prices overseas buyers pay for Africa's primary products like cotton, coffee and tea has often hardly risen in 40 years. In many cases the total output of commodities such as cocoa from Ghana or cotton from Uganda has declined as the market became more competitive. The breakup of East African community services like railways, post and telecommunications, and customs and excise has increased national costs while the behemoth trucks going from the coast to Rwanda have helped ruin many of the highways and spread HIV along its route.

Nevertheless, changes have occurred. In Ghana, for instance, electricity has spread to rural areas, more people have access to clean water, and some diseases like Guinea worm and river blindness have either been eradicated or are in steep decline. For better or worse, much of Africa has entered the international telecommunications age and computers, and particularly cell phones, are rapidly appearing, not only in cities, but also in way out rural areas far from any previous outside links. It's a cruel paradox that while Africa is being more closely linked to the outside world, it has, since the end of the cold war, become of less interest to most of the rest of the world.

Appendix

Fieldwork activities

England

1950   Blackburn, Lancs, assisted with mound excavations, director Frank Willett

1951   Somerton, Somerset, Roman villa, director Ralegh Radford

1951/2 Lenton Priory, Nottingham, medieval tile kiln and well

1952   Arcy sur Cure, France, Middle and Upper Palaeolithic cave sites, director Dr A. Leroi-Gourhan

1953   Hoxne, Lower and Middle Palaeolithic site, director Dr C. B. M. McBurney

1953   Wharram Percy, medieval deserted village, Yorkshire, director John Hurst

1953   Barclodiad y Gawres, Anglesey, Neolithic/Bronze Age megalith, director Dr Glynn Daniel

1954   Lamport Post mill, Northamptonshire, Lockington, Bronze Age round barrow, Leicestershire

1955   Swarkestone, Bronze Age barrow, Derbyshire
Ingleby, Derbyshire, Pagan Danish Cemetery

Kenya

1957   Olorgesailie, Middle Stone Age site Olorgesailie, Masai cenotaph burial mounds Kinangop, iron furnaces Lanet, Iron Age enclosure and houses

Uganda

1959   Nsongezi with W. W. Bishop. Bweyorere, Ankole, royal capital site-training school

1960   Bigo, Large enclosure and capital site-training school

1962   Nyero rock shelter, Late Stone Age and rock art

1963   Magosi, late Stone Age rock shelter with Glen Cole

1964   Lolui island, Iron Age cairns and field systems

2004–7 Dufile, West Nile, fieldwork and excavation of nineteenth-century military station

Tanganyika

1958/1961 Nyabusora, Kagera River, Early and middle Stone Age riverine site

1963   Kilwa, Medieval Islamic town, director Neville Chittick, directed field School

Ghana
1968   Jakpasere, Salaga, Gonja, site associated with legendary leader, director Duncan Mathewson, field school
1970   Fort Orange, Sekondi, associated settlement site, director Bernard Golden. Also Begho, Hani, Brong Ahafo, early modern town Brong Quarter, training school
1971   Begho, Kramo Quarter, training school
1972   Begho, Easter Dwinfuor quarter, Summer, B2 quarter, training school
1973   Cape Coast castle, slave dungeon. Director Doig Simmonds
1975   Begho, Easter, early Iron Age site, Summer Dwinfuor quarter, training school
1975/6 Fort Ruychaver, Dutch fort; Hani, twentieth-century trash heaps
1979   Begho, Market Quarter, training school
1980, 1983, 1984, 1985, 1989, 1995, 1998 ethnographic research at Hani

Jamaica
1980   survey of plantation sites with Douglas Armstrong
1981   Drax hall, slave village, director Douglas Armstrong, training school

Togo
1979   Archaeological survey of country with Philip de Barros
1981   Notse, Survey and excavation of town wall, training school
1985   Denou, stone circles, enclosures and terraces, with Dovi Kuevi, training School
1986/7 Notse, narrow strip weaving study

Somalia
1976   Survey and reorganization of museums and monuments

Benin
1991   Ouidah, 18th/19th town site with Ken Kelly

Note: Unless noted otherwise, all archaeological excavations were directed by Merrick Posnansky and all were of one week's duration or more.

Notes

Chapter 1: Family

1. The Pale, established in 1791, was 400,000 square miles (the equivalent in size of Texas and California) and eventually enclosed over 90 per cent of the Jews in tsarist Russia. It was the heartland of Ashkenazi Yiddish speaking Jewry. Strict controls were placed on movements in and out of the Pale. For administrative convenience Jews were compelled to adopt surnames; those without names were assigned them, some derived from their profession and others from geographical areas.

2. Spelt in that form. When the area was under German control in the eighteenth century the same name changed to Posen, but under Poland's influence it was Poznanski. The spelling of our name suggests it was adopted in the nineteenth century when Russia was in control.

3. There were several items in the *Jewish Chronicle*, published in London. The first described the inauguration of the first shul in Great Moor Street in 1904 and the last, in 1970, its formal dissolution in 1969.

4. Fernie Street has been referred to as part of Manchester's voluntary ghetto and was an area in which there were many glazers. See Bill Williams, *The making of Manchester Jewry 1740–1875* (Manchester: Manchester University Press, 1976) p. 177.

5. The family's pioneering role is embellished on boards listing *Chevra Kaddisha* (burial society) officers in Urmston cemetery, now nearing the end of its days (information from Valerie Eisner, my cousin).

6. When women began to replace coal carriers in the First World War, sack sizes were reduced from two to one hundredweight (112 lbs).

7. My cousin Sidney and several other relatives claim they died in a pogrom. This is unlikely because most pogroms were either before 1906, or during the period of disillusion and economic collapse following the November 1917 German armistice with the Bolsheviks, which was after our grandparents had died.

8. My brother Leonard left his children a very informative and anecdotal account of his youth and ancestry, with more details of distant relatives, the neighbourhood around Star Cliffs and our father's shop, against which I checked my own memories. My brother-in-law Sidney who is also my first cousin recorded his own personal history in a 2002 video, *Transformation and change: the Jewish community in Stoke-on-Trent* produced for the Staffordshire University Institute for Holocaust and Genocide Education and Research. I have also checked some of our own history with that of his father, my father's brother Morris.

9. For a time during the 1914–18 war this river formed the frontier between the German and Russian lines. It was during this back and forwards fighting that mustard gas was used for the first time in warfare in 1915.

10. When I visited in 1996 the graveyard was overgrown and it was only with difficulty that we found parts of three broken tombstones. All had been smashed during the war. The Christian cemetery, by contrast, was well cared for with little sign of any destruction.

11. See Krzysztof Jan Kaliński, *Z dziejów Bolimowa*, Bolimów, 1993.

12. Sharman Yoffie, 'Three Doras', *Downtown Brooklyn: a journal of writing*, vol. 10 (New York: Long Island University, 2001).

13. Food controls were an essential part of the war effort and price rises were restricted to less than 20 per cent over a six-year period. Rations were supplemented with special imports from places like the USA, especially after 1942, of dried eggs, dried milk, dehydrated fruits including bananas, and occasionally fresh fruit like oranges. For key commodities like sugar, meat, eggs and milk the British diet was restricted to about 60–70 per cent of what Americans and Canadians were consuming. See UK Ministry of Food, *How Britain was fed in wartime: food control 1939–45* (London: HM Stationery Office, 1946).

14. The name of a drink using sarsaparilla, a root found in tropical America, as a base.

15. Captain Lugard built the fort in 1890 and it served as his base while he attempted to appease feuding Baganda religious factions. On his visit to Uganda in 1961, Sir Mortimer Wheeler called it the 'last hill fort of the British Empire' because of its concentric banks and ditches. It was a special place for me because the small building in the centre served as the first Uganda Museum in 1908 and was known as '*Nyumba ya mayembe*', the house of charms or fetishes. In bringing order to Uganda after the 1900 Uganda Agreement, British protectorate administrative officers collected all the war fetishes from the ssaza and leading chiefs of Buganda and placed them in the museum. Some time before, the British had apparently burnt all the decommissioned cowrie shells there when they introduced copper currency. It later became the headquarters of the Boy Scouts. There was a beautiful view of Kampala from the top of the embankment and in those tranquil days lovers came there to get away from the tumult of the town.

16. A boarding school solely for the sons of chiefs was established at the royal capital of Mengo in 1905. This was not the first school, for Protestant and Catholic missionaries had set up schools, or at least special classes, at their missions soon after they arrived in 1877. An interesting feature of Uganda education that distinguishes it from many other African countries is that the first girls' boarding school at Gayaza was set up at the same time as Budo. See G. P. McGregor, *King's College, Budo: the first sixty years* (Oxford: Oxford University Press, 1967).

17. Eunice Posnansky, 'A mind unfolding in Uganda', in Roger Bannister (ed.) *Prospect: the Schweppes book of the new generation* (London: Hutchinson, 1962).
18. In the late 1950s and early 1960s coffee prices on the world market were relatively high. When we first visited the USA in 1966 a pound of supermarket coffee cost $2.50–3.00. The price of a basic motorcar, like a Volkswagen, was about $1700. By the end of the century coffee was selling at discount prices in the USA at under $2.50 a pound whereas motor vehicles were around $15,000. The same applied to many other imports from the developed world to Africa, which had risen in many cases tenfold whereas the prices of primary products like coffee, tea and cotton, had either stood still or declined. The story of the last quarter of the twentieth century was a story of the impoverishment of proud land-owning farmers.
19. Land she instructed should go to the grandchildren of her sister Faith, who died in 1996.
20. McGregor, *King's College, Budo.*
21. In going through her papers I realized that she had been aware of her condition because she would write notes to remind herself to ask the doctor about her memory loss. She also forgot several appointments or mistook the times or dates, for she would berate herself in little notebooks to which I was not privy at the time.
22. John Bayley, *Iris: a memoir of Iris Murdoch* (London: Gerald Duckworth & Co, Ltd, 1998).

Chapter 2: Education: England and Uganda, a mind unfolding
1. It was quite common to heap up root crops in the fields, cover them with vegetation for insulation, retain them within a ring of stones and cover the whole mound with soil and turf sods.
2. Sir Cyril Fox, *The personality of Britain: its influence on inhabitant and invader in prehistoric and early historic times* (Cardiff: National Museum of Wales, 1947)
3. Merrick Posnansky, 'The Pleistocene succession in the Middle Trent Basin', *Proceedings of the Geologists Association*, vol. 71 (1960) pp. 284–311; and Merrick Posnansky, 'The Lower and Middle Palaeolithic industries of the East Midlands', *Proceedings of the Prehistoic Society*, vol. 29 (1963) pp. 357–93.

Chapter 3: Education: Ghana and the United States
1. For a history of the university see Francis Agbodeka, *A history of the University of Ghana: half a century of higher education (1948–1998)* (Accra: Woeli Publishing Services, 1998). In 1967 when I arrived there were 2252 students in residence of whom one in seven were women; when I left the number was over 4000 with one in five being women, the faculty student ratio was a little under 1:7; in 1976 the ratio was a little over 1:7. The University of Ghana had graduated 833 students by the time it severed its

link with the University of London in 1962, compared with 527 at Makerere. Both these universities have grown substantially. Makerere is now more than ten times larger than it was and Legon eight times. Neither has adequate resources for so many students, making student life for those not resident on campus full of stress and involving travel from inadequate private housing.

2. Makerere now has a large bank but still no post office; its bookshop is small and mainly for textbooks. Makerere did, however, have a swimming pool and senior common room, providing morning coffee and bringing academics together from different disciplines.

3. The programme is aimed at juniors, though some seniors and graduates can participate under certain circumstances.

4. The reasons for this have often been debated. Some suggest that male students want to work to accumulate money or travel on their own, whereas women students prefer to have more structured travel, are looked after more by their parents or are more interested in using their holiday and a year of their time for travel.

5. Merrick Posnansky, 'Studying abroad in Africa', in Merrick Posnansky (ed.) *Proceedings of the Japanese/American Workshop for Cooperation in Africa, UCLA, 1992* (Los Angeles, 1994) pp. 239–49.

Chapter 4: Religion and race on three continents

1. There does not appear to be a vigorous orthography for Yiddish. In many books there are varying spellings of words such as chada or chaider for Hebrew school. Some words I thought were Yiddish were possibly creations of our own family. I have adopted spelling suggestions from David C. Cross, *English–Yiddish, Yiddish–English dictionary* (New York: Hippocrene, 1995).

2. Reverend Richards joined the armed services as a chaplain towards the end of the war and later moved to South Africa where he served in Port Elizabeth becoming a rabbi and retiring as rabbi emeritus of the Reform congregation in Durban.

3. This was all part of a very unequal colonial legacy. Even before the war European school children took nearly 30 per cent of the government education budget and Africans 47 per cent, yet Africans outnumbered white children in their separate schools by more than 50 times and their parents collectively provided more than three times the revenue provided by the European taxes.

4. See Eunice Posnansky, 'A mind unfolding in Uganda'.

5. Israel was the third country after Britain and the USA to establish a diplomatic mission in Kampala. The Israeli community comprised many agricultural and fishery experts. Ugandans were invited on short courses to Israel and day-old breeder chicks were imported to launch a poultry industry in Uganda. Other Israelis won road-building contracts and there was a close interaction between the Israel and Uganda military establish-

ments. Idi Amin was proud of the parachute wings he earned in Israel. Uganda was a useful sounding post on the Arab world and Ambassador Uri Lubrani made many contacts with southern Sudanese exiles in Kampala. The close relations lasted until the Israeli invasion of Egypt in 1973 at the conclusion of the Yom Kippur War initiated by Egypt.

6. It became the Church of Uganda after independence.
7. Selena Axelrod Winsnes, 'There is a house on Castle Drive: the story of Wulff Joseph Wulff', *History in Africa*, vol. 27 (2000) pp. 443–8.
8. The Reagan administration pulled out of both these international arms of the UN.
9. Commentary, 'African European Jewish Relationships', *African Sentinel*, vol. 6, June 1961.

Chapter 5: Career: preparations, excavations, museums and universities
1. Rex Wailes, *The English windmill* (London: Routledge & Kegan Paul, 1954).
2. Julian D. Richards, 'Heath Wood, Ingleby', *Current Archaeology*, vol. 184 (2003) pp. 170–3.
3. Merrick Posnansky, 'African archaeology comes of age', *World Archaeology*, vol. 13 (1982) pp. 344–59.
4. Glynn L. Isaac, *Olorgesailie: archaeological studies of a Middle Pleistocene lake basin in Kenya* (Chicago: University of Chicago Press, 1977).
5. Nsongezi (1959), Mweya (1959), Nyero (1962), Magosi (1963), in Uganda and Nyabusora in Tanganyika (1959 and 1961).
6. Merrick Posnansky, 'Rock paintings in Uganda', *Roho*, vol. 1 (1962) pp. 38–41.
7. Peter R. Schmidt, *Historical archaeology: a structural approach in an African culture* (Westport: Greenwood Press, 1978).
8. Merrick Posnansky, Andrew Reid and Ceri Ashley, 'Archaeology on Lolui Island, Uganda 1964–5', *Azania*, vol. 40 (2005) pp. 73–100.
9. J. H. Chaplin, 'The prehistoric rock art of the Lake Victoria region', edited, with additional material, by M. A. B. Harlow, *Azania*, vol. 9 (1974) pp. 1–50.
10. Merrick Posnansky (ed.) *Prelude to East African history* (Oxford: Oxford University Press, 1966).
11. *Actes du premier colloque international d'archéologie africaine, Fort Lamy 1966,* Institut National Tchadien pour les Sciences Humaines, Memoires I (Fort Lamy, 1969).
12. He visited Ghana in 1971, lectured to our students on the Sahara and invited me back to Hamburg where he persuaded the German aid corporation DAAD to support our department by providing radio carbon dates.
13. After the revolution in Iran David Stronach was offered a chair at Berkeley.
14. Hudson Obayemi, later known as Ade Obayemi, for a time taught archaeology at Ilorin and became director of antiquities in Nigeria. Previously there had only been a postgraduate diploma programme in the department taken by James Anquandah who became head of the department from 1981 to 1991.

15. Since then I have become more comprehensive in my approach to historical archaeology, including the rich oral memory that survives in African states.
16. Albert van Dantzig and Barbara Priddy, *A short history of the forts and castles of Ghana*, Ghana Museums and Monuments Board Series, no. 2, 1971.
17. Doig Simmonds, 'A note on the excavations in Cape Coast Castle', *Transactions of the Historical Society of Ghana*, vol. 14, no. 2 (1973) pp. 267–9. With the help of gifts from Danish institutions and a great deal of personal ingenuity Doig developed a fine museum with some good historical material. It was opened to the public in early 1974 but he was edged out in regrettable circumstances and the museum rapidly deteriorated. It was again rehabilitated, this time with the help of the Smithsonian Institution and a World Bank loan in 1994, but its adequate maintenance was not assured and it again began to deteriorate with the harsh coastal environmental conditions.

Chapter 6: Career: coming to America, new directions

1. Merrick Posnansky, 'Towards an archaeology of the black diaspora', *Journal of Black Studies*, vol. 15 (1984) pp. 195–205.
2. With 826 participants at the Williamsburg meeting the society in 1984 began attracting larger participation.
3. An early version of my paper 'Towards an archaeology of the black diaspora' was given at the African Studies Association in Washington in 1981.
4. James Deetz, *In small things forgotten: the archaeology of early American life* (New York: Doubleday, 1977).
5. Timothy F. Garrard, *Akan weights and the gold trade* (London: Longman, 1980).
6. James de V Allen, 'Swahili culture reconsidered: some historical implications of the material culture of the northern Kenya coast in the eighteenth and nineteenth centuries', *Azania*, vol. 9 (1974) pp. 105–38.
7. J. Desmond Clark, *The prehistoric cultures of the Horn of Africa* (Cambridge: Cambridge University Press, 1954).
8. Merrick Posnansky, 'An archaeological reconnaissance of Togo', *Nuame Akuma*, vol. 15, (November 1979) pp. 73–8.
9. Gayibor later became vice chancellor of the university in Lomé; Aguigah gained a Ph.D. in archaeology in France, became the first lecturer in archaeology in Togo and later became a government minister; Kuevi enrolled in a doctoral programme at UCLA, left to join politics, but advanced the cause of archaeology both at the university and culturally; Père François de Medeiros became head of the history department in Cotonou; Alexis Adande was the first Beninois to teach archaeology in Benin and Dr Metinhoue became a key minister in the Benin government.
10. The newsletter gained its name from the surprise that our first Togolese visitors had when touring Los Angeles on seeing signs outside restaurants and fast food joints advertising Food To go.

11.   Merrick Posnansky, 'Traditional cloth from the Ewe heartland', in *History, design, and craft in West African strip-woven cloth* (Washington, DC: National Museum of African Art, 1992) pp. 113–32.

12.   Fauziya Kassindja, *Do they hear you when you cry* (New York: Delacorte, 1998).

13.   When I revisited in 1990 the remaining bricks had been used to build a seaside hotel that had never been completed. Though one cannot mourn the passing of such a place it was nevertheless the last memento of its kind on the coast, a place equally as worthy of pilgrimage by black Americans cruelly transported to the New World, as the infamous forts like Goree in Senegal or the Gold Coast castles.

14.   He formed the subject for the novel *The Viceroy of Ouidah* by Bruce Chatwin (New York: Simon & Schuster, 1980) and for a travesty of a film version by Werner Hertzog Cobra Verde (1989) in which Ouidah was substituted by Elmina Castle in Ghana, an army of nubile Amazons was assembled and the kings of Dahomey lost their majesty and became tragic figures of ridicule.

15.   Merrick Posnansky, Agbenyega Adedze and Jessica Levin, 'Postal images of Africa: a new frontier', *African Arts*, vol. 37, no. 2, 2004, pp. 52–73. Papers have dealt with historical archaeology, with creating an awareness of archaeology in Africa and discovering which countries are most interested in promoting an awareness of African archaeology.

Chapter 7: Hani

1.   The Brong people are an Akan-speaking part of the Kwa family. Among other Akan peoples are the Asante who formed their state with the Asantehene as the head of a confederacy in 1701 and the Fante who live along the coast. The Brong probably were the first Akan to come into contact with the Islamic Mande traders from the north, perhaps as early as the fourteenth century AD. They established important city states of which Begho was arguably the largest, earliest and lasted until the early nineteenth century with several of its clans, and certainly its trading group, the Dunso, dispersed to towns like Bonduku in Côte d'Ivoire after the attacks by the Asante in the later eighteenth century. The villagers of Hani are the lineal descendants of the people of Begho.

2.   René A. Bravman and R. Duncan Mathewson, 'A note on the history and archaeology of "Old Bima"', *African Historical Studies*, vol. 3, no. 1 (1970) pp. 133–49.

3.   O. Davies, 'Gonja painted pottery', *Institute of African Studies Research Review*, vol. 7 (1964) pp. 4–11.

4.   Merrick Posnansky, 'Processes of change – a longitudinal ethno-archaeological study of a Ghanaian village: Hani 1970–98', *African Archaeological review*, vol. 21, no. 1 (2004) pp. 31–47.

5.   The villagers called the person from Techiman a 'witch'. Terms for such people are very difficult. Some years ago such a person was termed a fetish

priest. The term traditional healer or therapist is insufficient since many of these practitioners claim supernatural powers and they are credited with healing skills they do not possess.

6. The Pentecostal church in Hani is the Apostles Continuation Church.

7. There are many spelling variations of these names for the different Akan groups but the most prevalent are Sunday, Kwesi/Akosuwa; Monday Kojo/Adjua; Tuesday Kwabena/Abena; Wednesday Kweku/ Akua; Thursday Yaw/Yaa; Friday Kofi/Afi and Afua; Saturday Kwame/ Ama or Aba.

8. Nana Appau I ruled from around 1918 to 1938 and is credited with sending the first children to school and being very progressive and modernizing. It was in his time that the palace was built and the chieftaincy built up. There had been two interim chiefs before Kofi Ampofo was formally enstooled.

9. A similar situation obtained on the death of the chief in Notse in Togo, where I worked from 1981–92; his room was sealed and his wife was shut off from all his property including minor household items. Again I was asked to furnish duplicate photographs to replace those the elders had seized. The wife was then living in Lomé.

10. Dane guns are locally made, often with the same type of cylindrical metal used for bicycle frames. The gun is thus unrifled and normally uses a percussion cap firing system and lead pellets. A few farmers, including the then Chief Ampofo had twin-bore shotguns.

11. The Harmattan (similar to the Khamsin in Egypt) blew south from the Sahara every year bringing dry conditions, often as low as 5 per cent humidity, dust in the air and such poor visibility that on occasions flights had to be cancelled.

12. Normally stuffed with kapok from the silk cotton trees, cotton or occasionally straw.

13. Though Hani farmers were promised help, termed inputs, for both fertilizers and disease control, none of the farmers I interviewed in 1998 had received such aid more than once and few remembered the last time an agricultural extension officer had visited them.

Chapter 8: Africa: Kenya and Uganda

1. The Royal National Parks of Kenya had two archaeological divisions, one for prehistoric sites and the other for historic sites on the East African coast based at Gedi near Malindi headed by James Kirkman who had been working at the site since 1948.

2. I was fortunate because a few years earlier some Land Rovers had no windscreen wipers at all. Trafficators, when found on cars, were normally of the kind in which a little arm stuck out at the side. Compulsory indicators in the form of flashing lights did not appear as a regular, as opposed to optional accessory, until the late 1950s.

3. The Kabaka ruled with a series of regional or *Ssaza* chiefs below which were Gombolola subchiefs who governed smaller areas.

4. Mubende was the last area Buganda took from Bunyoro in the troubled times at the end of the nineteenth century. Under the Uganda Agreement of 1900 it was included in Buganda over the objections of its Banyoro residents. Relatively few Baganda lived there until the 1960s when it became a bone of contention. Its status was not settled at the independence negotiations in London but left for an official enquiry and ultimately a referendum to sort out. Mubende had no large urban centres and no special economic assets other than its agriculture, which was similar to adjoining parts of Buganda and Bunyoro.

5. We got to know Brigadier Opolot who was head of the armed forces from 1964 to 1966. He became Uganda ambassador to Ghana for about a year following his release from prison in 1971. Obote imprisoned him in 1966 on the suspicion that he was more loyal to the president than to him.

6. Ocheng's death from cancer may explain why he felt he had little to lose in leading the revolt against Obote. It was popularly believed that Obote may have hastened his death.

7. Kabaka of Buganda, *The desecration of my kingdom* (London: Constable, 1967).

8. Apollo Kagwa was the *katikiro* or prime minister of Buganda in the early part of the twentieth century.

Chapter 9: Africa: Ghana

1. It has been renovated, is grander than it was and is now known as the Britannia Adelphi.

2. An exception was Portland cement from Britain to build the cement motorway, the cocoa silos, new harbour and town at Tema, the new airport in Accra and many other projects. The Ghana government suffered from unscrupulous foreign and Ghanaian agents who took cuts from sales and sold the government too many simultaneous orders it could ill afford.

3. The equivalent of about $30 in 2005.

4. *Tro-tro* literally means three pence (or cents), the original cost of a journey.

5. Known as murram in East Africa, always red and made up of iron rich oxidized soils.

6. One had to wait until the 1990s for improvements, which was when Ghana acquired a satellite connection.

Bibliography

Actes du premier colloque international d'archéologie africaine, Fort Lamy 1966, Institut national tchadien pour les Sciences Humaines, Memoires I (Fort Lamy, 1969)

Agbodeka, Francis, *A history of University of Ghana: half a century of higher education (1948–1998)* (Accra: Woeli Publishing services, 1998)

Allen, James de V., 'Swahili culture reconsidered: some historical implications of the material culture of the northern Kenya coast in the eighteenth and nineteenth centuries', *Azania*, vol. 9 (1974) pp. 105–38

Axelrod Winsnes, Selena, 'There is a house on Castle Drive: the story of Wulff Joseph Wulff', *History in Africa,* vol. 27 (2000) pp. 443–8

Bayley, John, *Iris: a memoir of Iris Murdoch* (London: Gerald Duckworth & Co, Ltd, 1998)

Bravman, René A and R. Duncan Mathewson, 'A note on the history and archaeology of "Old Bima"', *African Historical Studies,* vol. 3, no. 1 (1970) pp. 133–49

Carlebach, Julius, *The Jews of Nairobi 1903–1962* (Nairobi: Nairobi Hebrew Congregation, 1963)

Chaplin, J. H., 'The prehistoric rock art of the Lake Victoria region', edited and with additional material by M. A. B. Harlow, *Azania*, vol. 9 (1974) pp. 1–50

Chatwin, Bruce, *The Viceroy of Ouidah* by (New York: Simon & Schuster, 1980)

Clark, J. Desmond, *The prehistoric cultures of the Horn of Africa* (Cambridge: Cambridge University Press, 1954)

Cross, David C., *English–Yiddish, Yiddish–English dictionary* (New York: Hippocrene, 1995)

Davies, O., 'Gonja painted pottery', *Institute of African Studies Research Review,* vol. 7 (1964) pp. 4–11

Deetz, James, *In small things forgotten: the archaeology of early American life* (New York: Doubleday, 1977)

Fox, Sir Cyril, *The personality of Britain: its influence on inhabitant and invader in prehistoric and early historic times* (Cardiff: National Museum of Wales, 1947)

Garrard, Timothy F., *Akan weights and the gold trade* (London: Longman 1980)

Goody, Jack, 'The Mande and the Akan hinterland', in Jan Vansina, R. Mauny and L. V. Thomas (eds) *The historian in tropical Africa* (London 1964) pp. 193–218

Isaac, Glynn L., *Olorgesailie: archaeological studies of a Middle Pleistocene lake basin in Kenya* (Chicago: University of Chicago Press, 1977)

Kabaka of Buganda, *The desecration of my kingdom* (London: Constable, 1967)

Kalinski, Krzysztof Jan, *Z dziejów Bolimowa* (Bolimów, 1993)

Kassindja, Fauziya, *Do they hear you when you cry* (New York: Delacorte, 1998)

McGregor, G. P. *King's College, Budo: the first sixty years* (Oxford: Oxford University Press, 1967)

Macmillan, Hugh and Frank Shapiro, *Zion in Africa: the Jews of Zambia* (London: I.B.Tauris, 1999)

Posnansky, Eunice, 'A mind unfolding in Uganda', in Roger Bannister (ed.) *Prospect: the Schweppes book of the new generation* (London: Hutchinson, 1962)

Posnansky, Merrick, 'The Pleistocene succession in the Middle Trent Basin', *Proceedings of the Geologists Association,* vol. 71 (1960) pp. 284–311

'Rock paintings in Uganda', *Roho,* vol. 1 (1962) pp. 38–41

'The Lower and Middle Palaeolithic industries of the East Midlands', *Proceedings of the Prehistoic Society,* vol. 29 (1963) pp. 357–93

Prelude to East African history (Oxford: Oxford University Press, 1966)

'An archaeological reconnaissance of Togo', *Nuame Akuma,* vol. 15, (November 1979) pp. 73–8

'African archaeology comes of age', *World Archaeology,* vol. 13 (1982) pp. 344–59

'Towards an archaeology of the black diaspora', *Journal of Black Studies,* vol. 15 (1984) pp. 195–205

'Traditional cloth from the Ewe heartland', in *History, design, and craft in West African strip-woven cloth* (Washington, DC: National Museum of African Art, 1992) pp. 113–32

'Studying abroad in Africa', in Merrick Posnansky (ed.) *Proceedings of the Japanese/American workshop for Cooperation in Africa, UCLA, 1992* (Los Angeles: UCLA James S. Coleman African Studies Center, 1994) pp. 239–49

'Processes of change – a longitudinal ethno-archaeological study of a Ghanaian village: Hani 1970–98, *African Archaeological Review,* vol. 21, no. 1 (2004) pp. 31–47

Posnansky, Merrick, Agbenyega Adedze and Jessica Levin, 'Postal images of Africa: a new frontier', *African Arts,* vol. 37, no. 2 (2004) pp. 52–73

Posnansky, Merrick, Andrew Reid and Ceri Ashley, 'Archaeology on Loui
    Island, Uganda 1964–5, *Azania*, vol. 40 (2005) pp. 73–100
Richards, Julian D., 'Heath Wood, Ingleby', *Current Archaeology*, vol. 184
    (2003) pp. 170–3
Samuelson, Maurice, 'My children will know', *Midstream*, vol. 37, no. 3
    (April 1991) pp. 34–6
Schmidt, Peter R., *Historical archaeology: a structural approach in an
    African culture* (Westport: Greenwood Press, 1978)
Simmonds, Doig, 'A note on the excavations in Cape Coast Castle',
    Transactions of the Historical Society of Ghana, vol. 14, no. 2 (1973)
    pp. 267–9
Trowell, Margaret and K. P. Wachsmann, *Tribal crafts of Uganda*
    (Oxford: Oxford University Press, 1953)
UK Ministry of Food, *How Britain was fed in wartime: food control 1939–
    45* (London: His Majesty's Stationery Office, 1946)
van Dantzig, Albert and Barbara Priddy, *A short history of the forts and
    castles of Ghana* (Accra: Ghana Museums and Monuments Board
    Series, no. 2, 1971)
Wailes, Rex, *The English windmill* (London: Routledge & Kegan Paul,
    1954)
Wilks, Ivor, 'Wangara, Akan, and Portuguese in the fifteenth and
    sixteenth centuries', in Ivor Wilks (ed.) *Forests of gold: essays on the
    Akan and the kingdom of Asante* (Athens: Ohio University Press 1993)
    pp. 1–39
Williams, Bill, *The making of Manchester Jewry 1740–1875* (Manchester:
    Manchester University Press, 1976)
Yoffie, Sharman, 'Three Doras', *Downtown Brooklyn: A Journal of Writing*,
    vol. 10 (New York: Long Island University, 2001)

Index